SAMSON RISING

SAMSON RISING

The true story of a Cornish lad who found inspiration
through sport and strength in adversity

John Hambly

FOREWORD BY DYLAN HARTLEY
FORMER ENGLAND RUGBY CAPTAIN

UNITED WRITERS
Cornwall

UNITED WRITERS PUBLICATIONS LTD
Ailsa, Castle Gate, Penzance, Cornwall.
www.unitedwriters.co.uk

British Library Cataloguing in Publication Data:
A catalogue record for this book is
available from the British Library.

ISBN 9781852001971

*Whilst this is a true and factual account of
the author's life, some names and occurrences have
been changed to avoid misunderstanding
or embarrassment.*

Printed and bound in Great Britain by
United Writers Publications Ltd.,
Cornwall.

Dedicated to my family,
friends and anyone
living with
Multiple Sclerosis.

Contents

Acknowledgements

Marion, Ellie, Meg, Grace and Cerys – I am of course hugely proud of all of them. Marion has always been so caring and resourceful and it has rubbed off on the girls. They have become impressive young women, possessing common sense, ambition, compassion and generosity well beyond their years. The ever-increasing restrictions that my condition has imposed and the focus required for me to help develop the Samson Centre has been all-consuming for long periods of their childhoods and could have stymied their outlook on life, but not a bit of it. Their unconditional love and boundless enthusiasm in embracing all that we have laid at their young feet have given Marion and I such joy and carried us through our darkest moments.

The Unsung Heroes – over the years I have felt flattered to receive so many accolades and awards in recognition of the setting up and development of the Samson Centre. In my heart of hearts, though, I realise that I have been blessed to have known or be introduced to amazing people from every walk of life who have given so generously, not only financially but also of their time and energy. There can be absolutely no doubt that the support from the rugby boys was instrumental in instilling the belief that my initial idea, viewed by some within the MS ranks as hare-brained, could be brought to fruition. However, momentum behind the project gathered pace so quickly that the charity could have been found wanting in terms of its infrastructure and key personnel once we had moved into the new centre. That's when our unsung heroes began to emerge. As I look back, I can appreciate more than ever the vital roles and selfless contributions that our trustees, volunteers and key members of staff have played in making the Samson Centre the success story that it is now.

Actonians RFC – to a man, during my toughest match, you have sustained and carried me across the Field of Dreams. I will forever be in your debt.

Malcolm – belief, patience and wisdom are a potent combination – thank you for bringing this story to life.

Michael Calvin and **Dylan Hartley** – I never envisaged this book having a foreword but once I had read your kind and insightful words, it was clear that they would set just the right tone for what follows.

Bruce, Phil and **James** – a huge thank you for creating such an amazing cover. I suspect that the book may be purchased purely on the basis of your eye-catching design!

Colin Moore – thank you so much for allowing Bruce and James to professionally 'plonk' St. Michael's Mount onto your stunning piece of artwork.

Brian Tregunna – thank you cuz, your gentle promptings and wise counsel instilled the belief to enable me to pen these words.

Matt – Python, sport, coffee and a fellow author – the perfect ingredients for the germination of a memoir! Thanks for listening to my aimless ramblings mate.

The Fountain Brothers – thank you for your incredible friendship, support and never-ending supply of rugby humour and anecdotes!

Rear-Admiral Stumble & the 16 Idiots – in causing mayhem on various bodies of water up and down the country your extraordinary fundraising exploits will never be forgotten. Shipmates, I salute you!

Dave & Jeanette, Piers & Mary, Andy & Lucy, and **Gea** – thank you all for your courage and candour in allowing, and assisting, me to recount your heart-breaking losses in the chapter *'Together'*.

Robert Snook – Bob, my first Actonians captain, how could I forget meeting you at my second training session, 15 years after we went our separate ways from primary school? Surely, a Cornish beacon for the sequel!

Richard Price – your enthusiasm, encouragement and understanding of what makes a page come alive were crucial in getting me in sight of the finishing line. I will forever be grateful for your kind and timely intervention, Richard.

The oval ball game – mother, this wonderful sport that you feared would cause me so much physical harm ended up fixing your boy!

Harvey Thorneycroft Ltd – my heartfelt thanks to Jane, Alice and Harvey for your vision and endeavour in promoting and marketing this story through a wonderful network of sporting and business contacts.

Photo Credits – thank you to Steve Porter Pictures, Graham Jelley, Sport Gives Back, Endemol.

Foreword
by
Dylan Hartley

I am proud to have captained England. The English rugby system moulded me after I arrived here at the age of 16 eager to build a new life, but I continue to hear echoes of my upbringing in Rotorua, on New Zealand's South Island. It is in Maori heartland, and we were taught to appreciate the significance of Mana.

This is a powerful, supernatural force, central to Melanesian and Polynesian culture. It comes from within people, places and even inanimate objects. It symbolises authority, influence, pride and prestige. Those who possess it are able to perform to their best in any given situation. It can be a force for good, or ill, but when used wisely it has healing properties.

Anyone reading this book will recognise that John possesses Mana. When we talk about courage in rugby it is normally in physical form, because it demands an ability to endure punishment and a willingness to lay your body on the line for the team. In John's case, responding to MS required a singular sort of bravery, the moral courage to think of others instead of yourself.

The Samson Centre, where fellow MS sufferers are able to manage their symptoms, stands as a symbol, not just of the solidarity of sport, but of the power of one man to make a difference. It is the product of sixteen years' planning and execution by a remarkable collection of individuals, drawn together through what John calls rugby's 'unique band of brothers'.

This is the story of a remarkable man, who initially found self-expression through rugby, before running a marathon and developing interests in cricket and horse racing. He captained the Old Actonians rugby club with distinction; I was fortunate to lead out Northampton and England. In that sense we are kindred spirits, because we both know, from experience, that leadership is multi-faceted and often practised away from the spotlight. Captains develop a natural grit, and instinctively never get ahead of themselves.

I knew talent was only part of the equation. I wasn't selected by Eddie Jones because I was his best player. I had to earn my place in his team every single day. As one of the oldest squad members, I had to set the best example in training. My disciplinary rap sheet, which is longer than *War and Peace*, testifies to my imperfections, but I committed to representing my team and my country in the best way possible.

My credit came from working harder, and longer, than anyone. Did I enjoy that? Of course not. It can be miserable doing additional training and attending strategic meetings with management and support staff when everyone else is enjoying downtime. But I'm thankful I did it all, because it enabled me to experience the highs of winning consistently and the satisfaction of leading from the front.

Sport reflects life, in that it is not a straight, smooth road. It tends to be defined by the ability to recover from setbacks and adapt quickly to sudden diversions. My England career petered out with a bout of concussion and the long term knee injury that eventually prompted my retirement, but it provided me with the gift of perspective.

An international squad consists of 30 boys in a bubble. It is not until you leave that bubble that you understand the scale of things, and the extent of the privilege involved. In what other job do you have the goodwill of millions of strangers? When I had to miss the 2019 World Cup I was struck by how many people approached me in the street asking how I thought the team would get on.

11

During my rehabilitation I met those with far more profound challenges than those I faced: children dealing with aggressive forms of cancer, parents attempting to generate as many memories as possible before they went blind. As a parent, that moved me, almost beyond words. As a player, it reminded me of the need to enjoy rugby for what it is; a game.

One of Eddie's strengths as a coach is his eagerness to share knowledge and stimulate thought. He introduced me to the philosophies of Urban Meyer, the legendary Florida and Ohio State football coach. He had three transferable but pivotal values, relentless effort, competitive excellence and the power of the unit.

I was intrigued by Meyer's equation, $E+R=O$. In other words, Event plus Reaction equals Outcome. Applying that to John's life and times is instructive. The event, his diagnosis with MS, led to an inspirational reaction, a junior rugby club and the wider community raising thousands of pounds. The outcome is a centre that cares, and will continue to care, for fellow sufferers.

Fantastic. To borrow one of Eddie's many texts: 'Relentless effort, not talent or intelligence, is the key to achieving great things in your life.'

Introduction
2015

"SO here am I sitting in my tin can. . ."

Someone laughs loudly and I awake with something of a start. Today's trip down Memory Lane is over and yet more vivid images of a forgotten past have been recovered from my cranial cutting room floor. I rub my eyes and glance up at the timer to see that there are 7 minutes to go before the bell tolls and the 606th session of my thrice weekly incarceration is over. I am inside a steel barometric chamber breathing 100% oxygen at twice atmospheric pressure through an uncomfortably tight face-mask. To some this dull claustrophobic ritual of self-encasement would appear to be utterly futile and pointless given that oxygen is freely available to us all 24/7. The simple fact is that, in slowing the relentless progression of a degenerative illness and by replenishing resolve, it has been my lifeblood in recent years.

It has now been over 15 years since I was given the hammer blow diagnosis of a chronic neurological condition which, in the intervening period, has continued on its own merry way, ravaging a once fit body and mind, impinging on every aspect of family life, work, rest and play. And yet, despite the devastating repercussions of this medical wrecking ball, the love and encouragement of my beautiful family and an incredible group of friends, particularly my beloved rugby club, have buoyed and sustained me through some of the darkest periods. The kindness and generosity of so many people has enabled me to discover previously unrealised inner resources and mental strength that, as a healthy individual, I wonder whether I would have felt the need or inclination to tap into. It may sound odd but so extraordinary and enriching has been the journey and the amazing achievements by so many along the way that I feel truly blessed.

Five hours a week in solitary confinement gives ample time for reflection; an opportunity to put thoughts on paper and try to make sense of life's game of dot to dot. In our helter-skelter world life rushes past, simply appearing to be a series of occurrences and coincidences interspersed with good or bad luck and missed or grabbed opportunities, but what if much of our time here on this mortal coil is interlinked with beacons guiding us along pre-prepared divine course settings? Fair enough, we deviate miles off course at times but maybe, just maybe, eventually our jumbled flight plan is revealed as the dots, our beacons, begin to join up.

Chapter 1

Grass Roots
1966-7

L IFE on a Cornish council estate in the mid 1960s was undoubtedly tough, but my parents worked feverishly hard in order to provide for my brother and I. At nine and four years old respectively, we were blissfully unaware of our plight and how well we were being cushioned from all the financial worries heaped upon a mother and father who had seen their fair share of despair and destitution throughout their young lives. We were by no means the worst off on the estate, and with my mother somehow managing to turn us out well dressed, we were probably viewed as being comparatively well off. Built just prior to the outbreak of World War II, despite the hardship, there was a wonderful sense of unity within the folk of Truro's Trelander Estate, although, inevitably, one or two families aspired to hold the mantle of tribal leaders. In particular, the Webb clan, with five boys and three girls, and father, John, running the estate football team, proved to be a powerful force on the scene. Whether it involved the cup finals, summer fêtes, firework nights or just a good old dispute with the Council, they were there fighting our (well, mostly their own) corner.

As far as large families were concerned, ours was up there in Division One, at least where my father's generation were concerned. He was one of eleven children and, sadly, although Henrietta and Reggie died as infants and Louis passed away from peritonitis in 1941, aged 21, whilst serving in the Royal Army Service Corps, most of the remaining offspring had failed to up sticks and move far, so new family branches had appeared on the estate. Having said that, my father's siblings seemed to bring a modicum of reality to 'livestock' numbers or, perhaps, it was just that a certain John Logie Baird had introduced a popular distraction into their lives!

As a child I was aware that my parents had had difficult upbringings, but to their great credit they seldom burdened my brother and I with past traumas and current trials and tribulations. My father, Cecil, especially, was tight lipped about his wartime experiences. I knew that he had been shot and lost a lung, but it was only some years after his death that I learnt that this had happened in November 1944, during the push towards Nijmegen in the Netherlands, when he was a gunner in the Royal Artillery at just 19 years old. I recall my Aunt Doreen, Cornish through and through and without doubt the family matriarch, telling me of her utter shock when he stumbled through the door having discharged himself from hospital.

"Aw my God, when he came in he looked so ill, I thought he'd come home to die, John. From a strapping great chap, he was just skin and bones."

In fact, he was so badly affected by his injuries, that for many years following the war he required regular sessions of electric shock treatment at Bodmin Asylum, which operated on the principle of disordering the mind and jolting war veterans out of their emotional distress. It is therefore all the more remarkable that despite his physical and emotional frailties, he was so warm and caring that I can barely recall an occasion during my childhood when he exhibited any sign of post traumatic stress disorder. He somehow managed to shield us from his inner turmoil and hold down a full time job at Harveys sawmill.

And then there was my mother, Guiseppa, who arguably had endured even greater levels of emotional stress during the war. Born in Malta in 1933, tragically her mother died two years later at the tender age of 26 following the birth of her youngest brother, Leli, and with her father away at sea for long periods, it was left to her grandparents to raise the four children. She was only 7 years old when Hitler and Mussolini resolved to bomb and starve the island into submission by attacking its ports, towns, cities and Allied shipping supplying the island. Malta was one of the most intensively bombed areas during the war. Strategically important to the Royal Navy and Royal Air Force and their campaign in North Africa, Malta endured 3,000 bombing raids over a two year period. My mother, big brother Nenu and older sister Rita, recounted the desperation of the islanders as they hand-excavated into the limestone bedrock to form bunkers. Night after night, the family of six would remain huddled, freezing cold and starving in their tiny subterranean void. It was, however, a wise move as their house took a direct hit and was flattened in 1941. On the 15th April 1942, King George VI awarded the George Cross to the people of Malta in appreciation of their heroism and devotion.

By 1950 my mother was working as a nanny to a naval family in Valetta, and such was her love and care for the two children, the commander and his wife sought permission from her grandmother to bring her with them to the UK. Grandfather had passed away in 1947, so it was not a cordial meeting with a grandmother in ill health and Rita doing their best to keep the family unit together. The truth of it was that my mother was so devoted to their family that, despite the class divide, they loved her too. Perhaps the arrangement also gave her the structure and stability that her young life had lacked until then. In May 1952, my mother arrived in Truro and immediately fell in love with Cornwall. She returned to Malta only once in the next 30 years; in 1955, to nurse her grandmother for four months following a stroke. Shortly after her return to Truro, she met my father at a dance in the Territorial Army drill hall and within 12 months they were married. Big brother Dave was born in May 1957, and over five years later I arrived to annoy him, which I strive to do to this very day! My sister, Marianne, was a complete shock to everyone's system when she joined us in 1975. The British Legion Christmas bash of '74 and countless Babychams can lay claim to that minor miracle!

Built in the mid 1930s on one of the steeper parts of the city, Trelander had less of the monotony usually associated with Council Estates despite the houses being of similar design with rough rendered elevations, single glazed metal windows, all capped with locally sourced slate-clad pitched roofs. At that time, the services were basic and devoid of today's creature comforts but, thankfully, for the families lucky enough to qualify for the accommodation, the new properties were a welcome departure from the city's squalid, rat-infested Victorian slums. Whether the Cornish architects had grand designs for the estate is highly doubtful, but at least someone had the vision to name the streets in accordance with the topography and orientation. So, there was a North, South, East, Highway, Vean and Barton, all pre-fixed by the name Trelander. Quite why there was no Trelander West is a bit of a mystery.

My memories of estate life in the '60s are surprisingly vivid. Perhaps it was the close proximity to the countryside and estuary, or the close-knit community where your parents could ask you to go and tap on almost anyone's door and ask for help, whether it be a cup of milk, tea leaves or flour, a spanner or just another pair of hands! Everybody mucked in, presumably in the knowledge that on any given day it could be them doing the asking. One other boon, although I wouldn't have appreciated it at the time, was that Trelander was only a stone's throw from Truro rugby club. My cousin, Derrick, would often take me to the club on a Saturday afternoon and although I didn't really understand what was going on, whilst he was in the bar, I would find a tree to climb and watch the game from on high. Once the match was over, I would then have the hazardous task of wriggling and threading myself through a mass of giants to find Derrick and scrounge a bottle of Vimto and some crisps. On reflection, that was probably the best part of the afternoon!

When not frequenting the rugby club on Saturdays, I would join a gang of kids and my cousin, Brian, who was just a couple of years older, to play footie in the street. Using streetlamps for goal posts gave us a 'pitch' about 40 yards long by 6 yards wide including the pavements. The latter could present a significant hazard with their granite kerbstones, although the concrete carriageway was the biggest problem when it came to sliding in for a tackle. Most of the lads wore tracksuit bottoms, but skinned knees and elbows were still all too evident. At four years old, I was too small to mix it with the bigger kids so invariably I was the car/bus monitor, combining this onerous task with the job of part time goalpost. As traffic was almost non-existent in those days, I was largely redundant, that is until the ball got booted under a parked car, at which point I was shoved head first beneath the vehicle.

On one occasion, whilst in the throes of squeezing myself between the road surface and chassis, I heard an almighty furore followed by the sound of scampering feet.

"Bleddy kids, look what they've done to my car, June!" screamed Fred Tregowan.

I could see his slippers and the bottoms of his trouser legs as he surveyed his beloved Singer Hunter, crunching broken glass from the wing mirror dispatched by a clubbing right footed volley from one of the Webb boys.

"I'll box all of their ears, June, I will. The little beggars!"

I must have laid there trembling for 30 minutes during which time poor old Fred probably circled the car at least half a dozen times, thankfully never stooping to look underneath. No sooner had he wandered back inside his front door mumbling to himself than three of the gang emerged from a neighbour's alleyway to drag me and the ball to safety.

"Comez on, Johnny boy, we've gotta get home for 3 o'clock. My dad says we're gonna win the World Cup today."

A year passed. It's now August '67 and you can imagine the level of excitement and effervescence within a five year old about to go away on his summer holiday. My father and mother had somehow managed to scrimp and save enough of their hard earned cash to book a week's break at a caravan park on the Lizard peninsula. Stan, our taxi driver, arrived spot on time with his dazzlingly polished black Austin of England. With bags and beach paraphernalia shoehorned into the boot, we were away, cruising majestically, although somewhat apologetically, through the estate down to the

A38. As usual our mates were playing footie in the road, but oblivious that some of their own were escaping. David, now reaching an age when any modicum of excitement was to be suppressed at all costs, lay slumped on the other side of the back seat; under no circumstances could our covert operation be exposed.

Our ninety minute journey from Truro to one of Cornwall's crown jewels was largely silent in terms of family banter. The old man chatted away with Stan whilst he and my mother turned the air blue, chain smoking their way through a packet of twenty Cadets. Why wouldn't they listen to my protestations? Far from my parents inhaling habits enticing me to wish for a drag, I had recently been soundly thrashed for stamping on the sacred fag packet one Saturday evening during the Dick Van Dyke Show.

With the caravan key collected and the relevant corrugated crate identified, Stan brought his gleaming charge to a halt and my father clambered out, allowing fresh sea air to flood my lungs, releasing me from my smokey entombment. The smell and sound of the coast rushed in like a bright awakening from the monotonous urban dream that was life on the Trelander Estate. The urge to fling the bags to one side and just jump straight into my swimming trunks was overwhelming; only to be dampened by the obligatory cup of tea, smoke and tidying up, something that had become a lifetime obsession of my beloved mother.

An hour later we strode purposefully down the craggy cliff path towards our favourite cove. We had holidayed at Kennack Sands the previous summer and fallen in love with the sheer beauty and majesty of the coastline. However, even at my tender age, the stillness and a foreboding sense of unease struck me, culminating in our emergence onto a virtually deserted beach. No golden sands peppered with happy skipping kids and parents asleep on their deckchairs, just desolation interspersed with what looked like vast tracts of dark black seaweed. Undeterred, I sped across the sand, bucket and spade clanking in hand, only to be halted in full stride at the sight of the rotting carcasses of sea birds, washed up by the morning's high tide. As I slowed and drew closer, I could see that the lines of black seaweed were in fact heavy clumps of crude oil covered kelp. I fell crest-fallen to my knees.

"Come on boy, up onto your feet. Let's see if we can catch a few trout up by the old boathouse," uttered my father as he slung a consoling arm around my shoulders.

"They're probably all dead too, Dad," I choked out, through streams of tears.

"They're alright boy, way up above the waterline. You wait 'n' see, they're clever but we're smarter. What's your Aunt Doreen always saying when things get tough?"

"The evening will crown the day, Dad," I sniffed. "But what does she mean?"

"Well, she's sayin' no matter how bad things are, be patient and in time things will improve."

"Hmm. . . does that mean that the beach will be back to normal in the morning then, Dad?" I chirped enthusiastically.

"Not quite, boy, but you've got the right idea," my father said smiling as he ushered me away from the carnage behind us.

The Torrey Canyon Disaster of March 1967 had left its indelible mark on the South Cornish coastline. There was to be no glorious summer beach holiday after all. My poor parents had been sold something of a duffer given the devastation to the environment. As a result, we spent the next six days traipsing around the countryside and campsite looking for things to do.

I would not have appreciated it as a child, but being able to accept disappointment and swiftly move on to the next point of interest would instil something in me that would stand me in good stead for later life. An ability to keep looking forward and not dwell on the negative would prove crucial.

Chapter 2

Gross and Grosser
1973-1976

BY the time I'd passed my Eleven-plus and been selected for Redruth Grammar School some ten miles away, my body was beginning to change at an alarming pace and, with it, my outlook on life. Between the ages of nine and eleven I had found an affinity for home cooking and TV, which my parents unwittingly encouraged in order to keep me and, to a lesser extent, my brother from mixing with the rest of the Bash Street kids on the council estate. The result was rapid weight gain and consequential loss of self-esteem. From an out-going, athletic and generally carefree youngster, without really being aware of it, I had become introverted and self-conscious.

A grammar school in an unfamiliar mining town without your junior school mates would be trial enough for any molly-coddled little fat boy, but throw in the spiteful antics of my peers and the school prefects, and suddenly there was a blackness to the start of every day. The sense of me retreating into my shell would not have been tangible to those closest at home.

"Maybe he's just a bit quiet because he's tired travelling to and from school and then having all that homework," would be the usual explanation.

The downward spiral was given a kick-start in week one when the aptly named Mrs Bulger, the school nurse, plucked Booth, Bee and myself from a parade of new inmates on the grounds that we were conspicuously rotund. At 5'2" and 13 stone, she probably had a point. My two counterparts each hitting the scales at 15 stone plus were clearly already in the super heavyweight league and resigned to their newfound infamy. We were given a good ticking off and sent away with specific dietary and exercise instructions; all largely meaningless to me and to my bemused mother who merely scoffed at the thought of her young buck being denied her daily homemade treats.

The trouble with the over-eating (and plenty of the 'wrong stuff' too) at that age was that I was in a bubble of ignorance and indulgence. My day would begin with a hearty cooked breakfast with stacks of toast or crumpets. It was then off to school on the bus with a packed lunch of sandwiches, pork pies, cakes and chocolate bars in hand. The school day would also be punctuated with mid-morning and mid-afternoon trips to 'Buck's', the school tuck-shop run by our crusty old caretaker, Mr Buckingham. He was as miserable as sin and made no attempt at conversation or expression to acknowledge his customers' presence, except perhaps to bark out the price and thrust out a large hand for the money. God help anyone who touched merchandise on the table and didn't commit to buy it!

Along the half mile walk back to the bus station after school, the appetite moth used to draw me to the flame, affectionately known to a few of us as Scratchies fish and chip shop, seeking batter bits liberally sprinkled on top of chips. An hour and a half later, I would be sat at home in front of the TV demolishing my mother's latest calorific catastrophe. Homework brought a two hour lull in proceedings but was followed by a supper of cakes, biscuits and Ovaltine. All in all, an incredible feat of gastronomic endurance which over the ensuing three years left me doing the proverbial coach party trick on the school scales, topping out at an all time high of 15 stone. Needless to say, with Booth and Bee also even larger than first identified, Mrs Bulger seemed equally perplexed and apoplectic!

Throughout this period of sustained growth my clothes struggled to keep up with the rate of expansion and I repeatedly found myself walking around with seams split asunder. My mother did her best to shore up the damage but in truth she was fighting a losing battle.

Grammar school uniform had to be worn and looked after with military precision, so it was with some relief that in the spring of 1976 our Head announced, with some resignation, that we would amalgamate with the nearby Tolgus School and become comprehensive in the autumn. Gone would be the teachers with black gowns and mortar boards and in would come a vast array of colours and fashions, both for staff and pupils. My mother seized the opportunity and re-attired me with a selection of clothes which can only have come from Truro's second-hand glam rock shop!

Whilst integrating with another school was both exciting and daunting, little was I to know that it would lead to one of several defining moments in my life – my nemesis was about to appear on the horizon, like a shark fin breaking the surface just off the beach.

Even at 15, Robert Stephens had the menace and air of a prize fighter strutting to the ring in the knowledge that he was untouchable and with a licence to do as he pleased with whoever dared cross his path. A good looking and well built youth, his self-confidence was boosted still further by the attentions of the school's female contingent and a band of mates equally adept at performing the Stephens's strut. With sporting prowess in abundance and no small amount of intelligence, Stephens had all the attributes to make him a leading contender in the WBA, World Bullying Association. And there was me, high up the weight division but seriously lacking in terms of sporting ability, looks and confidence.

My first inkling that life was about to take a major nose-dive to the canvas came as early as the first week of the new school year. The Cornish summer had been blisteringly hot and continued well into September. It therefore came as something of a jolt to the system to have to pack away my fishing tackle and go from the riverbank to the classroom. The end of the summer school holidays always had a feeling of inevitability from mid-August as I began to count down the days so, with the glorious weather, I had been extra keen to get to the river's edge each day and sometimes well beyond nightfall. There was something about the beauty and tranquillity of the river and its inhabitants that made the solitude feel so appropriate. The hours spent crouched behind the rushes trying to tempt native brown trout were now just a distant memory as I sat in Bernie Farquhar's maths lesson peering longingly out of the window as the bright autumnal sunshine cast its rays through the large metal casements highlighting the dust disturbed after six weeks of summer inactivity.

Bearded, stocky and brusque, Bernie was feared and respected by most of his pupils. In fact, so much so that maths actually got taught in his lessons without an obvious semblance of dissent or disruption. It may have been this regimented, almost monastic environment, that nurtured Stephens's notion of an undercover assault part way through the lesson albeit in full daylight. Initially, whilst startled, I just thought that I had suffered a muscle spasm in my lower back, but when the sharp jabbing pain was repeated three or four more times in the next five minutes, accompanied by the faintest of sniggers, I knew that I had been identified as prey and the target area firmly locked in on my buttocks and lumbar region. For the next twenty minutes I endured upwards of 30 direct hits. All inflicted without a squeak or a murmur from me, too frightened to face my tormentor and even more terrified of crying out for help through fear of disrupting Bernie's lesson.

It seemed as though a fat posterior extruding through a hole in a plastic school chair was just too enticing for a devious bastard like Stephens. Jamming a compass point between the sole and leather upper of his Dr Martens boot had proved an interesting experiment, but after the first right jab with no resultant counterpunch, the continued attacks became irresistible.

The bell signalling the end of my ordeal sounded and with the panic-stricken disorientation of a boxer emerging after a pounding on the ropes, I shuffled my way out to the boys' room to survey the damage. All done without a backward glance or a flicker of recognition of the assault. "Never show them you're hurting boys," had been our rugby master's advice, and having blanked him throughout the attack there was no way I was going to allow Stephens to see the physical and emotional turmoil he had just wreaked.

I locked the cubicle door and pulled down my trousers. The tail of my cotton shirt and the top of my white Y-fronts were speckled red, some of the blood coagulated and stuck to my skin. The strangest thing was not the concern about Stephens's multiple epidurals but what my mother would make of it. A born-in-the-blood worrier, I had no doubt that on discovering the evidence in the washing basket she would immediately jump to irrational conclusions – piles, rectal bleeding, etc., would be spouted before the inevitable physical examination which, of course, would reveal the random array of pinpricks. No, the evidence must be destroyed and self-applied first aid administered. That settled in my mind, I folded my hankerchief in two and hung it over the elastic waist band of my Y-fronts. Readjusting myself, I drew a deep breath in self-assurance of a job well done and opened the cubicle door.

My first realisation that all was not as it should be was when I noticed that the lobby door had been wedged from the inside.

'Mmm, strange not done by me and no windows open for a prankster to have escaped.'

"You took your time, you fat bastard!"

There was hardly time for me to spin around before Stephens grabbed my shirt and in one swift movement pulled my face to his whilst thrusting his knee into my groin. The look on his face was alarming; one of sheer hate, his features contorted into a weird mass of furrows, twitches, perspiration and acne, his eyes squint-like and black as coal. As my nether regions gradually radiated their trauma to the rest of my core I wilted and fell to the floor. Following one last knee movement to the kidney area my assailant parted swiftly, the inner lobby door closing slowly, silently and innocently, misrepresentative of the ill-wind that had just blown through. Rolled up into the foetal position, the excruciating pain caused me to throw up. It must have been five minutes before my senses ebbed back. I opened my eyes and, through the tears, took in the beauty of the marbled green thermoplastic floor tiles from my lowly vantage point.

"What the hell is going on here then, boy?" A voice echoed around the lavatory as the new school caretaker, on one of his break-time smoking raids, emerged heroically.

Having endured three years of Buck, I had never associated

compassion with the job so was relieved when he gently sat me up and got me breathing slowly and deeply.

"You've been had by Stephens, haven't you, boy? Nasty little bastard, that lad. Deserves a bloody good thrashing himself." My good Samaritan summarised succinctly as he passed me a paper towel to wipe my eyes and face.

"I'm not sure, sir. It was so quick, I didn't see his face," was my limp response.

"He'll only have you again boy, and the next time it will be worse. We'll go and see the Head now and we can put a stop to this."

"I really don't know, sir."

"Don't know it was Stephens or don't know that you want to grass?"

"I couldn't see for sure who it was, sir."

At that point the school bell gave its five second death rattle signalling the end of the break. The brief session of counselling ended without further comment or gesture. Like an automaton responding to a master's remote call, the caretaker was gone.

Had I missed my gilt-edged chance to chop this insidious growth at root level?

Chapter 3

Round 2

late October 1976

A S with most quarry, you are invariably completely unaware of being stalked until the hunter strikes. I hadn't forgotten (how could I?) the classroom assault and subsequent crotch crunching of six weeks before, but as the time passed without repeat incursions, I became less vigilant and began to believe that Stephens had moved on. Maybe he had, as I had spotted him from afar on a number of occasions pinning other unsuspecting victims against a wall, no doubt nicking tuck shop money or stationery or just 'dusting up' someone if they had a pristine schoolbag or trendy clothing.

However, what I had not factored into the equation was that Stephens was a multitasker and could hunt different prey at the same time; not simultaneous group beatings but isolated attacks on several individuals who were on his hit-list and just happened to stumble into his zone. I'm not saying that he was an assiduous planner but certainly his deeds had an element of forethought and planning. How, otherwise, could he have ended up with a protractor point in the front of his Dr Martens the last time he had fixed me as a target?

Despite his 'I don't give a toss' persona, Stephens was a highly intelligent, devious bastard who managed to do the bare minimum of school work, on most occasions having made one of his minions do the assignments. It was so obvious, but the staff just failed to haul him in and question his understanding of topics. Perhaps, being aware of his reputation, they were prepared to look the other way. His family were builders going back several generations and through decades of success, big players in the local community, both commercially and socially. Not exactly a licence to behave as they wished, but they had been known to obtain planning permission for development schemes where other applicants had been flatly refused. Stephens's air of supreme confidence and invincibility may have been nurtured from within a close-knit family unit so used to getting what they wanted but, even then, behaviour bordering on psychosis was difficult to understand. Not that his prey, whether skewered on the end of his boot or held by the throat or testicles, were in any position to query such a conundrum whilst in the throes of passing out.

When it arrived I was not ready for Round 2 of this one-sided affair. Having spent much of the lunch break on the far-most school field sitting playing Formula 1 Top Trumps, it was with huge delight that the end-of-break claxon remained silent – yippee, a staff meeting!

"Hey, Hambers, haven't you got a new pack of Top Trumps that we've not played before?" enquired one of the gamers.

"Yeah, but they're back in my locker and that's miles away."

"Not if you go through the trees and across the bottom rugby pitch. You'll be gone and back in five minutes."

"Good idea, I hadn't thought of that. See you in a bit."

Not quite knowing when the claxon might stir again, I bustled along until I reached the corner of the woods. The dense tree canopy meant that it was quite dark compared to the bright sunshine out on the field. I hesitated momentarily, but as it was only about 100 metres across to the rugby pitch I broke into a trot and pressed on. Midway through the woods, I thought that I spotted a figure dart back behind one of the large oak trees 20 metres ahead. Despite being in close proximity to the main school grounds, this place was still a haunt for students grabbing a crafty fag. Teachers were usually on patrol during school breaks, but today with the staff meeting they had other priorities. What better place and time for smokers to indulge themselves and stick two fingers up to the staff.

Intent on completing the first leg of my expedition as quickly as possible, I continued.

"Ha ha, fatso, you have incredible timing. Just the type of ponce I've been waiting for. Come here you slug and try this!"

I swept around to see Stephens step out from behind the oak tree, followed by Penneluna and Beswetherick, two of his trusty henchmen. Before I had time to think of making a bolt for the field, I found myself in the familiar position of inspecting Stephens's nasal hair as he grabbed me by the throat, forcing me up against the tree, my head hitting the substantial trunk with a resounding thud. His breath stank of nicotine and spearmint. Quite a curious flavour of chewing gum, I pondered for a millisecond, but one unlikely to be adopted by Wrigley's.

Cocking his head to one side, Stephens grunted at Penneluna and Beswetherick who positioned themselves either side of me.

"OK boys, let's have a bit of fun with this saddo. Just as I showed you at the Boys Club last night."

"Right on, Stevo. I've got the gear. What do you want to try out? Banger or Air Bomb Repeater?"

"Bloody hell, Bess, are you mad? We don't wanna launch the fat bastard into the Head's office!" Stephens sarcastically implored.

"OK, just a banger to get us going then, Stevo," Bes announced.

"What's your favourite fag, slug?"

"What? Uh, uh, I don't smoke and never have," I offered with obvious trepidation.

"Ooooh, we're a good little boy, aren't we? Well, don't worry, we'll get you started today, just the one, then you'll never want another. . . if you live, that is!"

Oh yes, Stephens was enjoying this immensely. A dark little spot with no easy way out, a terrified victim and two dim-witted assistants egging him on.

And with that, the grip around my throat tightened still further causing me to gag and gurgle.

"Open wide, fatty, time to light up my day," taunted Stephens, beckoning his grinning assistants to grab my arms. At this point and to my utter surprise, I completely lost it. There was no way I was going to let this sadistic son of a bitch blow my head off! Catching

Penneluna and Beswetherick off guard, I somehow managed to push both of them away. However, this only served to irritate Stephens who punched me hard in the stomach, knocking every bit of wind out of me. Reliving the desperate search for air induced by my chief tormentor in the boys' toilets the previous month, I fell to my knees and then onto my side, curling into a ball.

"You fucking chicken. Get up and take your medicine!" screamed Stephens.

Even if I wanted to, I couldn't reply. All I could muster was a wide-eyed, open-mouthed squeak as my diaphragm refused to budge.

"Right, now he's down and gasping for a smoke, shove that thing in his gob and light it up, Penny."

As my midriff began to release its stranglehold, the squeak became a gasp and I managed to get my first full breath. I was not going to suffocate after all. My wave of relief was short-lived as Stephens grabbed my hair and yanked back my head.

"Go on, get on with it!" Stephens gesticulated to Penneluna.

For the first time I detected an air of reluctance from his sidekick. My semblance of a fight back may just have delayed their best laid plans and, clearly, there was now some degree of urgency to get the deed done.

"Get on with what bit, Stevo?"

"The fucking banger, you idiot!" screamed Stephens, by now with prominent veins appearing on the side of his head, "Oh, for fuck's sake, just give it to me!"

Snatching the firework from a motionless Penneluna, Stephens stuffed his other hand into his bomber jacket, clawing for his matches, only to fumble, drop the part opened box and scatter the contents across me and the woodland floor.

Even from my perilous supine position, I could see that he was wobbling – not completely in his conviction to cause harm but, unmistakably, this tyro was losing his control. His much vaunted vice-like grip on proceedings and indomitable air of self-assurance was dissolving in front of our very eyes. Were the potential repercussions of this odious act suddenly dawning on him? He had come this far so why stop at blowing someone's face off? Perhaps

Stephens had a conscience after all or maybe, just maybe, this bungled operation had whipped away his cloak of invincibility and, with it, the malicious intent.

I had never considered myself a particularly fortunate person, but as the delayed lunchtime claxon finally sounded across the school grounds, I could not help but count my blessings. I was probably one of only a few pupils who were delighted to hear it!

The brief respite was brought to a crushing halt as a Dr Martens boot hovered over me for effect and then stamped down on the side of my head. The downward pressure stayed applied whilst he offered his final words of advice.

"One word about this to anyone, you sad shit, and you're dead meat!"

I said nothing as my senses dimmed.

Chapter 4

Fight, fight, fight...
mid-November 1976

IT'S strange how some incidences turn out to be so pivotal in one's life. The series of beatings at the hands and feet of my chief tormentor had left their marks, both physically and emotionally, but my defiance not to just roll over during his latest attack had, paradoxically, given me some backbone. There was no strutting about the place as if I'd slain the dragon and everyone should know it. After all, the ambush in the woods was a private affair, but the brief sight of Stephens's soft underbelly had somehow instilled a belief that I would no longer be his or anyone else's punchbag nor a figure of fun.

For weeks I had endured the most harrowing period of my young life. An ever present sense of blackness hovering over me was hardly the perfect grounding for my formative years. Perhaps the caretaker's words were wise ones. Grass up my arch enemy and that'd be it sorted out once and for all. The trouble was that I doubted that would be the case. In a lot of people's eyes, Stephens was untouchable and so vicious that retribution, whether on the school grounds or somewhere else, was considered a distinct possibility. I also worried that on discovering her boy's turmoil, my mother would erupt and do something completely irrational. Being of Mediterranean descent and feverishly protective of her brood, despite her diminutive presence, she would blow her top when the state of equilibrium was threatened. I just could not bring myself to put her or my father through that, so did my best to consign all the anxieties and darkness to the back of my mind once home. Whilst I was a reluctant sportsman, the grazes and bruises could always be put down to PE, plus an ability to focus on school homework would allow me to avoid addressing the issue. This in itself became the coping mechanism. Arrive home, mumble a few words as to how the day had gone, eat dinner, mumble a bit more and then lock myself away for hours, poring over assignments. Throughout this ritual, Stephens's face would intermittently pop up and interrupt my train of thought. At least here in my 9'x6' bedroom I was in control and, mentally, he could be pushed back into his dark little underworld.

Three weeks had passed since my latest pounding so I was vigilant but, understandably, on edge. One of my best friends from Trelander, Kenny Tregaskis, might have been aware of what I was going through but not the full extent of it. We had become great pals, living on the same estate and both sharing a love of fishing and trains. To top it all, we had both been selected for Redruth Grammar School so spent even more time together, including commuting the 10 miles from Truro.

Much to our delight, this had initially started with us using British Rail, only for this to be scuppered after Teague and Clemo upturned the waste bin at Redruth station. Nothing particularly dangerous in that, except that 'Pongo' Coles had been squashed into it and rolled screaming along the full length of the platform, arms flailing into luggage and innocent bystanders. To be honest, the ban had been a long time coming as previously Trego, in being encouraged to try his first cigarette, had inadvertently set fire to one of the carriage seats, and then there was Luckall's total obsession with the 'communication cord' which he sought to pull at least once a fortnight. In his defence, it did say "Pull the chain', albeit under the word 'ALARM'!

"Would the Truro train boys please stay behind after assembly," was a regular announcement by the Head.

After countless tight-lipped, shoulder shrugging huddles of thirty boys and the resultant indiscriminate canings, the powers that be

34

made the decision that the train was no longer for us and we were to travel to Redruth on Western National double decker buses. Not really a stroke of genius, given that Luckall now had several bells and an emergency door with which to fixate, Teague & Clemo discovered Pongo 'planters' aplenty at the bus depot and Trego delighted in the fact that he now had adequate cover to perfect his newfound habit as we were with Joe Public collectively chain-smoking the whole journey.

It was about this time that Kenny decided on an extreme makeover. Since our early days at the grammar school, he'd had a silky pageboy haircut which, combined with a prominent hooter, tall gangly physique and an unusually large triangular briefcase, meant Kenny already had a distinctive image. So, even after we had joined the comprehensive ranks, it came as something of a surprise when one Saturday morning he turned up on my doorstep adorned with a black leather jacket, white high-necked collared shirt, boot lace tie, high-waist drainpipe black trousers and leather creepers. To top it off, shorn of the pageboy locks, he proudly sported greased-up black hair combed back in a Teddy Boy style.

"What do you reckon then?" enquired Kenny, smiling broadly from ear to ear.

"Woh, what the hell happened to you Ken?" I uttered open-mouthed, completely taken aback by the vision in front of me.

"I've got Fonzarelli-itis, mate!"

"What, uh, the heck is that?"

"You know? The Fonz on Happy Days?" And as if to justify his bewildering transformation, splaying both feet and flexing at the knees, Ken stuck out his thumbs and offered a rather convincing, "Heeyyyy, Cunningham!"

"Oh, right, I get you now Ken. I thought you were trying to be Alvin Stardust!"

"Nope, The Fonz has arrived in Truro. Like the great man, I intend to conduct a similar moral code and stick up for those who can't defend themselves."

Inwardly, I welcomed the thought of my own enforcer working for good against evil but, given that Kenny was so mild mannered and kind-hearted, I wondered just how far his campaign could go.

Moderately reassured that I would be in the presence of a well meaning vigilante, on the Monday morning we set off on the 15 minute walk to the bus depot. We always got there early so that we could go upstairs and grab the front seats right above the driver's cab. Not only would we get the best view of the countryside as the bus wound its way around the villages of Chacewater, St. Day, Carharrack and Lanner picking up pupils from the mining and farming communities, but we could open the front fanlights and waft some of the cigarette smoke back to those who had produced it; invariably Sixth Formers who'd nabbed the back seats.

Forty-five minutes later, our trusty old Western National workhorse pulled up in the school car park and the process of unloading the unruly rabble from the top deck began. Our penalty for having the best seats was that no one from the back of the bus would ever let us onto the stairs before them so we had got used to staying put until everyone else had disembarked. Perhaps it was Kenny's Brylcreem-laden, gleaming bonce that proved irresistible but there could be no justification for the violation of his reinvented persona.

"Ouch, shit, I'm on fire!" shrieked Ken, flapping at his immaculately styled hair-do.

"Oh God, what's up mate?" I shouted, startled by his distress.

"Someone's stubbed their fag out on my head! Jeez, it hurts like hell." Ken grimaced.

"Who was it Ken?"

"I don't know. I just didn't see it coming."

"Even the Fonz doesn't have eyes in the back of his head, I guess."

At that moment I glanced down looking for assistance from one of the teachers on parking duty and caught sight of Trego standing in front of us flicking a V-sign. Call it red mist, call it black fog, whatever, something just grabbed me with such rage that I sprung to my feet, did a 360 degree turn off the bench seat, barged my way to the head of the stairway and sluiced past everyone down to the tarmac. Quick as my disembarkation was, Trego had already turned and was walking with a swagger towards the Sixth Form centre. I had seen that sort of mischief from him before but nothing so brazenly arrogant or hurtful.

By then I was trembling with a deep-rooted anger and, oblivious to all around me, broke into a sprint. Just as he'd done to poor Kenny, Trego did not see the attack coming from behind. Being two years older than me, he was bigger and stronger, but unable to withstand a tackle to the back of the knees. He fell heavily to the ground and, on reflection, rather fortunately landed on his school bag to soften his landing. 'Underhand' had never been a phrase laid at my feet but, whilst Trego was face down and clearly stunned, I straddled his back and rained down punches to his head. For once, my membership of the Fat Boys' Club would pay dividends as Trego remained prone. I said nothing. I heard nothing. I made no sounds. Was this out-of-body experience the sort of exhilaration that Stephens felt whilst delivering his bag of dirty tricks?

". . . . . . .fight, fight, fight, fight, fight, FIGHT!" the baying mass chanted as my senses slowly returned. As the mist dissipated, the punches diminished to powder-puff pats and I sat up, apologetically looking down at what I had done to Trego.

"What the hell is going on here? All of you get back out of the way!" screamed Harold Stevens, our PE teacher and rugby coach, from outside the ring of chanters.

Reluctantly they parted and into the makeshift arena strode Harold, bristling with irritation that his week was getting off to such an unsavoury start. The look on his face as I peered up, perched on Trego's back, was one of incredulity.

"You! You're the last person I'd expect to see scrapping like a yob. You're a church mouse on the sports field."

"I'm sorry, sir, but Trego attacked Kenny and, uh, er. . . I, uh, lost my temper, sir."

"Get up now and come with me to see the Head and explain your disgraceful actions, boy." Harold demanded as he grabbed my left ear and pulled me off a ranting Trego.

"Save your breath, son. The Head will want to see you too."

Trego stopped for a few seconds, but then, presumably to stave off complete humiliation, took a wild swing at me as he was getting up, catching me a glancing blow right under the nose. It was enough to split my nostril but, other than a slight stagger, I stayed upright glaring at Trego's illegal blow after the bell. As the claret began to flow down my shirt I couldn't have cared less. I had done it. For the first time, I had stood up to a hooligan. Kenny 'The Fonz', had found his assistant vigilante.

"Right, that's done it for you, Trego!" Harold shouted and in the blink of an eye he'd attached himself to one of my assailant's sideburns, lifting his head to one side. Trego immediately went silent with a cock-eyed facial expression signifying his total surrender.

Spotting his fellow sports master, Roger, getting out of his car, Harold shouted across for assistance.

"Roger, can you lend me a hand here, pard?"

Handing over Trego's sideburn to his colleague, he pointed in the direction of the main school building.

"He's OK, just a bit roughed up, but he needs to see Arthur and explain why he's taking cheap shots after I've told him to lay off. Add to that, he's reeking of fags."

"No problem, Harold, just leave him with me. We've had a few problems with you before, haven't we Treggers? I'm sure that Arthur will love to warm up his caning arm first thing on a Monday!" announced Roger as he turned to lead Trego away, still held by his facial hair.

"This one's a mess so let me see to his face in the sports hall."

Sitting in the sports medical room on a Monday morning with blood dripping off my chin felt rather surreal. Never had I felt so invigorated by my actions. There was not a shred of guilt that I had hurt a fellow human being nor was I the slightest bit concerned that I would inevitably be frog marched to the Head's office for a thrashing. Perhaps this was Stephens's drug and how he felt after each of his invidious attacks.

Harold had given me the silent treatment walking from the crime scene to the medical couch and then, stone faced, just left me there with a handful of tissues to reflect on what I'd done. Twenty minutes later he returned with a completely different demeanour.

"Right boy, I've had a chat with Roger who's just sat through ten minutes of Trego blubbing. Fortunately for him, and you, the Head is attending a conference today. Turns out that Trego had a total breakdown and admitted to smoking on the bus and hurting your friend with the fag end. Whilst I do not condone your response, I can understand your anger towards him, but can you explain to me why you assaulted him." Harold stood right in front of me and raised his greying eyebrows, inviting my reply.

"Sorry but I can't, sir. I just seemed to be on auto-pilot from the moment I saw Trego flicking two fingers up at Kenny after what he had done to him."

"That's not a good enough reason. You'll have to learn to control that blind rage or you're going to find life very trying."

This, I sensed, was the moment to get the monkey off my back.

"Not like Stephens then, sir?"

"What's he got to do with anything, lad?" barked Harold, looking puzzled by the sudden change of direction in his line of enquiry.

I dabbed my nose again as the congealed blood began to block the nostrils and, breathing in deeply through my mouth, I revealed the underlying thread behind my previous comment.

"He's been beating me up for weeks sir and, umm, I think, all the frustration just came out today."

"Well, that's news to me lad, but this is clearly your lucky week! Stephens got himself into real trouble last Friday after Mr Greenslade caught him lighting a banger in someone's mouth just around the back of the science block. Turns out they were all duds. Of course the poor lad, a fresher, had no idea and ended up soiling himself before fainting. He would probably have got away with it but for the intervention of Mr Greenslade who was in his lab and heard the commotion."

"Sounds kind of familiar, sir. Is the fresher alright?"

"Not sure lad as they kept him in Treliske Hospital over the weekend. Unfortunately, he'd whacked his head and had a fit."

"Oh my God, that's awful, sir. And what about Stephens, will he be off for long?"

"Regrettably, he won't be back here as the Head has said that this will be a permanent expulsion not a suspension."

My heart leapt at the realisation of a Stephens-free existence.

Chapter 5

Rugby Fledgling
early December 1977

DESPITE having been thrown the oval ball during my early grammar school days, rugby had never really grabbed me by the adrenals as it had done for so many of my testosterone fuelled peers and as a result I had never played a competitive match. However, the new comprehensive system meant that every Friday afternoon throughout the autumn/winter terms was dedicated to the game, which for me led to a disheartening trudge from the warmth of the sports hall onto the school pitches, invariably lashed by the Cornish gales and horizontal rain.

At the time, I was soft, overweight, lacking confidence and devoid of any desire to compete. Such fundamental inadequacies, of course, meant that I was corralled to the corner of the field with other lost souls. Harold, our coach, was an ex-County and Barbarians player and not inclined to suffer fools and donkeys. That said, he was very well-respected and had an uncanny knack of identifying and nurturing young sporting talent and melding the most unlikely rag-tag bag of individuals into winning teams.

Being almost sedentary and graced with the requisite ballast, I was about to be introduced to the dark underworld of front row forward play.

"Right, you look like a tight head," Harold declared, pointing to me, after reinforcing the rules, objectives and ethos of the game and running a couple of non-contact sessions of simple ball skills.

'Tight head,' I mused, sounds nice and tidy, perhaps even warm and dry, the sort of place where I could get away with doing very little and keep my pristine ironed kit clean and dry. Certainly it had more of an allure than 'loose head' and 'blind side' that went the way of Bee and 'Doris' Sleightholme respectively, who both looked equally bemused to think that they had any place to play in this rugby pantomime. How appropriate those positions were though, as in the coming months, Bee would regularly lose his head and go absolutely demented when his face got planted in the mud by his opposite number and Doris, despite having a fine engine, unfortunately had the vision of a badger. I simply lost count of the number of times he screamed 'mine' under the high ball only for it to land 20 yards behind him!

And so the day came when Harold's Odds and Sods were to go into battle. Gone were the days of touch tackling, uncontested scrums and hot potato passing routines. Harold found time out of his busy 1st and 2nd XV schedules to preside over a full contact 3rd v 4th XV trial match, just a week before our real baptism of fire. We all knew each other quite well and my simple logic suggested nothing worse than a game of British Bulldog in fancy kit.

When it came to my first scrum, I was pleased to see Booth, my old mate from the Fat Boys' Club, packing down behind me. The only problem was that as he proceeded to lean his considerable bulk against my rear end, the combined weight and energy from the opposition pack led to me experiencing an extraordinary close up examination of my scrotum accompanied by a strange gurgling sound from within my midriff! This mind-boggling feat, achieved with me some three foot off the ground, took no more than five seconds to complete and ended with an ultra-concerned Booth gently lowering me to my feet.

"What the hell happened there, Hambo?" he asked quizzically.

"No idea, but can you lean on someone else next time Booth!"

At this point Harold emerged on my right earlobe, puce with rage, snorting like a sergeant major who had just caught two squaddies slacking on manoeuvres.

"For heaven's sake you two, this is not an audition for Come Dancing! You're meant to push horizontally not vertically!" he shouted, nigh on a force 8 on the Beaufort Scale, which merely served to force me closer to Booth's consoling frame.

"Now get yourselves over there and join the rest of this shambles."

"Yes sir, sorry sir," was the reply in unison as we set off in search of team mates afar.

". . .and both of you stay behind and see me after," rumbled Harold as he sped off, having spotted that a scuffle had broken out during his absence.

"Beeeeeeeeeeeeeee, put him down, lad!!" screamed Harold.

Fifty minutes of heavy panting and numerous re-inspections of my testicles later, I stood crestfallen on parade in front of Harold. Booth, for some reason, was summarily dismissed without so much as a swipe across the back of his legs with Harold's whistle.

"Son, I've seen your sort many times before and haven't bothered to waste my breath," Harold started, not even bothering to look at me initially. Then, fixing his eyes on mine; ". . .but, despite what you did to Trego the other week, there's something in you that I like."

'Like!' I thought. 'What had I done to deserve that?'

"You took a total pasting out there boy, but got on with it and actually started to get the hang of it. If we can harness that latent aggression and get some of that puppy fat off you, we might just get you to enjoy the benefits of this wonderful game. Get yourself showered and changed, and don't forget: 4pm kick-off next Friday – you're playing tight head prop for the 2nd XV!"

Chapter 6

Derrick
early December 1977

THROUGHOUT my childhood, I had been blessed by the love of my immediate family and, thanks to my father being from such a large family, a wonderful clan of aunts, uncles and cousins. As owning an automobile was at a premium, most of the kids on the estate tended to stay put and amuse themselves on the playing field or out in the glorious Cornish countryside which provided an abundance of natural playgrounds of great beauty and fascination. However, as a teenager, due to my almost total loss of self-esteem, I tended to hang around with my older cousins. Their level of maturity at least allowed me to get involved in whatever they were doing without the inevitable snide remarks and physical abuse I had had to endure from my own age group.

Out of this band of 'brethren' emerged the most unlikely, but very welcome, broad shoulders of support. I say unlikely only because my cousin, Derrick, was seventeen years my senior, worked alongside my father at the sawmill, and when not immersed in his world of jigsaws, Clint Eastwood videos, country and western music and football, could be found sampling the dubious delights of Truro's many hostelries. A huge man in stature but, at times, immature at heart, Derrick was a wonderful character, perma-clad in his beloved red Liverpool FC tracksuit. Our Der singlehandedly coached every young lad on the estate who showed any semblance of footballing ability. Out there in all winds and weathers, the finest football brain ever to come out of Trelander could be seen directing hordes of youngsters hither and thither; a logistical nightmare for any FA qualified coach let alone a guy whose encyclopaedic tactical nous had been gleaned from Match of the Day, *Shoot* Magazine and a sheer fanaticism for the game.

"I'm gonna lose some of this weight and get my coaching badge, Cuz," would be his weekly mantra. We all knew him well so, despite his undoubted desire and dreams, no one was surprised to hear that Derrick had once again been found curled up on a park bench after another beer and spirit fuelled binge.

Why, it occurred to me, could this intelligent, funny and ultimately very caring and generous man let his demons out of the bottle so often? Utterly focused and devoted to his beloved footie, how could he so completely lose sight of the ball? Most people in the town, who just knew him as Louie (his middle name was George so I wondered if it came out of respect for his Uncle Louis who died during the war) viewed this delightful man as almost childlike in his mannerisms and outlook on life. Yes, OK, he had an affinity for coconut mushrooms and Mars bars and a propensity for rat-a-tat one line joke telling, but he was no fool. Maybe his generosity, humour and caring nature, intertwined with his dishevelled appearance, occasional recklessness and fixations, contrived only to skew people's perceptions of him. And yet out of this habitual madness came a key phase in a young boy's formative years.

"What's up Cuz, you look like you've got the weight of the world on your shoulders?" enquired Derrick, at the same time holding out a crumpled bag of coconut mushrooms.

"No thanks, Der," I said, holding up my hand firmly to deflect the pull of temptation.

"Blimey, you are off colour, Cuz. Come on, tell me what's happened."

"Well, nothing really. I suppose it's what might happen that's the problem," I offered quietly, head down and shoulders slumped. "I've got to play rugby for the school this coming Friday."

"Well that's great, what an honour. What's so bad about that?"

Derrick enthused whilst tossing a few more mushrooms down the hatch.

"I'm too fat, too slow and worried that I'll let them down. Harold's a good coach, but to be honest I haven't a clue what I've got to do."

Derrick thought for a moment, chomping throughout.

"Right, I tell you what, Cuz. We are both going to start to get into shape here and now. We'll show 'em all. I'll do that FA coaching course and you'll prove your rugby teacher's faith has not been misplaced."

And with that Derrick rolled up his bag of mushrooms, stuffed them inside his tracksuit, pulled up his trackie bottoms revealing an alarmingly large white paunch, and made off for the exit from the playing field.

"Come on Cuz," he beckoned without turning. "We are going to go for a run around Four Acres."

'What, me. . .' I thought, *'. . .and you, Derrick, running together? People will think we are bonkers!'*

And that's how it all started. Maybe not every day in Derrick's case, as he'd be just too distracted by the lure of the estate football pitch, but certainly for me daily runs out through the country lanes upon returning from school became routine. The first few weeks, particularly that first day, were extremely hard but utterly hilarious. There we were, a small rotund boy lumbering alongside a jolly red giant. Throughout the wheezing, belching, farting and frequent stops to admire the views, came an almost non-stop stream of one liners that even Bob Monkhouse would have been proud of. Humour aside, frankly, it was quite alarming to pull up at the end, look back and see Derrick's hulk-like frame barely shuffling forward, tracksuit drenched in sweat and a face so red that you'd have believed he'd been around the two mile circuit at least 20 times.

"Are you alright, Der, you look awful?" I said as he staggered to a halt some minutes later.

"Dodgy beer last night, Cuz. Giving my guts hell," he huffed, letting out yet another colossal belch. "Don't worry, this is just the start. It's always hard training up a thoroughbred from scratch!"

"Let's sit on the swings and get our breath back. Maybe plan a better way of getting that horse back to fitness," I offered, genuinely concerned that he wouldn't be able to walk that far.

"Yeah, good idea Cuz. Fancy a coconut mushroom?"

That one run did little for my short-term fitness and certainly contributed nothing towards my performance in the rugby match at the end of the week. What it did, however, was instil in me a sense of freedom and achievement, no matter how small, and an overwhelming desire to cast off my self-imposed shackles. A sort of awakening, I suppose. Not really just a faint realisation that my physical being could be as good as anyone else's, but a meteoric rise in levels of self-belief.

The rugby for the remainder of that term continued in a decidedly Sunday League vein, but there were tell-tale signs that this cheap basement store was about to yield a bargain. Gradually there would be less walking about the park, gasping and looking for the school clock to work out when the final whistle would come, and certainly a lot less apprehension about locking horns with bigger lads of my age.

Spring turned to summer, and those two mile trudges turned into five and six mile varied and structured runs, and always through the most breathtaking havens of natural beauty. The waters of the River Fal encroached twice daily into the upper reaches of the estuary just three-quarters of a mile from Trelander. The smell of the tidal water and blossom making a potent, intoxicating and re-energising mix as I ran along the waterside track with the sun glinting through the tree canopy. For the first time in my teenage years, life felt good and, with a much fitter Kenny taking over as training partner, my body began to respond by shedding the pounds. The layers of darkness that had shrouded me for so long began to fall away.

Chapter 7

Chrysalis
early September 1979

ANOTHER autumn term commenced, and the long haul from Truro to Redruth began again in earnest, but this was not just another regular school year for me, as I had experienced a metamorphosis over the previous 12 months, particularly the spring and summer of '79 when Kenny and I trained hard almost every day. I distinctly remember the looks as I wandered into lectures after the summer break, not only from my peers but also my tutors. The quizzical 'what the hell's happened to him' double-takes were plentiful. The obvious thought may have been 'gosh, he's shot up', but the fact was that the shedding of three stone from a young stubby frame had triggered a vertical release to such an extent that I was comfortably over six foot tall.

Rugby was again to intervene and reinforce my newfound status. Sporty teenagers in our area tended to either mass as surfers, footballers or rugby players so, broadly, you needed to slot in with one of those groups in order to get respect. Aside from my physical appearance, Harold, with his astute eye, had seen the change in my confidence level and set about his next project with gusto.

"Got your head sorted then, John?" he enquired with the hint of a knowing smirk as we gathered for the first of the season's training sessions. Just to be on first name terms with Harold signalled a quantum leap upward in his hierarchy.

"You look lean and fit; although you're bordering on being too light for the front row now so we'll need to bulk you up!" was his next offering as he circled me, surveying the emerging physique with almost forensic precision.

'Oh great,' I thought, *'I've just spent six months sweating my rocks off and here's Harold planning a calorie-fest!'*

"Weights and plenty of hill work, that's what you'll need to do for a while. Get off the rest of your puppy fat and beef up your upper body and legs. Running is all well and good, but you're not here for cross country events, John."

A few weeks later, there we were on a wet and windy October afternoon looking up at the long imposing grass slopes which divided three levels of the sports pitches. I say 'we' as Harold had asked the full 1st XV squad to stay on after college. I did, however, think Harold's judgement had gone awry by including me.

Up until now he had never revealed his hand, but standing there in the stiff south-westerly, bobble hat atop his rugby worn face, he announced: "You lads are here tonight because you are going to form the core of the under 18 team that will win us the County Cup this season. In recent years, no side has got anywhere near to dethroning Truro School. Well, that is going to change."

He paused for effect.

"What's more, and I want you to remember this throughout this session, some of you are good enough to represent the County Under 18s side and really put Redruth on the map. It won't fall into your laps but, with hard work, it will happen."

'Me, part of a core group? He's lost it this time!' I thought for a fleeting moment, but the truth was that I was ready and, for the first time, I really wanted it.

On that bleak Cornish evening several of the squad emptied their stomach contents and ended up completely wasted after a gruelling hour. "Nothing more than a series of shuttle runs," Harold had said, but add in the 1 in 4 gradient, numerous exercise stations, and long piggy-back runs, and it was a relentless beasting.

"Good lads, that's the worse one over. It'll get easier over the next five or six weeks," Harold reassured us, his bobble hat now half tilted across his forehead like some mad old seadog.

Mad seadog or not, as a coach, he had what it took all right. Six months later, there we were lapping up the adulation of our school mates, teachers, families and friends in front of the County Ground grandstand. Truro School vanquished, County 18 Group Cup aloft, we had delivered for our beloved Harold.

The combined smell of Cornish sea air, pungent clawing mud, liniment and sweat, and the sound of metal studs on the concrete changing room floor, nervous retching, shouts of encouragement interspersed with expletives, pounding of chests and stomachs and, of course, the customary warm up chant, all made for an intoxicating mix. In Adrian Curtis, we had a skipper of immense ability and respect. He had already been an England trialist at several age groups, but now, at 18, had recently broken into the senior Cornish County side. Ruggedly handsome, supremely fit, graced with great pace and rugby instinct, his 'call to arms' before each game would bring an immediate hush to the pre-match fidgeting and preening.

Encircled by us, arms intertwined tightly, shoulder to shoulder, over the next five minutes in front of our bulging eyes, Curt would transform himself into a snarling rage, grabbing shirt collars, face slapping indiscriminately, spitting and screaming out instructions. The culmination of this ritual being a hair-raising synchronised run on the spot, all studs in time resonating menacingly from the changing room out across the pitch. A message that Harold's charges were enraged, pumped and primed for battle.

The immense pride I felt that day could never be erased, but a few days after the County Final it was bettered when Harold pulled me aside to tell me that I had been selected to play tight head prop for Cornwall against Pembrokeshire in an 18 Group fixture at Redruth. Cornish folk have always been very passionate about their county rugby teams, whatever age group, so I was not surprised to see that a decent crowd had turned up on a Wednesday evening. Harold, one of the selectors, handed me my county tie and badge and then the black and gold Cornish jersey.

"Well done, John, you've earned your selection. Now go out there, suck in the atmosphere and give these Welsh lads a good seeing to." Harold, looked me right in the eye and simmered with pride.

In between the barking of team instructions across the dressing room, I could hear the expectant murmurings of the crowd and the announcements from the tannoy. With five Redruth lads in the team including Curt as skipper, and our hooker being Colin Groves, a fellow Truro Colt and another destined for England honours, the line-up had a familiar feel. That was all brought clearly into focus when Curt began his rousing pre-match ritual, this time with even greater intensity. This was not just for Redruth, this was for the whole of Cornwall!

Redruth's ground has for decades been the scourge of unsuspecting touring teams. Sloping markedly downwards to the southern extremity of the pitch, most Cornish fly halves had perfected a long raking kick to 'Hellfire Corner' from where the forwards would take over, scrummaging and mauling their opponents into submission. On wet and windy days this was the place to be, not out in the backs freezing off your proverbials! Whilst conditions were much more springlike that evening, old habits die hard and, much to the delight of the baying crowd, we still gravitated towards Hellfire, which yielded a brace of tries. In a tight game during which Pembrokeshire gave us a running rugby lesson with their Welsh wizardry, it was the Cornish forward dominance that just held sway.

In the immediate aftermath, I sat quietly satisfied, soaking up the atmosphere. I had just entered the exalted world of Cornish representative rugby. There could be no doubt that it was a huge step up in class, and for much of the first quarter I had my hands full against a strong, squat loose head intent on head butting me into oblivion. Fortunately, my fitness was good and after a lengthy spell at Hellfire late in the game I had felt the fire in his belly subside. In any sport, sensing the moment to drive home the advantage is a huge plus, but in rugby it is paramount when you have established a key field position. Grovesy knew the point at which we had them on toast.

"Come on Hammers. This is the one, get under his chest. Curt has called for an eight man drive."

Tight across the front row, crouching, we felt the weight of the locks and the flankers bind on. There was no head butt this time, more of a nestling gently into position. A mighty call of escalating volume from Curt on the open side flank made the hair on the back of your neck stand up.

'Ready, ready, readyyyyyyyy. . .' And, at the point of the scrum half feeding the ball into the tunnel: "DRIVE!"

The roar of the crowd in the corner said it all. The whole of the Welsh front row lifted off the ground and, with the power coming through from behind us, their scrum folded back over itself. Totally exhilarated (as if the County Final hadn't provided enough), I was well and truly hooked on the game now. That sensation would stay with me week in, week out for 20 years until ending abruptly. Plenty of time though, for a wonderful sport to influence so many facets of a life that until then had been blighted by shyness and acute physical and emotional insecurity.

Chapter 8

Bruv

late April 1980

FROM a very young age, there can be little doubt that I was an irritating distraction for my brother. Except for rainy days spent at home before he was at senior school, we might get on for an hour or two playing Subbuteo or Monopoly with cousin Brian until the point where I'd lose the plot and throw the board in the air after landing on Mayfair with a hotel! The five year age gap was always just too wide to bridge. I loved being around my big brother, but as he began to mature and go off out with his mates, my mother's pleas of "Go on David, take your brother with you," regularly fell on deaf ears. I would sense that he was about to go off somewhere and try to stalk his every move, only to realise too late that he had in fact snuck out of the back door having said that he was going to the loo. The sight of him and his mates on their bikes disappearing over the hill would be the trigger for a total inconsolable meltdown. No amount of colouring books, Fuzzy Felt or painting by numbers could coax me back to normality. My mother despaired and invariably my brain would need recalibrating with a swift backhander, but, in hindsight, as his teenage years arrived, who could blame Dave for his increasingly ingenious Houdini-like disappearances.

However, by the time I was 10, the age gap was narrowing, not numerically but from an escapology angle – I had a bike! A red

Moulton Mini with shopping basket to be precise. With its tiny wheels, disproportionately long frame and tall handlebar/seat stems, it would not have looked out of place in a circus, but I didn't care, I was mobile. Granted, even pedalling like a hamster on steroids, I had absolutely no chance of keeping up with the bigger lads on their racing bikes complete with 5-speed derailleur gears, but I had perfected such an effective style of ear-wigging that I was very happy to let them steal a march. On one occasion my intel caught wind of a fishing expedition down to picturesque St. Clements about a mile from the estate. Playing dumb, I retreated to my bedroom, sneaked a look from behind the curtains and, sure enough, there were the fishing rods tied to the crossbars as the party set off at speed with my brother glancing back a couple of times to check that he hadn't been rumbled. I gave it thirty minutes so as not to alert my mother, grabbed the sandwich on offer and then set off on the understanding that I was just going up to the park for a kick about.

Aside from the stunning river views at St. Clements, there was a large lagoon about half a mile from the village along a dirt track. For decades, kids from our estate had ventured there in search of silver eels, mullet and anything else spring tides had left stranded. Shrouded by trees and rushes, the lagoon provided wonderfully secluded pitches. Unfortunately for Dave, steep fields on two sides meant that even normal voices reverberated back across the water, enabling the source to be pinpointed from the track. Having found a spot near but out of sight of the gang, I scaled a tree and sat patiently watching them fish. Although I was only young, thanks to my father and cousins, I had been fishing for a while with a fair degree of success. On the other hand, Dave had not really done much fishing, preferring football and following his mates' band. After an hour or so, they had drowned a few worms but caught nothing. For one, they were being too noisy for the mullet and secondly, not fishing deep enough to lure the eels from the muddy bottom. Unable to resist my urges any longer, I shimmied back to the ground and wandered nonchalantly across to the group.

"Oi, Dave, look who's here?" announced one of his trusty crew.

"Eh? What?" murmured Dave, who was in the middle of

attending to yet another tangle, glancing around almost as an afterthought.

I had probably been watching too many cartoons, but I am convinced that his eyes protruded on stalks on catching sight of me.

"Oh no! You little shit, how the hell did you find us all the way down here?" blurted my exasperated big bruv.

I said nothing and just sat quietly smiling to myself, biding my time, trying to gauge the right moment for my next move. After five minutes, I sensed that I could speak without fear of being thrown in.

"I'll untangle your bird's nest for you David."

"Get lost! You're in big trouble. I bet Mother doesn't know you've followed me."

Another five minutes passed, during which time the bird's nest took on albatross proportions. I posed the question again.

"Oh, for God's sake. Here you are smart ass, sort that out then!" At which point his rod and reel, complete with its avian creation, landed across my lap and Dave stomped off towards the trees.

He had certainly created a particularly challenging mess. However, following fifteen minutes of painstaking stripping back and untangling, I had the reel fit for use and with brother out of view, decided to alter the tackle. I cadged a barrel lead, swivel and a smaller hook from one of the other lads.

"What are you using as bait, Lionel?"

"Worm."

"What sort?"

"I dunno, they're worms from my Dad's compost heap. Why?"

"You want ragworm for the mullet and the eels will take anything that wriggles if you stick it on the bottom." I cautiously offered without wishing to sound like a know-all. "I'll go get some rag from the mudflats."

Twenty minutes later, I cast out for the first time, nervously looking around for a reprimand from Dave. I need not have worried as I caught sight of him mucking around at the other end of the lagoon where a small overflow tunnel allowed water to cascade down to the tidal water. No sooner had I put the rod onto its rest and crouched down expectantly, than the line tightened and the rod tip arced over to one side. On striking, I knew that I was in trouble. This was no tiddler. If I did manage to get it to the bank and Dave realised I had been using his gear, his trademark heavy punch on the upper arm would be almost inevitable. Whilst I knew that there were time constraints as I had spotted that he'd moved along the lagoon, I was not prepared to rush playing the fish as the equipment was clearly creaking under the strain.

"Blimey, have you got something big on there, Johnnie boy?" remarked Lionel, as he shuffled across between the reeds.

"Yeah, I think it's a big eel, but you'd better take over as David will kill me if he spots me using his rod."

"Don't worry, he's at the other end of the lagoon and, anyway, I won't say anything. Go on, bring it in."

"OK, but if you see him coming please grab the rod off me, Lionel."

With my lookout on high alert, I got back 'in the zone' and over the course of the next 5 minutes gently coaxed my quarry to the bank. Just at that point, I could hear voices coming down through the trees.

"Lionel, quick, take it," I urged, almost throwing the thing at him, just as David emerged onto the waterside.

Cool as they come, in one motion Lionel dropped his tackle and single-handedly caught the rod, and then drew the fish toward the bank.

"Sorry Dave, I couldn't resist re-doing your rig and throwing out another line whilst you were mucking around over there," triumphantly announced Lionel, holding up an impressive silver eel of around 3lbs, winking at me in the process.

"Wow, that is a corker, well done mate."

David seemed genuinely happy, but in a split second normal service had been resumed.

"You still here, you bloody pest!" he directed pointedly at me.

"Yeah, but I was just about to go when Lionel hit into the fish and asked me to help him land it."

"OK, job done. Now bugger off before you get a whack!"

Cycling home I couldn't help but smile. I had temporarily infiltrated David's inner circle, caught their best fish and escaped without repercussions. I'd always liked Lionel!

*   *   *   *

Inevitably, however, the five year age gap would continue to be an unbridgeable impasse for the next few years, particularly during my early teens when normal communication made way for grunts and shoulder shrugs. Combined with the dark days of self-doubt and introversion, many strange traits and habits were beginning to emerge. From the inside looking out, I had no sense of the bizarre, but looking back it's easy to see why there were so many stares and sniggers. Take, for example, one warm September evening in 1975. I had long yearned for a large cassette/radio; the khaki coloured military style ones that preceded the ghetto-blaster. Through my Saturday job, over the best part of a year, I had managed to save enough money to warrant a trip to Currys and the deed was done. After a few evenings entrenched in my bedroom, studying the manual from cover to cover and fiddling with every lever and button, an overwhelming urge came over me.

"Where he goin' boy?" enquired my father, as I trudged off out the back door with my pride and joy perched on my shoulder, arm curled around it as if carrying a piece of lumber from his sawmill.

"Just going out for a walk to test out the reception. Anyway, there's nothing on the telly."

"Daft bugger, why do you need to do that? We're on top of a hill here!" My father looked on incredulously.

Undeterred, off I went. Not somewhere quiet like the middle of a field or by the river. Oh no, this bit of kit was worthy of a full public viewing. For the next two hours I strode purposefully, but in reality aimlessly, around the streets of Truro with my incongruous earpiece blaring out Radio One. Even if passersby or those sitting outside pubs or restaurants were unoffended by the mobile DJ, my attire may have been more of a cause for concern. Tank tops and Oxford bags were all the rage. In the case of the latter, the more buttons on your waistband, excessive bagginess in the legs and voluminous pockets, all the better. Imagine then, the vision of muggins coming down the main street – purple, black and white hooped tank top (complete with belly) shrouding a high collared turquoise shirt, bottle green 9-button bags, white socks

56

and blue trainers. And I had never even seen Tommy in the Pinball Wizard!

Oblivious to the looks I was attracting, I continued my Forrest Gump-like tour of Truro's back streets. Emerging from Cathedral Lane I was 'exposed' briefly onto the main shops of Boscawen Street, before darting left into Squeeze Guts Alley, St. Mary's Place and right down Old Bridge Street to peer into the river, looking for trout drifting in and out of the shallows. Unfortunately for me, this beautiful vantage point where I had spent hours fishing from the bridge with Kenny was smack bang opposite the Barley Sheaf where Dave and his mates happened to be sitting outside the pub. Already fuelled by several pints of Devenish ale, my unexpected arrival merely provided a joyous opportunity for heightened mickey-taking.

"What the hell do you look like, Razzie Mouse?" shouted one of the group (my brother's nickname amongst this group being Razzie), "You auditioning for some sort of village idiot competition?"

It was only then that I spotted Dave with his head down, gently shaking it from side to side, before jumping to his feet and running over to me with a look of utter disbelief.

"Why me! Why the hell did you have to turn up here, you complete prat?" he implored. "Have you got any idea how stupid you look? Now bugger off home and act like a normal person."

In that instant, standing looking at my reflection in a shop window, I realised how weird I must have looked. Resigned to my fate as the butt of his mates' jokes for eternity, I slowly lowered my treasured hi-fi, turned it off and bolted. I finally burnt out my engines about 400 yards from home, slumping to the ground, knees up to my chest and back against the estate's telephone kiosk; the earlier innocent indulgence and pleasure gone, bludgeoned by a sharp shock of reality and ridicule. In dwindling sunlight, I sat there slumped with my head down for a good twenty minutes.

"What's up, cuz? Has someone hurt you?"

The very welcome towering figure of Derrick stood over me. He may not have been everyone's idea of a guardian angel, but he did have an uncanny knack of popping up when I most needed someone's shoulders to cry on.

"No, I've just made a total idiot of myself. No one else's fault but my own." I blubbed, wiping the tears away with the back of my hand.

"Don't worry about it cuz, I do that virtually every day of my life! As long as you're happy and not doing anything wrong, don't listen to the beggars. They'll end up no better than you or I." Derrick consoled me. "Here, have a coconut mushroom."

Willingly, I dipped my soggy hand into the crumpled paper bag. As we walked home slowly, Derrick deflected my negativity and inner turmoil by running through the previous weekend's football results – simple life coaching at its best.

By the time I was approaching 15, there was definitely a thawing of our polar opposites. Whilst Dave and his mates were all in full-time jobs, evenings and weekends were a time for sport or following Aggie Pascoe and his band. Slowly but surely I was being allowed to tag along without my mother having to plead. A huge step forward appeared in the form of a brand new Gray Nicholls cricket bat as a birthday present. Dave must have parted with at least £40 of his hard earned carpenter's wage packet. I had been dropping hints for months but thought that they had fallen on deaf ears. I absolutely loved that piece of willow, to the point that I didn't really want to hit a cricket ball with it, preferring instead to apply linseed oil on it most weeks and sit back and admire it. This couldn't last as the temptation to show it off to the rest of the estate boys became overwhelming. This was a big mistake. Whilst I was putting on the pads (yes, I had pads too), David Webb grabbed my cherished blade and banged in the stumps with the main face! Clearly, I was still heavily traumatised when cousin Brian roared in from the Cemetery End and uprooted my middle stump. To the bemusement of all, I tucked the bat under my arm and walked off home, complete with gloves and pads! Not exactly Don Bradman-esque.

At 17, rugby was beginning to bring me more and more into Dave's domain. He was playing prop for Truro's 1st/2nd teams and I had got into the Colts side. Yet the fixture list and multitude of after-match drinking holes around the county somehow kept us apart. That is until Dave Johnson, the Colts coach, called me over after Monday training in late April and asked me if I would be OK playing second row for Truro 2nd's against St. Ives on the Wednesday evening. My confidence was on the rise and I accepted the invitation without hesitation.

At that time St. Ives were one of the top sides in the county, along with Redruth and Camborne, and possessed some formidable forwards, so I knew that it would be a tough game. Word had clearly got around the club that Dave's little brother was making his senior debut. As I hesitantly walked into the changing room, a sea of beards and oversized sideburns greeted me along with many comforting grins.

"Aye, aye, Horiz, trouble's here!" announced Muscles, one of his front row colleagues and general partner in crime. "Sit your arse over here boy, I need to run you through the line-out calls."

"Bleddy hell, Muscles, give the boy a chance to smell the liniment!" piped up John Nightingale, a club stalwart with a rugged, weather-beaten look of a man who had just conquered Everest.

"Can't take any chances with these cocky Colts, John," chirped Muscles, the 2nd's longstanding hooker who took his rugby very seriously, despite his diminutive stature.

I took my instructions, got myself changed and kept my head down whilst I waited for the team talk and warm-up.

"Right, fags out. On your feet," was a somewhat unconventional opening gambit, at least compared to what I was used to, but the sheer intensity and ferocity of the short warm-up gave every indication that there was a huge challenge awaiting. As we left the clubhouse and jogged through the supporters across to the pitch, Dave drew alongside me.

"You'll be alright, we've got a good side out tonight so St. Ives won't have it all their own way."

'Oh, my God,' I thought, *'Dave's actually spoken to me like we're equals!'*

Ninety minutes later, we were truly brothers in arms. Despite getting smacked across the jaw for fringing, I thoroughly enjoyed my first taste of senior rugby. At 6-6, it was by no means a classic for the spectators, but given the standard of the opposition, we received a rousing round of applause as we left the pitch. Dave slung an arm around my shoulder.

"Well done Bruv, you did well out there."

I was chuffed to bits. Dave probably never knew what that one simple word – 'Bruv' – meant to me.

In the showers afterwards, Brian Chenoweth, the final piece of the front row triumvirate, leant across, "Oi, Vertical, you were alright tonight. Well done boyee."

"Thanks Brian, but why is everybody calling me that? Is it because of my line-out jumping?"

"Christ, no boy, blame your brother for that one. He's Horizontal! Give it a couple of hours in the bar and you'll see why!"

Chapter 9

Langdon's
1975

AS a young lad, my father would take me down into Truro most Saturday mornings. It entailed a well trodden route – Horwoods turf accountants to put on his bets, Tamlyns tobacconists for his smokes, John Langdon's field sports shop for a potter around and finally the British Legion for a few beers (in my case, Corona and crisps on the step outside!). For me though, the highlight had to be the point at which we walked down the wooden ramp into Langdon's. Stacked from floor to ceiling with a vast array of fishing equipment, guns, models, bicycles and tools, and situated on a narrow side street in the shadow of the cathedral, it was an enchanting and hugely popular place. Many, like my father, just ventured in, in the hope of meeting friends and old acquaintances. For me, it was simply a case of wonderment. Glass cabinets with a mesmerising kaleidoscope of colours lined both sides of the shop, seemingly as far as the eye could see, but it was the aroma that gave you the full Langdon's experience. The combined smell of gun oil, fish bait, epoxy resin and general mustiness made for an alluring mix.

In the summer of 1974, my Maltese cousin, Tony, introduced me to trout fishing on the River Allen, which ran across the moors near his housing estate right into the centre of the city. From that point on I was well and truly hooked! Apart from the obvious benefits of

61

spending more time in a healthy countryside environment, it gave me a good excuse to visit Langdon's on a more regular basis. As a result I got to know Paul Taylor, the proprietor, quite well. Apart from his ownership of Langdon's, he ran an insurance company in the city and was also a Justice of the Peace. It was the latter, in his capacity as a magistrate, that we got chatting about the possibility of establishing a club for the young lads who fished the three rivers that converged on Truro. Many came from Trelander and, through cousin Tony, I knew a lot of the lads from the Rosedale Estate who fished the nearby River Allen. It seemed like a really exciting idea, but neither of us could have foreseen how it would develop. Once I'd mentioned it to Kenny and got him on board it quickly gained momentum. The Truro Trout & Freshwater Fishing Club was formed and within a year we had 40 members; all juniors.

At a time when I was woefully short of self confidence, it was my first taste of how creative teamwork could be such a shot in the arm. Monthly meetings were held at Langdon's after closing time with chairmanship duties alternating between Ken and I. In fact, at various times we also acted as Club secretary, treasurer, recorder, press officer and events organiser. Paul, as President, was wonderful in the way that he supported almost everything that we proposed. In effect he had helped us form an alternative type of boys' club with a diverse range of activities. Granted, fishing, in the form of monthly competitions, was very much to the fore, but it was the community work, including charity fundraising events, that regularly got us mentioned in the *West Briton*. The first time we hit the papers followed a weekend when the Club set about cleaning up the lower reaches of the Allen where it snaked through the centre of Truro. Fed up with snagging our lines on all manner of discarded paraphernalia, much to the amusement of the general public, four teams of six, clad with wellies and waders, set about dredging the river. By the end of the task the local photographer had us all lined up next to a large trailer heaped full of builder's rubble, bottles, plastic and scrap metal, including an old bedstead and the obligatory shopping trolley! It was a job well done, but that was only the start of the rise of our public profile.

A few months after the clean-up operation disaster struck. Our much loved little river got badly polluted when a massive quantity of detergent escaped from a local laundry. Ken and I just happened to be hanging around town and decided to venture over to Old Bridge Street to peer down into the river and spot trout. The scene that greeted us was heartbreaking. The crystal clear water we were so used to seeing, swirling and bubbling as it emerged from under the buildings, was eerily silent. The river was dark purple, almost black in the deeper pools, with a sinister grey foam blowing around in the wind. And then, amid our despair, dead or dying fish rolled lifelessly in the current. Our despair was quickly replaced by anger. Thankfully Paul, on one of his days at the shop, was just the right person for us to unload our findings. In addition to all his other skills he knew how to help us put together a campaign and lobby the right people in this sort of situation. Within a matter of days we were talking to the South West Water Authority about the incident. I am not entirely sure what action was taken against the laundry, but for us the priority was in getting the river restocked with brown trout. Ken and I must have been a right couple of irritants as a month later we received confirmation that the Authority had agreed to our request. All great news except that we hadn't quite bargained for several hundred ravenous pellet-fed reservoir monsters being dumped into our cherished rivulet. Word soon got around and most of the stock fish were caught within a matter of weeks, but it provided a great buzz within the Club, added a few new members and once again got us an article in the *West Briton*.

Shortly after that coup, Paul approached Ken and I to see if we would be interested in working at Langdon's on Saturdays and during school holidays. We should probably have played it cool, but it was the proverbial no-brainer for two fishing mad kids. After a brief glance at each other, we grudgingly accepted Paul's offer! On and off, for the next six years we lived the dream. If we had appeared bewitched as customers, it was nothing compared to being on the other side of the counter and having unrestricted access to the shop's inner sanctum. What we could not have realised was that the old property was twice as wide as the frontage would suggest and contained a labyrinth of hidden rooms interconnected by rickety wooden staircases. Behind the hustle and bustle of the shop there was a sense that time had stood still. Oak desks and metal storage cabinets covered in dust and cobwebs were crammed full of vintage sporting goods and associated paperwork. Were it not entirely fascinating, the ambience could have been spooky. Rather than go into Truro for our lunch, Ken and I would grab a pasty and sit in one of the abandoned rooms happily rummaging through the 'artefacts'. If only Ebay had existed back then we'd have made Paul a small fortune!

That was nothing, though, compared to what the property was about to yield up. When new manager, Neil Hall, was brought in to put some energy into the business and refresh the image of Langdon's, a decision was made to extend the shop sideways towards the labyrinth. If floor plans of the property had existed I guess there would not have been too many surprises. I was serving a customer at the fishing counter when I heard a commotion in the adjacent storeroom. I apologised and made my way through just to check that all was well. I could make out Neil, shrouded in dust, hands on hips, standing in front of a large hole where a stud wall had been pulled down.

"Well, will you look at that?" he said, smiling contentedly, Indiana Jones-like.

The air slowly cleared, revealing rack after rack of antique split cane rods and vintage fishing tackle which, alone, would have covered the cost of the building work. Tantalisingly, in the corner, another set of wooden kite winders hinted at the possibility of yet more riches above. The mystique of Langdon's was spellbinding.

Chapter 10

Bert
Summer 1977-1980

BERT Monk hobbled, rather unremarkably, into Langdon's late one Friday afternoon in June 1977, his gnarled silver-capped walking stick clicking metronomically on the concrete floor.

"Good evening young man, I'd like some advice about how to sea fish and where to go. Are you the person to help me?" Bert enquired in a bold London accent as he addressed me at the fishing tackle counter.

He would have been oblivious to a captive audience of Truro Sea Angling Club members who, at that time of the week, inhabited a corner of the fishing section. Rather astutely, Paul had extended our opening hours until 6pm and set up a row of chairs, a kettle, mugs and beverages – in effect, it was an open invitation to come and chew the cud and, of course, spend some of their end of week pay packets! Our sea anglers were a strange bunch. Many would come to Langdon's on a Friday after work to swap tales of 'the big one that had got away', enhance their bragging rights, or just buy a few live ragworm for the weekend, rather than go straight home for their family dinner.

"Yes sir, not a problem. I'd be only too happy to help. What kind of gear have you got?" I enquired, acutely aware that the mob in the corner had already begun their murmurings.

"Well, nothing at all for this neck of the woods. You see, I've just moved down here from Purley and all I have is carp fishing tackle." Bert said, now a little more hushed having detected the nearby snorting.

Perhaps because of my own circumstances, even at 15, I could sense his unease at the presence of our resident bully boys. My next line surprised not only myself but also took the wind out of the mob's sails.

"Tell you what sir, we're about to till up for the evening, but how about you meet with me and my mate, Kenny, down at Dynamite Quay this evening? We can show you the gear we've got and the methods we use and we can take it from there. What do you, er. . . reckon?" I paused briefly, wondering if I had been a bit too forward.

"Bert Monk," he announced and stuck out his right hand. "That'd be absolutely splendid."

For the next three years, this unlikely trio became inseparable when weekend sea fishing competitions were held. It turned out that Bert was 78. A retired civil engineer who had just had enough of the Big Smoke and decided to fulfil a lifetime dream and resettle in Cornwall; a venue for 50 years of happy family holidays. As teenagers, Kenny and I were incredibly fortunate to hitch up with such a kind, considerate and wise old boy. Heaven only knows how our team must have looked to other competitors registering for the events.

There was Bert with his hunched frame sporting a full length waxed coat, chest waders and braces, Tweed deerstalker hat and black thick-rimmed glasses astride his hangdog face which also accommodated a large white moustache and his trademark Lee Van Cleef style pipe. To cap it all, and here was the big surprise, Bert drove a bright green 3-litre Ford Cortina Mk3, complete with tinted glass, spoilers, go-faster stripes and oversized alloy wheels. A real eye-opener and bird-puller; that is, until Bert opened the driver's door and invariably fell out, accompanied by his customary cursing of "Bugger, bugger, bugger!" from the kerbside.

And then there was Kenny. No longer Arthur Fonzarelli patrolling Truro's backstreets, but, still the fashionista, now more

Elvis Costello-cum-Showaddywaddy. With our shared roots on the estate, at school, on the waterfront and now Langdon's colleagues, we spent hours and hours together. Despite the impression given by his ever changing attire and persona, Ken could be very focussed and, as a natural academic, extremely helpful when it came to maths, physics or chemistry homework. His ability to crack abstract algebra, whilst crying with laughter as we watched Fawlty Towers, was quite extraordinary.

The Truro Sea Angling Club 'All Night' Cornish Open of October 1978 was a flagship event for the organisation. Those who had regularly weighed in large specimen fish at previous competitions would strut their stuff, weighing up the opposition at the sign in before disappearing off to some mystery spot (for all we knew, it could have been home to bed and then to a friendly fishmonger the following morning!). On this occasion, as it was such a miserable Saturday night, Team Bert opted to stay in the Fal estuary and, although this would most likely lessen our chances of decent sized fish, we would at least get some shelter and be able to hear ourselves above the roar of a howling south-westerly. Understandably at his age, this was the right thing for our Bert. Huddled away with the Tilley lamp glowing bright in our estuarine hideaway, mugs of his wife's soup in hand, we listened intently to stories of life during the Second World War, his later fishing escapades and London life. We loved it and, judging by the warmth of his delivery and the relaxed tempo of the puffing on his pipe, Bert did too.

Approaching dawn, about an hour and a half before we intended jumping back into Bert's Green Machine, Bert and I simultaneously struck into fish, a pollack and spotted ray respectively. They were not huge, but possibly both big enough to weigh in. To top it all off, ten minutes later Ken foul-hooked (by the tail) what must have been one of the Fal's most unfortunate lesser spotted dogfish. We needed to have a minimum of three specimens to register points in the competition. Would Bert's first ever line caught sea fish be big enough?

Wandering into the weigh-in at 08:50 on that Sunday morning

was somewhat surreal. There were less 'big-hitters' present than usual and there were decidedly quizzical looks on the faces of those present when they caught sight of Team Bert ambling, side by side, across the woodblock floor of Truro City Hall.

"Hello Bert. Unfortunately there was no point in you and the lads pitching up this morning as there's nothing to see," dismissively remarked Tony Hawkins, the Club Recorder, "that south-westerly did for all the teams, wiping out both coastlines – just unfishable."

Bert stood still, puffing quietly on his Lee Van Cleef, and said nothing. I glanced at Kenny. We both smiled. Now in his latter years, Bert may not have had the presence or cut and thrust of a young man, but here was a guy with a real sense of occasion and timing. The minute hand of the City Hall clock clicked over to 08:58, two minutes before the close of the weigh-in, and with the poise of a gunslinger, Bert slowly unbuttoned his coat and flipped one flap aside, revealing a black bin bag knotted and hanging from his chest wader braces.

"Well, best you test out your scales with these then, Tony," Bert announced with authority as he ripped open the bag allowing the fish to slide on to the recorder's table, followed by a satisfyingly long draw on his pipe.

"Where 'ee been 'en, Bert? Sent one of your boys down to Cock's fish shop have 'ee?" shouted Arthur Pascoe, a Club stalwart and another Langdon's employee.

"Just weigh these please, Tony. They're bona fide catches alright," Bert asserted politely, blanking out Arthur's taunt.

A hush fell over the hall as word rapidly spread that Team Bert were, for the first time, about to weigh-in at a county competition. First, the spotted ray.

"4lb 2oz – that's good enough to qualify as one of the three," Tony declared, looking over his spectacles at Bert who was now shrouded in a huge cloud of smoke.

Then, the lesser spotted doggie, forlornly looking out of the weigh-master's tray, still with a mark on its tail where lassoed by Ken.

"2lb 3oz – that's OK for the second," Tony announced, hesitantly looking around at the murmuring throng.

Nervously, I looked over at Kenny. His wide youthful grin receding and an anxious frown forming below his hairline which, owing to the previous night's buffeting, was now more Ken Dodd than Elvis Costello. Bert's fish was to be last on the scales. The three of us knew that his pollack would be close to the minimum eligible weight.

Tony raised up his head and peered at the three of us.

"You'll be lucky if that poor thing is more than 2lb, fellas."

By this time the whole room had congregated around the scales. Could the unimaginable be about to happen? The 'professionals' floored by the amateurs – the 500-1 rank outsiders.

"Bloody disgrace! Fish stocks are low enough without the antics of this sad lot," someone blurted out, hidden away at the back of the hall.

"OK, OK, let's just settle down and wait to see what the scales say," asserted Tony, holding up a hand as he placed the fish on the tray. The mumblings gently subsided and a hush fell on the room. The scales teetered around the 2lb mark as Tony adjusted the sliding counterbalance with gentle flicks until the needle came to rest. Removing his glasses, rising slowly to his feet and rubbing his eyes, almost in disbelief, he announced.

"The third fish, a pollack, weighs in at, uh. . ." unintentionally pausing for effect, ". . .uh, 2lb 1oz. As official Club Recorder, it is therefore my duty to declare Team Bert as the winners of the team competition."

Bert remained unmoved, puffing away quietly, until the faintest of smiles emerged.

"Well done lads, you've just made an old man very happy. Little fish do, indeed, taste very sweet."

Almost two years later, during a bright, uplifting September lunchtime, the three of us are sat around a small round wooden table at the Barley Sheaf. Bert with his customary mild and bitter, Ken and I, still training together, supped half shandies. Despite the gaping age difference, conversation with Bert had never been difficult, perhaps just a bit suppressed during the recent cooler nights on the coast when Ken and I could tell that Bert's 80 year old body was feeling every one of the single digit degrees as the thermometer plummeted in the early hours. Today, however, was different. Each of us hamstrung by the awkwardness of our reason for being there. The sense of something rather unique and special coming to an end completely outweighed the anticipation of new chapters about to begin. We all knew that those wonderful Cornish dusks and dawns spent together watching the sun fall and rise were all but over.

Both Ken and I had obtained good grades at 'A' level and whilst we had initially taken the easy option of full-time posts at Langdon's in late August, it had been Bert in his inimitable manner who had pointed out our misjudgements.

"Langdon's is like an old sweet shop, very seductive, not only for the customers who indulge themselves, but also for you chaps working there. Fishing, shooting, models, bikes, etc., are all great fun, but remember that they are only hobbies and in years to come you could look back and think why didn't I use my education to better myself? My grandson is desperate to get to university and almost inconsolable that he's got poor grades and is now having to retake his exams. He would do anything to be in your situations."

Hardly a dressing down, but by Bert's standards it had been pretty seismic and prompted both of us to rethink our career settings. Ken managed to get enrolled on a 13-week training course with Devon & Cornwall Police and I was off to study for a Building Surveying degree. As always, wily ol' Bert had been right, we'd both been accepted without hesitation.

It was Bert who broke the silence, but only after an uncharacteristic wobble of his jowls.

"Here's to you, boys. You've got the world at your feet now. Go out and make something special happen."

The three of us clinked glasses.

"Thanks very much, Bert, we really appreciate that," I said, taking up the role of spokesman, but pausing and wishing I could summon something more meaningful, more poignant, more consoling. "We'll both be back in mid-December, so we can get out to Newquay headland and have a few cod and whiting sessions.

Kenny's driving now so we'll be able to leave the Green Machine at home and chauffeur you for once!"

"That'd be grand, boys. Something to really look forward to." Bert broke into the broadest of smiles as he fired up the Lee Van Cleef.

We never did that trip. Sadly, Bert suffered a massive stroke six weeks later and died the following year. God bless you, you old buzzard. Your calming influence and wise counsel would not be wasted.

Chapter 11

Crossing the Line
1980-3

B ERT'S wise words were all well and good, but actually getting away to study for a degree proved more difficult than I could have imagined. Initially, my mother just would not talk about me leaving home. David had recently married Nikki and flown the nest, and with my father so unwell I could understand why she was reluctant to entertain the thought of me departing too. The fact that they would still have five year old Marianne at home to occupy their minds had a bearing on relieving the impasse, but there was one key condition to be met. As I had only been out of Cornwall once in my life, I had to go to Leicester!

Why Leicester? Obvious, really. It was where Rita, my mother's older sister, lived. Although it wasn't said at the time, I later gathered that my parents felt that it would be the best way of introducing me to life outside of the county. That may have been partly true, but on reflection it was also an arrangement that would allay their fears that I might fall in with the wrong types and get led astray. However, whilst they may have had their suspicions, what they would not have fully appreciated was that the genie had already been let out of the bottle on many occasions. Ken and I, when not fishing, would go into Truro of a Saturday night, usually have a skinful and then finish things off with a dodgy Chinese takeaway on the top floor of the multi-storey car park, teetering on the parapet

Father aged 18,
before going off to war.

Mother aged 22, 1955.

Mother and Father's
wedding day, 1956.

Bruv watching over me,
1963.

Me at Tregurra Estate,
1965, before we moved
to Trelander.

Tremorvah Hall Infants, 1968.
I'm 7th from left on the back row and
Robert Snook is on my right:
see acknowledgements!

Bruv and myself at
Kennack Sands, 1966.

Bruv and myself with mother, 1967.

Coming back after a long
day at Kennack Sands.
Summer 1968.

Me on the beach at
Kennack Sands, 1968.

A Sunday trip with Aunt
Doreen and Uncle George, 1968.

Me and my trusty Moulton
Mini, 1970.

Cousin Marlene's
wedding, March 1972.

Beginning to fill out at 12
years old, 1974.

Soccer nets £26 for
fish club youngsters

Truro Trout & Freshwater
Fishing Club fundraiser
c1976 – Ken and myself are
the two tallest in the back row.

A nice ballan wrasse;
on the breakwater at Sennen
with Julian Bellamy, 1977.

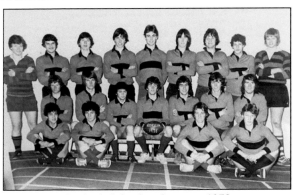

Redruth School rugby team, 1978.

Leicester Polytechnic rugby match,
1981.

In a familiar pose,
trout fishing, 1982.

Studying the form with Father in
the late 1980s.

Marc and myself cod
fishing in Norfolk, 1987.

Mr Cool in St. Ives, 1988.

Kempton Park
Half Marathon, 1986.

Night out with Mother and
Marianne, 1987.

Greece, 1987.

One fish to feed the 5,000!
Greece, 1987.

Greece, 1987.

Heavy ball, not one for the coaching manual!

Completing the Bridges Run, Putney; pre-season training with Jean-Bernard, August 1990.

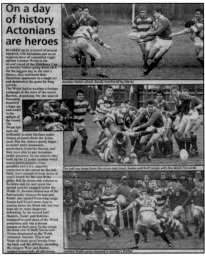

Middlesex Cup, Actonians v London Welsh, 1990.

Drinking the yard of ale at Truro Rugby Club.

Brown Willy Tour, 1990.

Leading the lads off against Truro on the Brown Willy Tour.

Admiring the silks of Derby winner Nijinsky at the Peter Harris stables, summer 1992.

Elvis is still in the building, 1991.

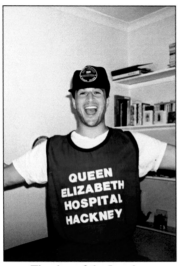

The day of the London
Marathon, 1991.

Overcoming the wall at the finish
of the 1991 London Marathon.

Our first holiday.
Summer 1992.

Myself and Marion at Lucy and
Tony '2 shirts' wedding, 1992.

wall overlooking the River Allen. Throw in the rugby social scene and it wouldn't have taken a genius to work out that I was drinking too much for a 17 year old. Yet somehow I would make it home, stagger upstairs and reassure the folks that I was fine (on the other side of a very flimsy partition), before slipping into a deep slumber. No matter how rough I'd feel in the morning, an early run to sweat out the alcohol and re-awake my senses would complete the masquerade.

Late September soon arrived and, amid an unsettling sea of emotion, I set off for the railway station. As the first in the family to go off to university, or in this case a polytechnic, I should have been proud, but instead I almost felt ashamed that I was causing such unrest at home. Truro to Leicester was a long tortuous train journey, so I had plenty of time to contemplate what might lay ahead. Whilst anxious, I did not have the overwhelming dread that had accompanied me on the journey to grammar school seven years earlier. Perhaps the folks' proviso that I live with family rather than on campus would prove to be a blessing after all. The warm welcome I received from Aunt Rita, Uncle David and my three beautiful Maltese cousins, Anne, Margaret and Marion, served to reinforce this.

However, within a matter of a couple of weeks, and in spite of the love and affection of my 'second' family, it became fairly obvious that being based 5 miles from all the student action would inevitably lead to a familiar sense of isolation. I even missed out on a little known group, Duran Duran, at the Freshers' Ball! Nor was I comfortable with my choice of course. I had not done my research into what BSc Building Surveying would actually involve. I had certainly not envisaged Economics, Law and Computer Studies being major parts of my academic life. As for those taking part in the course, they were an eclectic mix of older guys with years of construction experience, corporate sponsored or overseas students, plus a smattering of chaps like me, who had come straight from 'A' levels. The disparity in our respective abilities was comically illustrated in the first assignment, when we were tasked with reproducing a fairly simple mechanical drawing of a spherical garden fountain complete with freehand annotation. Given that I had never seen, let alone held, specialist drawing equipment, my effort was predictably lamentable and described by my lecturer as 'the work of an inebriated spider'! Of course, Messrs Ip and Lee from Hong Kong, and the band of bearded elder statesmen on the course, produced exemplary pieces of work that merely rubbed salt into the wounds. Putting ability aside, a slab of blockboard laid across my lap with a rickety wooden T-square and a leaky old drawing pen were simply no match for the swots and their swanky drawing boards with parallel motions and a vast array of draughtsman's equipment. Nevertheless, somehow, probably by way of sympathetic marking of a rookie's first assignment, I scraped a pass. Even so, it still left me feeling way out of my comfort zone. Why the hell was I putting myself through this?

One foggy evening shortly afterwards, I made up an excuse that I was meeting a fellow student for a drink and went walkabout in Leicester Forest East in an attempt to clear my head. It bore all the hallmarks of my evening rambles around the alleys of Truro; just my trusty commando radio/cassette was missing. About half an hour into my mystery tour, I found myself drawn towards the glow of bright lights along the A47 Hinckley Road, some way away from the residential area. As I got closer I could make out some unmistakably familiar sounds and smells which, like homing signals, prompted me to quicken my step. The trees lining the main road gave way, revealing a single storey brick clubhouse with floodlights overlooking a well manicured main pitch and two others further out towards neighbouring fields. I had arrived on a training night at Old Newtonians RFC and in no time at all I was sat in the bar chatting with a lovely old guy, Roy Catcheside, the club's president. Directly and indirectly, the club would play a major part in influencing the course of my stay in the East Midlands over the next three years.

Established in 1904, the club had become a force in the county by the 1950s when they were playing (and losing only narrowly) against the likes of the Leicester Tigers. Times had clearly changed by the time I rocked up. Whilst regularly fielding three or four teams, their standing within the regional rugby hierarchy had faded somewhat. However, the Old Newts still possessed some good

74

players and a cohort of wonderful characters who, at a time when I could have easily thrown in the towel and gone home to Kernow, collectively played a key role in changing my mindset for the better. Within just a few training sessions I was selected to play for the 1st XV. I would like to think that this was based on pure ability, but there was undoubtedly a novelty factor in my selection. As far as I could ascertain, with the club being so far out of town, they had not had many student players and most definitely not an 18 year old Cornishman who could play anywhere in the pack from tight head prop to No. 8. I was quickly welcomed into the bosom of the club (given the moniker of 'Cap'n Ross', after *Poldark* which was currently showing on the Beeb) and with that came some heavy after match drinking sessions. Aware that I was still under the watchful eye of Aunt Rita I would try and make sure that I didn't arrive home in too much of a state, but on one occasion it was pretty obvious that I was worse for wear. An intoxicated youth staggering to the loo in just underpants whilst sporting a full blown shiner would not have been a welcome sight to Aunt Rita. Throw in the fact that she had a chronic back problem requiring surgery, my behaviour merely accelerated the inevitable. A couple of days later, a watery eyed Uncle David took me aside and suggested that I seek out alternative student accommodation.

Just before Christmas 1980 I moved into Gimson Hall, a student hall of residence, right in the centre of the city. Even though my room was barely bigger than a broom cupboard I immediately sensed that I had fallen on my feet. The student social life that I had been so hankering for the previous ten weeks suddenly arrived and, with a seasonal twist, the ambience was seductive. Gimson, with its huge communal dining hall, lounge, TV room and snooker hall, and close proximity to the city's bars and clubs, was conducive to student bonding. Within a matter of days I had hitched up with Martyn, Huw and Eamonn, three like-minded guys more intent on enjoying life than studying! Disinterested in the student union scene and the city's nightclubs, our friendship was nurtured in the 'spit and sawdust' backstreet pubs where real ale was king. The more obscure the venue, the better. Initially, landlords may have been sceptical about our patronage, but once it was apparent that we were more interested in good beer, pool, darts and conversation we were soon accepted as regulars. Within the Gimson collective we may even have had an air of mystique as to where we were disappearing each evening, but a trend did eventually emerge when The Globe on Silver Street became our regular final watering hole. Everards 'Beacon' at 22p a pint and a Galaxian arcade machine may have had something to do with it. In time word got around, so Friday nights at The Globe regularly saw a fair gathering of Gimsonites. With rugby the following day, even though everyone was going for it, I always remained disciplined enough to ensure that a thumping hangover would not impair performance. However, by 5 o'clock on Saturday evenings the shackles came off and what were to become ritualistic binges began. It would be the same on Wednesdays when playing for the Polytechnic. I kept myself fit, but my studies and finances started to unravel towards the end of my first year. Without wealthy parents to bail me out I decided that I had to get myself a part time job. Marking the odds board at Ladbrokes bookies started off as just a few hours a week, but quickly escalated to around 25 hours, which meant that I was having to skive off lectures and rely on others to share their notes. Matters were not helped by the fact that Martyn and I regularly attended Leicester races on Mondays! I led this double life for the next two academic years.

Towards the end of the Gimson experience our gang of four secured the tenancy of a scruffy terraced house in Forest Road on the outskirts of the city. Socially it promised to be an exciting second year for us, that is until I rolled up to a riotous end of year student party. I had been seeing Ali, an effervescent Cornish girl, whilst at the hall of residence, although neither of us viewed it as a long term relationship. Effectively we were free to conduct our social lives as we pleased. With me preferring rugby, real ale and the company of the lads, I was not really interested in playing the field. It was therefore something of a surprise to find myself dancing (and bear in mind that all previous attempts at dancing had been confined to excruciatingly awkward pogoing as a sweaty fat boy at village hall discos!) with Tasmin Bramley, an eye-catching blonde. I had been a big Debbie Harry fan since the mid 1970s so, through beer goggles, that may have helped spark my initial interest, but within just a few weeks it was clear that we were an item. The break for the summer holidays put a temporary hold on us being together, so by the time September came around we were all over each other, to the extent that I spent more time at Tasmin's new digs on the opposite side of the city than at my own. I managed to meet up with the lads in The Globe from time to time, but there could be no escaping the feeling that I was upsetting the applecart. On the upside, I was drinking less and managing to catch up on some of my coursework whilst still working at the bookies.

Halfway through Year 2, Tasmin and I took the plunge and moved in together. I had not anticipated the reaction that this act would induce from my mother. In hindsight, the anger and desperation in her voice could probably have been averted if I had actually told her that I was going out with Tasmin! After a series of telephone calls fraught with emotion, the penny seemed to drop. I was no longer the chubby little boy that she could control, especially from 285 miles away. As proof of her reluctant endorsement of my new living arrangements, a huge cardboard box full of second hand kitchen utensils and general household paraphernalia unexpectedly arrived a week later. I suspected that Bruv and my father may have sat my mother down and made her see sense. However, it was not the end of the matter, not by a long chalk. My mother was (and still is) dangerous when wounded!

For the next six months life felt great. Tasmin and I were very happy together and even chose to stay in Leicester for part of the summer break whilst we earned money to help reduce our student overdrafts. It was a baking hot summer and in the end I cracked and headed home to see the folks and get to the coast. Tasmin went back to her mother's country pad in Storrington, West Sussex for a few weeks and then came down to Cornwall to stay with us at Trelander. It had never occurred to me that she might feel uncomfortable in our tiny little council house. In fact, whilst with us, I detected nothing untoward at all. Then, early one evening, all hell let loose. My mother accused Tasmin of being two-faced and looking down her nose at us. Within minutes the situation had escalated into a full blown eruption and my mother threw her out. I just could not fathom what was happening and for a brief moment I froze. Should I phone a taxi to take Tasmin to the train station and stay with the folks to defuse matters, or should I go with her and leave my mother to reflect on her outburst? Despite being worried about the effect my sudden departure would have on my father, I gathered up my belongings and, through the ongoing commotion, followed Tasmin out the door. Over the ensuing weeks, the Cornish volcanic activity subsided but the damage had been done. My relationship with Tasmin had been radically changed. I saw a different side to her. Mention of my family consistently drew snide remarks and there were always sneers when I went off to the telephone kiosk for my twice weekly calls home. Perhaps my mother's intuition about her had been right.

However, in my case love was blind, particularly with Tasmin being my first serious girlfriend. I ignored her sniping and suggested that we find some new digs in the misguided belief that a change of scenery might clear the air. Rather surprisingly, given her deprecatory attitude to most things, she agreed, so I set about finding a house that I hoped would enable us to rekindle our relationship. After a couple of weeks I found a nice three bedroom terraced house that we would share with three other students, all of which were campanologists. Bell-ringing meant nothing to me, but they seemed like very normal people so we took the plunge. My mistake was in not telling Tasmin that the property was only about five minutes from the lads on Forest Road. I had no intention of getting back into the old days of obscure pub reconnaissance missions, but chose the location as it was close to my usual branch of Ladbrokes. I say 'usual' only because the branch managers had started to vie for my board marking skills which had diversified into a sideline of topical sporting cartoons that the punters appeared to enjoy. However, inevitably, when Tasmin was on an evening out with her friends, I would end up trundling around the corner and nipping out for a beer, or five, with Martyn, Huw and Eamonn.

Halfway through my final year, it suddenly dawned on me that I had better knuckle down. And I did, to the point that I became a bit of a recluse whilst catching up on coursework prior to getting stuck into revision. As Tasmin had another year to go she was under less pressure and left me to it. Once in the zone, I usually had the ability to totally immerse myself. However, in so doing, I accepted the fact that Tasmin would go out most nights and regularly stay over with friends on the premise that she wanted to give me space. I was grateful for that and gradually began to turn things around. The lads up the road, who should also have been preparing for their finals, still carried on with their evening strolls but, for the moment, they did so without me. A couple of weeks after submitting my final pieces of coursework I got summoned by the Head of Surveying. My stomach churned. I had a feeling that this was not going to be a congratulatory pat on the back.

"Take a seat." Ray Tates's perfunctory greeting confirmed that it was indeed going to be squeaky bum time. "It has been brought to my attention that your recent attendance record has been very sketchy and, to back that up, much of your latest coursework indicates that you have not grasped what is being asked of you. What has been going on?"

'Bloody hell, I've been well and truly rumbled!' Inwardly I panicked. *'Try and dig yourself out of this mess, smart ass.'*

Complete honesty would probably have made my situation indefensible, so I quickly opted to be economical with the truth. I couldn't possibly own up to the fact that my absences had been going on for over two years.

"I'm very sorry, sir, but I've got myself into a bit of a hole with my finances and had to take a part time job this year."

"Well, frankly, that is just not good enough." Stern faced and virtually emotionless, Mr Tate seemed to look straight through me. "I'm inclined to show you the door right now, young man."

He took off his glasses and sighed heavily. My heart pounded, knowing that I was on the brink of expulsion. His next comment momentarily threw me.

"So, how long have you been an Old Newtonian?"

"Uh, I'm sorry sir, how did you know that I play for them?"

"I recognised the edge of the club emblem peeping out from under your jacket."

"Ah, yes, I'm with you now, sir." I relaxed a little as his line of enquiry moved onto more familiar territory. "This is my third season with them."

"Good for you lad, they're a fine club."

I was tempted to pursue the subject further but, sensing that the niceties were merely a brief stay of execution, I kept silent.

"Listen, I cannot disguise how unimpressed I am with the way you've approached this course," he paused and for the first time looked me in the eye. "However, all things considered, I am prepared to let you complete the degree, but on the understanding that you redo the last three pieces of coursework. Are you prepared to do that lad?"

"Of course, Mr Tate. I will turn this around." My relief must have been tangible.

"OK, glad to hear that. Do not let my judgement appear misguided."

On trembling legs I stood up and turned towards the door.

"Please give my best regards to Roy Catcheside when you next go up the club."

It was the first time that rugby, indirectly, would come to my rescue.

Having arrived at the last chance saloon, I had little option other than to throw all my energy into redoing my failed coursework whilst at the same time revising for my final exams. It was a formidable task requiring 18 to 20 hours work each day over a six week period. Everything else in my life had to be put on hold, but a week before my finals I felt that I was winning the battle. Invited on a night out with the lads, I gladly accepted the opportunity to get out for a change of scenery. Unlike our usual nomadic ramblings around the city's backstreet pubs, we stayed more central, eventually ending up at the student union bar which was a rare venue for us. Knowing that I would be back at the coalface the following day with my head buried in books again, I had very little to drink, so took to people watching as the rest supped away. In spite of the impending pressure of exams, I felt relaxed and content in that, against the odds, I stood a chance of salvaging something from the debacle I had created. A casual glance across the dance floor threatened to jeopardise all of that.

Ten minutes later, Martyn and several 'heavies' from the rugby club released their grip on my limbs and lifted me up on to a sofa in a room away from the main student union area. Disorientated, exhausted and soaked in sweat, it took a while for the mist to clear; the same red mist that had descended when Kenny had been assaulted by Trego six years earlier. The rage that Harold told me to harness and use to my advantage had welled up and overwhelmed me again. I probably should have seen it coming, but a combination of self-inflicted stress and sheer naivety meant that I had not spotted the signs that ultimately would lead to this latest meltdown. The sight of Tasmin in a tender embrace, kissing one of the guys from the Poly rugby club had provided the catalyst. I later learned that she had been in another relationship for months. Her deceit and betrayal were as destructive as the physical abuse I had endured as a teenager. As before, through tears of anguish, I would need to muster strength from adversity.

Chapter 12

The Prodigal Son
Summer 1983

H AVING somehow completed the degree course whilst
stumbling through an alcoholic and emotional haze, I retreated
back to the fatherland for some R & R. As the exam results would
not be released for a few more weeks, I found myself a casual job
picking daffodil bulbs near Truro. The early Cornish summer had
been untypically warm so conditions on the farm were hot, dusty
and, frankly, soul destroying. I badly needed the cash, but
scrabbling about in the dirt, hour after hour, when I could have been
at the coast ate away at my resolve. The ordeal was made worse by
the fact that you were required to fill a huge wooden crate before
receiving a meagre £15. On Day One I had designs on filling two a
day and creaming in £150 a week, but by the end of Day Three,
having just filled the first, I sat slumped against the crate, re-
evaluating my situation. So, I deduced, 8am to 6pm for three days –
30 hours for £15 equated to 50p/hour! Combining that depressing
realisation with rampant fingernail splits and skinned knees, I
rapidly came to the conclusion that a farm labourer's life was not for
me.

"Well, what are 'e gonna do with yourself 'en, boy?" enquired
my father as I arrived home announcing that I'd jacked it in. "What
about getting back down to Langdon's? I'm sure Mr Taylor will give
you back your old job."

"Yeah, I suppose I could go and see him, but if I get my degree I had better look for a proper job."

"Langdon's is a proper job. You could go all the way there, boy."

"It's hardly a career move in keeping with a Building Surveying degree though, Father."

"Yeah, but it'll tie you over for the time being, then you can look around for a surveyor's job down 'ere."

I knew that my father's health was deteriorating and sensed he was pretty keen to have me back in the fold. Having lost the lung in the war and been a lifelong smoker, his chest was a mess. As a small child I'd put the pillow over my head to muffle the sound of his daily ritual of cursing, coughing and spitting out phlegm. And yet he had managed to work at the lumber yard until he was 52 before succumbing to the effects of chronic airways disease and taking early retirement. Now his life was very sedentary, largely housebound on a cocktail of drugs and nebulisers. However, through his love of horse racing, he still had a reason to get up early and spend hours poring over the form in the *Sporting Life*. Over the years, watching Grandstand and the World of Sport, this had rubbed off on me, and together we had formed a great bond, comparing notes and fancies, sharing the glory and the despair and plotting the next big coup. Even whilst I was away at college, I would find a telephone kiosk and reverse the charges so that we could speak regularly and exchange 'vital' information.

Now that I was home again, I became his paperboy, statistician, bookie's runner and general partner in crime. I say crime, as initially that was the way my mother viewed our deliberations and clandestine activities. Whilst she was always very happy when a pile of £5 notes appeared on the kitchen table, the dry spells were the times when talk of wasting the housekeeping surfaced. If only she knew how good he was at having a flutter, she'd have had the faith and said nothing. I lost count of the number of times that he turned a 5p yankee into a £100, and with it would come a warm smile and an immediate uplift in his spirits.

When all was said and done, the Cornish economy was badly depressed through the collapse of the tin mining industry and decimation of the sea fishing sector through ludicrous EU fish quotas. The bottom line was that I would be unlikely to find a post-grad surveyor's job in and around Truro. Therefore, with something of a heavy heart, on learning that I had actually secured a degree, I announced that I was going to look for my first position in London. Bert's final words of advice from three years before were echoing loudly in my head.

As I sat in the reception of Mortimers Recruitment agency in Holborn, WC1 on a stifling August afternoon, I felt like a fish out of water. Sporting a distinctly naff brown pinstriped three-piece suit and oversized brogues that my mother bought for me from a charity shop, I had travelled up to the Metropolis via a friend's home in Hampshire. I fidgeted, fretted and perspired, longing for the mesmerising sound and smell of the sea. The Fal estuary would be utterly beautiful and spellbinding on a day like this. The sun glinting off the gently pulsing tidal waters at Loe Beach, dinghies darting in and out of tree-lined creeks, children giggling and chirping along the water's edge waving at the *Enterprise* as she serenely ferried folk from Falmouth to Truro.

'Aaargh, what the hell was I doing here in this maelstrom of humanity?'

After what seemed like an age. . .

"Mr Hambly, please go through to the conference room now. Mr Mortimer will see you in a moment," smiled Hermione Thompson de Mallett, her name emblazoned across an enormous badge covering much of her chest.

'What on earth were her parents thinking when they came up with that particular combo?' I mused, as I stood fumbling with my papers in the confines of a room fit only for a conference of two!

"Good afternoon, Mr Hambly. I'm sorry to have kept you waiting. I've had a look through your CV and, aside from your unusual background, I think we may have something that will suit a graduate Building Surveyor. Please sit," asserted Mr Mortimer, simultaneously eying me up from top to bottom.

OK, the flairs were voluminous and the leg length too short so my strides may have looked odd, but there was nothing wrong with my heritage. I resisted the urge to rise to the bait.

"Thank you, Mr Mortimer. That sounds great, sir."

"Oh dear, I feared that might be the case."

"Hmmm, sorry Mr Mortimer, sir. Is there a problem?" I enquired, confused that such a short sequence of words could lead to, what appeared to be, an about-turn. Surely my trousers weren't that offensive.

"Your accent. . . your dialect. . . umm, well, your West Country burr is very distinctive, is it not?"

"Never occurred to me, Mr Mortimer. Why would that matter, sir?"

"Well, to be brutally honest, Central London practices are looking for well-spoken, well-presented graduates."

"I am well-spoken, sir, just from a different part of the country," I was equally stunned and offended, "but that will not prevent me doing a job up here. Just look at what Richard Trevithick achieved."

"What are you talking about, young man?" quizzed Mr Mortimer, with a semblance of irritation.

"Richard Trevithick, sir. He was Cornwall's finest engineer and transformed mining all over the world, and built the first steam locomotive in the 1800s."

"Bizarre, I've not the faintest idea what you are talking about lad. If this was your interview you'd already be on the way out the door with that sort of impertinence. But, I suppose, you're at least showing a bit of character!"

I felt insulted by the fact that Richard Trevithick was apparently anonymous in this hell-hole.

"Now look, enough of this, it's late, but if you get your skates on, this gentleman will see you before the end of business today. Philip Andrews are a small private practice on Duke Street, behind Selfridges, off Oxford Street. You'll need to be there by 4.30pm and ask for Alan May. Got that?"

"Yes, sir, I have, but where's Duke Street and what time is it?"

"Oh, death of an empire, Lord please give me strength!" Mr Mortimer pleaded, looking skywards. "It's 4 o'clock."

Two minutes later, having been ushered down two floors to street level clutching an introductory letter, my increasingly irked promoter pointed left along a bustling Oxford Street.

"You need a No. 98 bus. Get off at Selfridges just past New Bond Street tube and then turn right up Duke Street. Philip Andrews are on the left before Manchester Square. Pass this introductory letter to Mr May."

A pregnant pause followed. He could just as well have been talking to me in Swahili!

"Well, off you go laddie and, for God's sake, do your bloody tie up before you go in. You're not in the students' union anymore."

And with that he was gone, leaving me totally disorientated.

'Blimey, did this bloke actually want a commission or had he just given up so that he could make a quick getaway to some vast country retreat?'

After several buses with the wrong numbers went gliding past, I made the decision to leg it. I'm not quite sure how many job interviews begin with a 20 minute run along a crowded city high street on a sweltering summer's day. Amazingly, having sidestepped innumerable bewildered shoppers with my high knee action as I attempted to avoid tripping over in my 'clown' shoes, breathless and sweating profusely, I stumbled over Philip Andrews's front door threshold and careered into their plush foyer.

"Oh dear, you look lost. Can I help you at all?"

At last, a friendly smile and calming voice amongst a mass of automatons.

"Phew! Apologies for bursting in like that, but I've just run from Holborn. I'm here to see Mr May for a 4:30 interview."

"I'm sorry, but Alan's been called out to deal with an urgent site matter and will not be back today," said Charlotte Kennedy, bearing a somewhat smaller name badge than Hermy Whatshername. "Would you like a drink whilst you recover from your exertions?"

"No, no but thank you all the same," I muttered as I adjusted my trouser legs to their maximum length to cover my blue socks and tightened my tie as commanded by Mr Mortimer. "It's a pity because I'm going back to Hampshire tonight. Can I leave you this letter from the recruitment agency for Mr May to read?"

"OK yah, that's fine. I'll do a memo and leave it on his desk for tomorrow. He tends to get in early to miss the traffic."

"That'd be great, thank you. I should go now as I've got a long way to travel home. Thinking about it, I'd better leave you my temporary telephone number."

At nine the following morning, as I'm tucking into a full English breakfast served up by June, my friend's mother, the phone rang. I thought nothing of it and ploughed on through my cholesterol challenge.

"John, it's Alan May for you," shouted June from the hall, causing me to choke on my third Cumberland sausage.

"Oh wow, really, already? Just a second, I'm coming June," I said, hurriedly dusting crumbs off my T-shirt as if that would have any sort of bearing on the conversation to follow.

Clearing my throat and taking a deep breath I took the handset from an expectant June.

"Good morning, Mr May. How can I help you?" I enquired stiffly.

"Good morning, John and, firstly, please drop the formalities and call me Alan."

"Yes, sir. Sorry, I mean Alan."

"Charlotte Kennedy left me a memo following your impromptu visit yesterday afternoon. I've had a quick look through your CV and wondered if you could come up to Duke Street for an interview."

"Yes, no problem at all. I'd be delighted to do that," I announced with just a hint of trepidation.

"Good. Would next Monday at 10am suit you? An early start, I realise, which means you'll have to catch a train this time rather than jogging!" chuckled Alan.

"Of course, that makes sense, Alan. I will look forward to meeting you then."

"Very good, me too." And with that he hung up.

"Well, that sounds positive." June stood smiling in the kitchen doorway.

"Hmm, yes, it is. I've got an interview in London on Monday. I'm just a bit baffled as to why he thought I'd run there!"

Chapter 13

London Calling
Mid-October 1983

SIX weeks on, it's 9:15 on a Monday morning and I'm sat in a small third floor office, peering out across a sleepy West End. It's my second week at Philip Andrews and still I'm familiarising myself with job files which, in all honesty, mean nothing to me. Half of the surveying team, including Alan, are away on late summer holidays, so I'm largely alone and my only conversations each day have been with Charlotte in reception. Over copious quantities of caffeine, we had agreed how wonderful the West Country was and how ghastly London could be.

As the brown bakelite clock ticked on past 11, I was close to imploding with boredom and the sense of what I was missing at home. So much for London being the best way forward for my career. The combination of an almost troglodytic office existence and a desperately rundown bedsit in Twickenham, made for a miserable first working week. Each day I had been mystified by the thousands of faceless people scurrying from home to work and back again, during which time most managed to avoid eye contact. Whatever happened to a good old fashioned 'Morning, pard' if you'd spotted someone more than once or, at worse, a nod to acknowledge your very presence. Undoubtedly, the boys at Langdon's were having a whale of a time, recounting glories from the weekend's fishing and planning their next trip to the coast, in all likelihood that very evening. Even life as a hard up student miles from home was more invigorating and fulfilling than this drivel. Perhaps this was just the way working life and being an adult was meant to be.

Tick, tick, tick. . . noon finally arrived and with no further improvement on the human interaction front I decided to take an early lunch and find a park. Having taken sandwiches into the office the previous week, I thought that this move might prove a masterstroke, a chance to explore and, dare I dream, to talk to someone other than the lovely Charlotte. Bright, warm autumnal sunshine hit me as I emerged onto Duke Street.

'What now? Whereto 'en boy?' My father's voice drifted into my head as I stood on the front step contemplating my next move.

Five minutes later, as I strode purposefully to the end of Duke Street, glancing right I spot the urban oasis I am seeking, nestled amongst a desert of concrete, bricks and mortar. I had to admit, I was pleasantly surprised. Grosvenor Square had been well manicured and, surrounded by mature London Plane trees and shrubbery, it allowed a modicum of seclusion to seep into one's senses. At the North West corner, standing imperiously, I looked up at the statue of Dwight D. Eisenhower and then across to the front elevation of the US Embassy crowned with a massive gilded bald eagle.

Acutely aware of my limited time, I wandered into the square and looked for a park bench. Not a chance, as it appeared as though the whole of the West End had chosen the venue for an early lunch. Reminiscent of Perranporth beach on a sunny summer's day, I tiptoed my way between the revellers until I found an expanse of grass large enough to set myself down. No, it was definitely not the Cornish Riviera, but actually quite reassuring to feel part of the human race again.

Having tucked into a gourmet meal of cheese and onion crisps, corned beef and sweet pickle sandwich, and a banana, I felt pretty relaxed so lay back on the grass. I reckoned I would have twenty minutes of chilling out and then get back to my hermit-like existence for the rest of the afternoon. Whilst woefully short of my accustomed seaside sights and sounds, the warmth of the sun, the cacophony of voices and the rumble of the city was surprisingly soothing. Sam the Eagle gently drifted from view as I slid into slumber. It had been a difficult few days so forty winks would do no harm at all.

I awoke with a start. It was darker, cooler, quieter, the sun had gone in. Bleary eyed, I glanced at my watch.

"Shit, it's 2:50pm, I've been lying here for two hours!" I announced to no one.

I was on my feet in seconds, probably too quick, as a wave of nausea hit me and I swayed like a lunchtime drunk. After a couple of deep breaths I had recomposed myself and bent over to pick up my jacket. It was only then that I noticed my pinstripes had turned a crazy psychedelic pattern of grey, green, brown and white, interspersed with purple spots. I rubbed my eyes, fully expecting the hallucination to disappear. It didn't. Rather emphatically, I'd experienced my first encounter with the rear end of one of the capital's one million over-nourished pigeons!

On a par with my entrance six weeks earlier, I stumbled dishevelled into the reception.

"Oh no, John, what happened to you? We've been very worried as Mr Andrews popped in to introduce himself to you at 1pm. Have you been on site and knocked over a paint tin?" enquired Charlotte, clearly astonished at my 'piebald pinstripes'.

"Not quite Charlotte. A large pigeon, I think!"

"Well, you know what they say about bird poo and luck, John?"

"So much for luck, Charlotte, I think I'm dead meat. I can't meet the senior partner looking like this, can I?"

"John, don't panic, it's OK. I told him you were on site checking some plans. Mr Andrews has gone off to a meeting in Kensington so will see you tomorrow.

The next day, clad in my only remaining suit, a shiny green New Romantic jacket and trousers (usually reserved for weekends at Secrets night club in Truro), together with brown brogues, I appeared to have inadvertently discovered the way to get my fellow commuters' attention. Perhaps they all thought I was from a thrusting pop group or, more likely, judging by the smiles, a London 'fresher' who had got dressed in the dark! The situation did not improve upon reaching the office, as Charlotte simply greeted me with an open-mouthed "Oh dear!" and Candida Dyson-Smythe, Mr Andrews's PA, cut to the quick and told me to leave the building because I looked inappropriate.

Biting my tongue I smiled, turned tail and headed off to my top floor cubby hole to re-read job files. Upon reaching my desk, I was panic stricken to discover a handwritten note from none other than Mr Andrews.

"John Hambly, please see me."

Almost instantaneously I turned clammy.

'Oh shit, shit, shit! Surely, he knows I had a three hour lunch break yesterday. Hey ho, this has been crap whilst it lasted anyway.'

I took a deep breath, straightened my tie and headed off down to the first floor. A sneering Candida D-S sat guard, typing outside Mr Andrews's office.

"What are you doing down here?" demanded the dubiously delectable PA, in the process picking up and drawing heavily on a cigarette.

"Actually, Mr Andrews wants to see me, Miss."

"Looking like that? I would very much doubt it, and don't call me Miss. You're not in primary school now!" snorted Candida.

"Well, here's the note, missus," I announced and triumphantly waved it in front of her. At which point. . .

"Candida, if that's the new man, let him through," demanded John Andrews, calling off his rottweiler.

"Yes, Mr Andrews. I'll send him in," Candida offered richly, belying the chewed-up-toffee face she was pulling at me.

Drawing myself up to my full 6' 2", I strode nervously into our senior partner's domain.

"Good morning, sir. I am very pleased to meet you."

"Ah, John Hambly, we meet at last. Very good to have you on board," boomed Mr Andrews; tall, bespectacled and balding, with a voice so loud and deep-seated that I had a fleeting image of him having swallowed a microphone!

"Thank you, sir."

"Please have a seat whilst I look through this matter I need you to assist me with."

As I sat cross-legged, I took the opportunity to glance about the room. Centrepiece was an over large but immaculately organised rosewood desk behind which our supremo sat gently rocking on a black leather swivel chair, the size of which would not have looked out of place at the helm of the *Queen Elizabeth II*. A substantial chimney breast with ornate marble fire surround complemented the high ceilings with egg and dart cornices and storey-height French doors opened onto the front balcony, itself beautifully adorned with well-stocked plant tubs.

Throughout his contemplations Mr Andrews made unsettling guttural grunts, each one accompanied by a scribbled note using a gold fountain pen. After what seemed an age, he finally raised his head and looked at me over his metal rimmed spectacles.

"Hmmm, this will be a nice job for you, John Hambly. Do you know what a rent review is?"

"No, not really, sir." I resisted the urge to try and bullshit my way through his opening gambit.

"Well, that doesn't surprise me. Do they teach you anything at university these days? If you're going to get through your test of professional competence you'll need a broad breadth of experience."

Leaning forward, Mr Andrews handed me the file with his notes.

"6 Red Lion Yard is a small mews property south of Grosvenor Square. Do you know the area?"

At mention of the latter, my stomach did a somersault.

'Oh my god, he's onto me and knows of yesterday's antics. I bet Candida D-S winkled the info out of Charlotte and grassed me up. She is going to be such a. . .'

"Well? Do you know where to go or not?" blurted Mr Andrews, abruptly bringing me back to the real world.

"Yes, I know Grosvenor Square very well, so with a London A-Z I will be fine, sir."

"Good, that's reassuring. We don't want you wasting time getting lost, do we?"

"Absolutely not, sir."

"Right, well, you're going to need a rod and cloth tape to measure the property and prepare simple floor plans for me to negotiate the rent. Charlotte on reception has the keys to the property. OK, off you go then."

Discontinuing eye contact, he bowed his head and wafted his left hand. Clearly, I was being dispatched.

'Phew, I'd made it through without mishap.'

"Thank you, Mr Andrews."

I gathered the paperwork and stood up, completely unaware that my left leg, having been crossed for twenty minutes, had gone to sleep causing me to lose my balance and lurch alarmingly towards the fireplace, throwing the papers across the room as I desperately reached out for a handhold.

"My God, man, what the hell is wrong with you?" shouted a startled Mr Andrews.

"I'm so sorry, Mr Andrews, but my leg. . ."

"I don't care! For God's sake just get out and get on with the job man!"

Hopping and hobbling like a sprinter with a pulled hamstring, I stooped to retrieve the notes and crabbed my way to the door.

"And one more thing, Hambly. In future, make sure you come to work appropriately attired. This is a prestigious West End surveying practice not a bloody discotheque!"

For a millisecond, I was inclined to explain about my introduction to the city's feathery inhabitants but, suspecting that Mr Andrews was about to blow, I just nodded and made a swift exit and closed the door.

"Hot in there was it, HUMMMBLY? You look very red and sweaty!"

I did not even look back to give the rottweiler the satisfaction.

The reality and bluntness of adult working life had arrived in no uncertain fashion.

Chapter 14

Forbearance
March 1984

WITH London life proving almost unpalatable for the first six months, I made every effort to get back home to Cornwall on Friday nights. I had not been provided with a company car so would walk from Duke Street to Paddington Station and catch the train to Truro. It was good to keep in touch with the rugby boys and to see the folks regularly enough to dispel their feelings that I had emigrated! My father's health was poor, but with my mother nursing him through the bad days and my little sister, Marianne, proving a heart-warming distraction, they were usually in good spirits. Initially I made sure that I gave them my time on a Saturday during the day, running errands in the morning and then sitting with my father to watch the sport in the afternoon. We both enjoyed the coverage of the horse racing, particularly the ITV7, which was followed by wrestling from Preston or motorcycle scrambling. However, Saturday nights were my pressure release valve and I would shoot up to the rugby club for a few beers before running amuck in the town. Being under the influence of alcohol, it was inevitable that before too long I was going to be coerced into playing again.

A couple of weeks later I got a run out for Truro 2nds against Redruth Albany. I had kept up a reasonable level of fitness by jogging around the streets of Twickenham, but there could be no substitute for actual game time in terms of strength and hardness.

Selected at flanker, I would need to be fairly quick to the breakdown but, thankfully, would not be propping and taking on Albany's extra large front row. Nevertheless, in the finest tradition of Cornish rugby, it was a very physical encounter with plenty of niggle going on off the ball. Truro, being the county town, in fact, city because of its magnificent cathedral, were probably viewed as the 'toffs' so there were a few cheap shots to evade. Both sides had large packs of forwards so, even with decent early spring weather, it was never going to be a try-fest with the ball rarely being moved wide to the wingers. However, halfway through the second half, against all the odds, it happened! The ball got through our centres' hands and it looked like our winger would get into the corner, but he was collared, literally, by the opposing winger and scragged just short of the line. There was then a frantic ruck to win the ball, with their winger on his back caught on the blind side pinned under a pile of bodies. I arrived late having been involved at the last breakdown. As I drove into the ruck to clear bodies away from the ball, I was aware that there was a player lying face up so kept a wide base to avoid contact. Squatting lower to get under one of the opposition forwards who had flopped over the ruck, I completed the clear out and found myself looking straight down at the prone player who was frantically trying to free his arms to protect his face.

'Don't worry mate. I am not the kind of bloke who relishes meting out a stamp on the head,' I thought, but almost as if my own well-being was in jeopardy, random images from the past flashed through my mind. I had been here before but never as the aggressor. His panic was understandable, he was helpless to protect himself. Seven and a half years earlier so was I. His eyes were fixed on me, imploring me not to raise my boot. Even then, he hadn't recognised me. The sense of defiance I had felt in the woods all that time ago resurfaced. Anger reared its ugly face.

'No one will see. Get the bastard back. Go on, do it!'

Involuntarily, I lifted up my left leg and my Cotton Oxford with its metal studs hovered six inches above my nemesis of old. All he could do was close his eyes, turn his shaven head and brace himself for the pain. We both knew how to play out this scenario. It's just that our roles had been reversed. I sensed the all-consuming toxicity of a deep-rooted anger and the first shimmer of red mist. Yet, despite the years that the resentment had lain dormant, there was no real hate, no fuel to ignite the fire within me. Harold's words, 'control the rage', brought me back from the brink. My boot hit the turf, nestling gently next to Stephens's left ear.

'Unlike you, you sad little man, I will not stoop to your depth of brutality.'

One simple act of self-restraint and we were equal. We would never meet again, not even in my dreams.

Chapter 15

Bricks and Mortar
1984-88

HAVING rather drifted my way into the building industry after almost flunking my degree, and hating every minute of my first six months in London, I was eventually let loose dealing with site matters and began to feel a little more settled. Another stroke of luck was that, for the first two years of my professional training, I was put under the watchful eye of Marcus Godwin. Initially, Marc was rather blunt and preoccupied with his own heavy workload to take much interest in a trainee surveyor, but after we were put into the same office, the barriers started to come down and he began to involve me in running some aspects of his schemes. Whilst he was 11 years my senior, we found that we had a lot in common through our interest in sport and fishing. Marc also had a very dry sense of humour and, being reluctant to align with all the yuppies at the practice, went out of his way to be unconventional. As something of a misfit myself, I loved the way that he would turn up at the office with a tatty old leather bag stuffed full of files and fishing magazines and the *Morning Star* wedged under his arm. I don't think he was an out and out socialist but did it more to irritate the partners and the likes of the Rottweiler!

For all his idiosyncrasies, Marc was a brilliant surveyor; technically very correct and superb on the drawing board, he could produce building specifications and plans in such detail that there would invariably be less arguments and issues with costs when the job got to site. Clients were happy, contractors less so! He was firm but fair, throwing a degree of humour into the mix which seemed to enable him to gain the utmost respect from most of our builders. At times, listening to him tell a burly foreman to remove and redo substandard building work was akin to a rugby referee standing toe to toe with a mouthy 20 stone prop forward before marching his side back ten metres. When it came to client meetings, Marc was the epitome of the modern property professional in establishing the brief and transforming the subject property into the finished article. Our clientele had a broad range from the public and private sectors, with the instructions varying from small domestic maintenance jobs through to large commercial refurbishment schemes. Without doubt, I was extremely fortunate to run into a mentor as good as Marc just as I was contemplating jacking in London life and possibly even a career in surveying.

As with many phases of my life, humour was important in helping to sustain me through difficult periods. The construction industry was full of characters and circumstances would so often contrive to create hilarity. In addition, with me being so wet behind the ears in the first few years of my career, I would be the butt of many pranks or just simply put my foot in it.

Probably my first faux pas occurred when Marc asked me to accompany him to a meeting at Kensington Housing Trust where we would be discussing three large residential schemes with their development team. No problem there, as I was attending more for experience than my input. The meeting started mid-morning and went on and on for hours, with one particular manager labouring over every point. By 1pm I was not only bored but absolutely starving. Thinking nothing of it, I delved into my jacket pocket and found a partially flattened Mars bar which I noisily removed from the wrapper and proceeded to devour, as I had done since childhood, by nibbling away all the chocolate, licking away the caramel and then chomping through the nougat centimetre by centimetre. Savouring every morsel, I was completely oblivious to the astonished looks from the rest of the people in the boardroom and the fact that the discussions had stuttered to a halt. Marc looked equally aghast but managed to lighten the mood.

"I must apologise, but John's from Cornwall and we've only just starting training him in basic etiquette!"

Thankfully, under his tutelage, over the next few years I managed to smooth off some of my rough edges, although my West Country twang was always the subject of much ridicule. However, my next cock-up, only a few weeks later, had nothing to do with how I spoke but was more a case of the country boy just being let loose on the roads in a very big city. Tasked with making an impromptu inspection of a new site intended to keep a tricky contractor on his toes, I enthusiastically bounded off to Montague Mews West, near Marylebone, to jump into Marc's company car. All the partners and surveyors left their vehicles in a basement car park at this property but what I had not been told was that the parking arrangements were the equivalent of sardines. Upon opening the heavy double doors to the garage, my knees nearly buckled. Not only was Marc's red Ford Escort tight to the rear corner, but there were two new 7 Series BMWs and a large pristine Volvo shoehorned in around it, all with their keys in the ignition. As Marc was usually first into the office, he would have been used to extricating his motor by moving the partners' cars onto the side road, before pulling out the Escort and then returning the other cars to the garage. I had not driven for months, nor had I ever sat behind the wheel of a prestige car, so I had good reason to feel nervous.

I was so grateful that the garage was tucked away, as I must have looked pathetic inching each car back and forth until finally, around 10am, I was in the Escort and out onto George Street.

'Right,' I reassured myself, with the London A-Z at the ready, *'55 Ladbrook Road, here I come.'*

London driving for a lad used to country lanes was a nasty awakening. Quite simply, you could not hesitate nor give an inch. Judging by the frequency of blaring horns directed my way, I was either going far too slow or cutting up other drivers, or both! My performance behind the wheel was not helped by the fact that I had no idea where I was going and kept glancing down at the A-Z open on my lap. Nevertheless, after two hours of wrong turns and stops to reassess my route, hugely relieved, I pulled into Ladbrook Road, SE25.

Clipboard in hand, I tapped on the front door of No.55 and waited for a surprised foreman to appear. After a minute without response, I knocked a little more forcefully. Still nobody appeared, so I peered through the front bay window. There was no sign of building work having been started. It was still carpeted with a few bits of old furniture and net curtains. The lack of a skip and any rubble sacks were further evidence that there was nothing doing on this site.

'Well,' I thought smugly, *'it's been a bit of a slog getting here, Mr Considine, but you've been rumbled!'*

The return trip was only moderately quicker, so by the time I had parked up at the garage, grabbed a sandwich and walked back to the office it was almost 3pm. Keen to grass up the contractor's non-activity to Marc, I ran up the stairs to our 3rd floor office, only to find him on the phone. It was clearly a difficult call, as he kept holding the telephone receiver well away from his ear as someone vented their anger at the other end of the line. Eventually he hung up and turned his attention to me.

"Mr Andrews has been up three times looking for you. Why have you been gone for six hours, Hambers? Down in Cornwall visiting your folks?"

"Yeah, I'm really sorry Marc, but I got a bit lost."

"A bit lost! You only had to turn left and head off on the Westway to Notting Hill! Where have you been?"

"55 Ladbrook Road, like you asked me to. Just as well I went though, because Considine's have done nothing. They weren't there. The previous tenant's furniture and carpets hadn't even been stripped out." I announced triumphantly, waiting for some praise.

"You total prat. I said Ladbroke Grove! If you'd picked up the file, even you would have found it. No wonder Considine's men weren't there." After his previous telephone conversation, Marc was clearly on edge.

"I'm sorry Marc, it won't happen again."

"It had better not, and make sure you have a plausible explanation when Mr Andrews comes looking for you again," demanded Marc.

We sat in silence for a good hour whilst I did some drawing work and Marc proofread all his correspondence. Never one to bear a grudge for very long, Marc eventually chirped up.

"Do you know, Hambers, in all the years I've worked in North Kensington I don't think I have ever come across a Ladbroke Road. What was the postcode?"

"SE25, I think," was the sheepish reply.

Mystified, Marc nodded slowly as he fingered his way through the office A-Z before roaring with laughter and spluttering out a remark.

"Ah, that particular Ladbrook Road. You do realise that you went all the way to Crystal Palace to look into someone's front living room!"

As the weeks and months of experience accrued I started to get the hang of the surveying game and began to feel like a valued member of the team. The biggest problem I had was that, apart from Marc as my immediate boss, there were also three partners, all dropping work onto our desks. Marc just knuckled down and was incredibly productive. Perhaps, understandably, I was less effective in terms of the amount of work I churned out, but it was a good learning curve and with that came confidence and ambition. We worked hard and played hard. That said, as the office was in close proximity to some good old fashioned watering holes when time allowed, usually after a long day, Marc and I would frequent the Devonshire Arms, aka the D.A's Office, during which time we struck up some good relationships with guys from other businesses in and around Manchester Square. It was important to let off steam, but on occasions the rugger bugger in me probably took it too far. Marc liked a beer but would not get quite as carried away as I did. On one of the few occasions when we over imbibed during a lunchtime, Marc who was none too good himself, got Charlotte to lock me in the boardroom to protect me from the wrath of the partners! The culture of lunchtime drinking was different back in the 1980s and, undoubtedly, would not be tolerated these days.

That was not the worst of my antics though. The Christmas office parties were usually held in a plush West End restaurant, where most of the staff and even the partners had their fill. They were great fun, so when it was announced that the 1987 party would be held in the office boardroom starting in the late afternoon, after all the hard work we had put in throughout the year, I felt that it was a snub. For once, I got a real gob on and the alcohol merely fuelled the fire in my belly. I was never one for surveying small talk, particularly when confined to a room with a few too many chain-smoking, Bollinger-quaffing, double-barrelled yuppies. The only thing that temporarily lightened my mood was seeing the horror on the face of the Company Accountant, as the senior partner picked out the Ex-Lax, disguised as homemade dark chocolate during the Christmas Lucky Dip, and then proceeded to munch several mouthfuls. Subsequently I gathered that he had had an unpleasant train journey home!

I was never good with drinking champagne, it made me irritable. This occasion was a case in point. Quite what possessed me to stand up, walk across the room and whip off one of Alan's shiny black slip-on shoes as he sat cross-legged, is still beyond me. In a flash, tucking his shoe into my jacket pocket, I was out of the front door and away into the West End seeking more upbeat seasonal revelry. The heavy rain did little to dampen my desire to visit as many of our regular haunts as I could. Beer and champagne were not a good combination, so by the time I had made it back to the D.A's Office around 7pm I was most definitely worse for wear.

A couple more pints passed my lips before Alan finally caught up with me. Clearly he had had a skinful too and, swaying right in front of me with his soggy left foot, set about giving me an expletive laden verbal volley. Never had the term 'demon drink' really applied to me, generally I was a happy, mischievous drunk, but in that moment it did. Even today I am ashamed to say that I tried to head-butt Alan. Luckily, as I was looking at two of him, it was an air shot and all that happened was that I fell over, and with it the shoe conveniently dropped next to its rightful owner's foot.

"You're in such a deep pile of shit, Hambly!" shouted an irate Alan, pointing his finger into my face. "Just wait until we get back after Christmas. You're out the door, asshole."

In defiance I turned my back and carried on drinking as Alan fell out of the door to stumble across the road to the office, only to sidle up next to me two minutes later.

"I'm sorry I had a go at you mate," he slurred, "but I've been hopping from pub to pub looking for my shoe. I love that effing shoe."

"Yeah, I knew that Alan. That's why I took it as a hostage. I wanna a pay rise!" I slurred back.

"Well, tell you what, I'll get you a huge one if you let me into the office. I've left my keys and case in there and everybody's gone. I'm gonna get really told off if I don't get home soon mate."

"OK, a £5000 increase and a new car or else no key." I even surprised myself with my forthright negotiating stance.

"You've got a deal. I've always liked you, mate," murmured Alan as he slid further down the bar.

Standing in the rain outside the office, I fumbled through my pockets for the third time.

"Come on, I'm getting bloody drenched here. Do you want a new car or what?" pleaded Alan.

"Sorry, can't help you, I've lost my keys Al." I chuckled as the mischief resurfaced; "Tell you what, make it £5k, a car and a swivel chair like John Andrews's, then I'll get you in."

"You know something? You're an effing West Country cowboy. I haven't even got a chair like that!" Alan was getting desperate.

"Well, 'tis yer call, pard. What'll it be, 'en boyee?" I said reverting easily to my finest Cornish vernacular and enjoying every moment of Alan's dilemma.

"Yeah, yeah, alright. Just open the frigging door, will you!" Alan clearly wasn't really up for playing anymore.

"Proper job, me anzum. Just hold this a sec, will 'e?" I smiled and handed him my sopping wet jacket and set off back towards the D.A's Office.

"Where the hell are you going now?" Alan called out, totally perplexed by my retreat towards the pub at the conclusion of our 'high brow' negotiations.

"Don't worry, I just need to psyche myself up. Get off the step, Al."

"Eh, what are you talking about now?" and then, realising my approach to his problem, "Oh no, no don't. . ."

One quick arm roll, a deep intake of breath and I was away. Like an epic slow motion scene from *Chariots of Fire*, I recall seeing a bedraggled Alan standing aghast as I passed him just prior to hitting the heavy wooden front door around shoulder height. The impediment to his Christmas journey home duly yielded but not without collateral consequences. In my drunken stupor, I had failed miserably to undertake a full survey of the building components for which I had been commissioned. The electric door release mechanism hung forlornly from a single wire and the frame into which it had been housed looked decidedly unwell, having a huge split in the timber and a chunk lying on the floor. As I assessed the damage, Alan ghosted passed me with his briefcase and whispered, "The deal's off, asshole." At that point I started to sober up!

'Right, don't panic. Think straight and everything will be fine.' I said to myself, trembling at the thought of Mr Andrews throwing the book and my P45 at me in the New Year.

It took me a while to come to the realisation that my brain was so addled that nothing useful could be done at that point. Thankfully I found my keys on my desk and at least had the clarity of thought to secure the door by throwing the deadlock. As I made my way home on the Tube, just before drifting off to sleep, I caught sight of my reflection in the carriage window. I looked an absolute mess. Alan had been right all along. I was an asshole.

The following morning was far worse though, as my head pounded and the severity of my misdemeanours turned a very sensitive stomach inside out. I reached out to the only person I thought would be able to help.

"Marc, it's Hambers. How are you today?" Was a weak opening manoeuvre, as I sensed his annoyance at being woken at 8:30am.

"What have you done now?" Was his curt but perceptive retort.

"Nothing really, Marc. I was just wondering if I could borrow a few tools."

"Sure. When do you need them?"

"Umm, you're going to laugh, Marc."

"I wouldn't bet on it," Marc sighed heavily. "Spit it out, will you."

"OK. I'm sorry, but I broke open the office door last night and need to start fixing it today."

"Today! What the hell is the matter with you for God's sake? I'm about to go off to Essex."

I said nothing. How could I? After all, it was Christmas Eve. An excruciatingly awkward impasse ensued.

"Get to the office for 10am," was all Marc said and then the line went dead.

At 10:15am, to my relief, Marc's red Escort screeched to a halt outside 2 Duke Street. Almost in one motion, he leant across, opened the passenger door, flung the tool bag onto the pavement, shouted, 'Grow up, you waster!' closed the door and sped off. I was left in no doubt that it was time to do just that.

Having spent several days putting right what I had so recklessly damaged, I eventually made it home for a few days. Still chastened by Marc's stinging comment and reflecting on my selfish stupidity, I spent a quiet New Year without alcohol before returning to London, half expecting to find a letter of dismissal laying on my desk. Fortunately there wasn't, but both Alan and Marc made it clear that they were unimpressed with my behaviour. Unsurprisingly, I didn't get that pay rise nor a new company car (not even a swivel chair!), but my subdued outlook on life was about to change for the better.

I first met Jane when grabbing a very late lunch in the office kitchen which coincided with her preparing afternoon tea for her colleagues. I was aware that her company, specialising in hospitality events, had taken a suite in the building, but our paths had not really crossed owing to the fact that I was either on site or entrenched in paperwork. We agreed to go out for a drink, and within just a couple of months we were living together in Harrow. Our relationship blossomed so quickly that when an opportunity to buy an unmodernised flat in Hanwell, near Ealing, came along soon after, we took the plunge. It was a massive undertaking, as the property needed gutting and a full refurbishment which ultimately meant that we had to move in with Jane's parents in Hertfordshire, but for the first time in a while I was happy and there was love and stability in my life again. I would be staying in the metropolis after all.

Chapter 16

Field of Dreams
late August 1987

WEATHER-wise, the summer of 1987 had been a particularly good one and I had spent most weekends back down in Cornwall enjoying sun-drenched days in the surf or fishing the North Coast. My weekly ritual of leaving the Big Smoke at 3 o'clock on Fridays had become particuarly necessary as my father's health had continued to deteriorate. So much so that I would often get a midweek call from Dave to say that the old man had again been admitted to Treliske Hospital with breathing and heart problems and he may not make it through the night. Philip Andrews were incredibly supportive so, by working four very long days, I was allowed to shoot off early on Fridays and tackle the M4/5 weekend gridlock arriving at the Daniel Arms around 10pm; just time to have a few beers with the rugby boys before turning in.

Throughout the 1984/5 season, I had begun playing for Truro again, not every weekend, but often enough to hold down a regular second team place without being present during weekly training sessions. It was great to keep my links with the club going whilst at the same time spending precious time with the folks. However, it was pretty clear that the 14 hour round trips over a 48 hour period were taking their toll and I would quite often fall asleep in the car between site meetings during the week. With something of a heavy heart, I came to the decision that I would have to limit my

Cornish sorties to once a month unless one of Dave's midweek calls arrived.

London rugby therefore beckoned, but with no real rugby roots laid in the capital I was forced to look around for advertisements asking for players in and around West London. Whilst there were plenty of rugby posts dotted about the area it was difficult to know whether they were school/college pitches and, besides, I was keen to find a 'proper' club with decent training facilities and a clubhouse that matched the family feel I had grown used to at Truro. After several fruitless weeks, I happened to take the Piccadilly Line Tube into work one hot sticky morning and, on walking through Acton Town station concourse, by pure chance spotted a small ad announcing boldly, 'Your Club Needs You', in the style of Lord Kitchener's 1914 rallying call. Being in close proximity to Queens Park Rangers, Fulham, Chelsea and Brentford football clubs, I seriously doubted whether the locals thought of the Old Actonians as their 'club' but it was an inspired move by the rugby club committee, not only because it caught my eye but, over the next few years, droves of Kiwis, Aussies, Boks and other rugby playing nationalities would stumble off the plane at Heathrow and board the Piccadilly Line looking for work in London. How so many found that little poster in a relatively obscure out of town station is beyond me, but what began there was a glorious period of sporting camaraderie, high jinks and the creation of lifelong bonds so strong that only the parting of body and soul could break. The cherished memories of that special togetherness served to strengthen our collective resolve for life's challenges later on.

I felt optimistic as I walked through the gates of the Old Actonians on a late afternoon in August 1987. I had none of the previous anxieties associated with the first day at school or a new job, there was just a welcoming air about the place. The rugby club formed part of a large sports association, so for a complete sports nut the sight of a large well-maintained clubhouse and pavilion, football pitch, cricket square, tennis courts, bowling green and various pieces of rugby paraphernalia made for sweet viewing. Only one anomaly; there were no rugby posts!

Undeterred, I ventured into the clubhouse only to be met by, well, no one and total silence. Granted, I was there about an hour before the 7pm advertised start, but there seemed nothing wrong with being keen. The main bar was fairly typical of a junior rugby club; the aroma of stale beer and tobacco, sticky vinyl floors and, in one corner, an overriding smell of damp mouldy kit emanating from abandoned bags randomly slung onto slatted racks. In addition, there was a large notice board haphazardly interspersed with formal committee announcements heralding the arrangements for the forthcoming season, hurriedly scrawled team sheets for the pre-season trial matches which were peppered with insults/hieroglyphics and, of course, tour photos proudly showing past conquests and beer-fuelled naked antics. All mildly amusing, given that these images sat next to a photo of another player who was particularly well groomed and adorned in club blazer and tie, proudly shaking hands and exchanging pennants with a startlingly large committee member from another club. I leant forward to read the wording on the pennant. . . 'Benidorm 86'; and briefly pondered future international tours.

"Oi you, what do you want at this time?" proved a sharp awakening.

"Oh, uh, sorry, yep, uh. . . I saw the ad at the tube station and thought I'd have a look around," I spluttered.

"Don't know what you're talking about! What ad and what do you need to look at anyway?" came the blunt retort.

In innocently perusing the clubhouse, I had unwittingly stumbled into the domain of the Association's head steward. Brusque and generally accusatory in his tone, over the coming years I would come to know him as a bit of a curmudgeon. Bespectacled, clean shaven and well attired with tie, he looked the part, but perhaps at 60 he was past caring about common courtesy.

"The rugby club are looking for new players, so I thought I would come along and give it a go."

"Well, bad luck, they're not here!"

"Oh, sorry, have I got the wrong night then?" I enquired, trying not to rise to the antagonistic promptings.

"Did I say it's the wrong night? No, I said they're not here and that's because there's pre-season practice over in the park and you're too bloody early anyway."

"Fine, I'll get warmed up and make my way over there. Where are the changing rooms?"

"Over there by the pavilion," he pointed without looking up as he rearranged the beer mats.

Summarily dismissed, I headed off in the direction of the pavilion intent on getting changed and warmed up before the expected battering from pre-season drills and gruelling fitness sessions. The changing rooms were on two floors and, even being generous, they were spartan in terms of appearance and facilities. Besides that, there was the comforting whiff of sweat, mud and liniment together with the almost obligatory abandoned jockstrap hanging limply from one of the few remaining coat hooks. The downstairs rooms were so small I wondered whether a full team could actually be accommodated. Mooching around, I wandered up to the first floor. Now, this was more like it, two large, relatively plush changing rooms; one having an external door onto a balcony, imperiously overlooking the grounds – clearly, the home team's pad!

Having changed into my training gear, I plumped for boots with moulded studs as opposed to high cut Cotton Oxfords with metal studs. The ground was particularly firm after the hot summer so any prolonged sessions in the latter would just produce the most horrendous bloodied blisters. Seemingly too early for other players to show up, I decided to warm up by jogging around the Association's grounds. Compact, roughly rectangular and comprising football, cricket and, presumably at some point soon, a rugby pitch, it ticked all the right boxes. I set off alongside the netball courts and cricket nets, heading away from the clubhouse, before turning through ninety degrees along the top side of the pitches. No sooner had I turned than out of the corner of my eye I sensed activity back near the clubhouse. Oh good, I thought, someone else has seen fit to turn up for training. After all, it was now 6:30pm, only half an hour before the scheduled start.

"Hey, you, get off my turf! What the hell are you playing at?"

'*Oh no, not Victor Meldrew from behind the bar again,*' I thought, but before I'd gone another 20 paces the perpetrator of my latest verbal volley was virtually upsides, arms waving around like some deeply offended landowner.

"This pitch ain't ready for training!"

"Hang on a minute, I'm only. . ."

"You're only what? . . . Mucking up my re-seeding programme, that's what!"

Having had quite enough of this unsavoury club welcome, I drew to a halt and squared up to my latest adversary.

"No signs, no roping off? I'm meant to be clairvoyant, am I?" I replied sharply, tinged with a tone of irritation.

Two robust rebukes within half an hour of arrival. Hardly the greetings I'd expected of a 'Club That Needs You'.

"Well that's my business. I'm the club groundsman and if I say 'don't train on the pitches', you need to go somewhere else."

Drawing on my dwindling reserves of civility, I stuck out a hand and in the broadest Cornish brogue announced.

"Sorry, but we don't have a problem growing grass where I'm from, Mr. . ?" I enquired.

"Uh... it's Frank," came the hesitant reply. "Are you having a laugh at me, son?"

"Nope, just apologising, Frank." Following which his large callus covered right hand, somewhat reluctantly, met with mine.

By my estimation Frank stood about 5 foot 9 inches tall and looked to be in his early 50s, although years of over exposure to all extremes of weather could have meant that he was in fact in his mid 40s. Dressed in wide-checked cotton shirt, multi-pocketed khaki canvas strides and cross braces, with heavily worn brown leather boots, Frank looked every inch a groundsperson.

"We're not used to people warming up here. Are you the new coach then?" Frank enquired, clearly thawing after his frosty reception.

"No, I'm interested in joining the rugby club. I was impressed by the flyer at the Tube station."

"Good luck to you, as they've been struggling in the last few years. More beer than brawn if you ask me," he announced with a restrained laugh. "Still, they're great for bar takings!"

"Well, good to meet you and sorry about the misunderstanding," I apologised again before setting off diagonally across the ground to avoid Frank's embryonic turf.

Twenty minutes later, having collaborated with another rookie, I found my way over to Gunnersbury Park. For West London this large tract of parched grass surrounded by plane trees provided welcome relief from the hustle and bustle of the nearby M4 flyover, various railway/Tube links and the sprawling residential areas of Ealing, Chiswick and Brentford. First impressions had always meant a lot to me in terms of whether I started and then persisted with something. Today was to be different though. The chaos that initially presented itself would normally have had me doing a 180 degree turn back out through the park gates. There was no training equipment as such, just half a dozen scraggy old rugby balls, mismatched training bibs and a few traffic cones strewn haphazardly across a wide area, with most of the players clumped together laughing and joking. Some, Kiwis I guessed, given all the fancy ball skills, had broken away for an impromptu game of touch rugby. A few others had taken to light stretches, shoulder rolling and jogging but, in general, the first impression was one of herding cats! And yet something made me stay.

After an hour of basic ball skills and fitness work, my initial hesitancy had been dispelled. There were actually quite a few good players amongst the group and once the 'coach' had separated the Possibles and Probables away from the remainder for a 30 minute trial session involving full contact, it became clear that the club had the bedrock for a decent side. In particular, the Antipodean lads were some way superior when it came to moving the ball around the park although less adept at making an impact when it came to scrummaging and mauling, something that Cornish rugby had taught me well. Having been blessed with good upper body strength, grappling and ripping the ball at close quarters had become

112

a big part of my game. I was thrown an orange bib and asked to line up for the Possibles.

Going into the last fifteen minutes, the Probables were a couple of tries down and under pressure inside their own 22 yard line. A quick tapped penalty by the Possibles' scrum half got us to within five yards of the try line, after which a messy huddle of tired bodies formed. Most people were leaning on, but I managed to burrow my way into the maul and get an arm over the ball enabling me to rip it downwards and force my way over the try line. From there on the Possibles proceeded to win comfortably. So much for the Probables making up the bulk of the 1st XV in a few weeks time.

As the session finished, reasonably pleased with how it had gone, I collected my gear and started to make my way back towards the club.

"Hello, I'm Roger Lee, the Club Captain. What's your name?" enquired Roger, appearing in front of me with the offer of a handshake.

"Hi Roger. Pleased to meet you. I'm John Hambly."

"You played really well tonight. If you're not rushing off, I'd like to buy you a beer and perhaps you can tell me where you're from and who you've played for."

"That'd be good, thank you Roger. I'll meet you in the clubhouse after I've showered."

It would prove to be the first of many long rugby-related conversations that Roger and I would share over the coming years.

Chapter 17

Skipper
February 1989 – April 1994

IN late February 1989, Simon Taylor, the 1st XV captain, was about to move away from the area for work reasons and asked me whether I would be prepared to take on the role for the remaining part of the season. Having been at the club for less than two seasons, I was both flattered and honoured that he had asked me and willingly agreed to take up the challenge. And it was just that, as despite the club growing in number and the rest of the teams performing well, the first team had really struggled in the newly formed Middlesex leagues. True to Simon's rousing captain-elect's speech the previous April, we would get out of Middlesex 4 – we were relegated to Middlesex 5! This was not a fair reflection on Simon who had done his best to pull the side out of the doldrums but more a case of shortcomings in the set-up at the club. We now had plenty of players, so a 3rd XV was regularly fielded, but the coaching was left to one or two senior players, and when they were unavailable training usually just involved some basic fitness drills followed by a short game before retiring to the bar. It was hardly the sort of regime that would propel us up the league tables.

If there was one thing that my professional career was beginning to show me, it was that the devil was in the detail. In the case of the Old Actonians I saw our failure as being largely attributable to our coaching methods, or more to the point, the lack of them. I therefore spent many hours poring over rugby magazines and training manuals, devising a fresh approach that I could first put to Roger and then roll out on Tuesday and Thursday nights. On top of my work commitments, it was a huge undertaking but I truly believed that the club had massive potential. Even during the time of relegation, spirits within the ranks never faltered, so when pre-season training started in late July 1989 I was not in the least bit surprised to find that a core group of players were as determined as I was to turn around the club's fortunes.

I had got to know the guys well, and in particular those who were willing to put it in on the training nights and leave nothing on the pitch come game time. Within that group I had strong allies in Roger, Andy 'Robbo' Robins and John Seeler, who were all very comfortable taking coaching sessions; each with their own style. Roger, as Club Captain, took his responsibilities very seriously and many may have viewed him as a bit of a disciplinarian but, owing to the fact that he seldom got wrecked after a game, he was a great ambassador, extremely good at 'working' the clubhouse to welcome new players and could even be relied upon to schmooze the match officials! He was also a strong prop forward who could play either side of the scrum as well as second row and No.8 when required. Once the season was underway, Roger would make a point of ringing me every Sunday around six o'clock to discuss the previous day's game and what we would need to concentrate on at Tuesday night's training.

John was not the biggest second row I had ever played rugby with, but being a New Zealander, he had an astute rugby brain and, perhaps just as important, shared our burning desire to get the club back on track. Even though he was relatively slight in build, he was athletic and had a real engine. When others were flagging, John would be right in there making a nuisance of himself at rucks and mauls whilst still holding his own at scrum time. When the number attending Tuesday training grew in excess of 40, I had no hesitation in asking John to take a group of guys aside to do warm-up drills which he did willingly without the need for preparation.

Robbo and I joined the club around the same time and with both of us being of West Country stock we immediately hit it off.

Formerly in the Royal Navy and Portsmouth's field gun crew, Robbo had a steely determination, trained very hard and expected everyone else to do likewise. Having spent the previous summer training together, it was clear to me that he would make a terrific fitness coach. His no-nonsense, and at times monosyllabic, approach would be just what we needed to identify the guys who were ready to roll up their sleeves and put in the hard yards. Robbo's particular speciality was the 'speed circuit', a sort of bleep test with diminishing recovery times between exercise stations, some of which included free weights. In the first few weeks you could spot exhausted players looking at each other with expressions that said 'Is this for real?' However, as the weeks went on and fitness levels improved rapidly, there was more teamwork with people encouraging each other and lots of banter and laughter. The club was not blessed with a changing room full of giants, so the coaching team decided early on that our main emphasis would be on a fast fluid game based on superior fitness, thereby enabling us to move larger teams around the pitch to the point that they were less effective in the tight. Robbo's drive and input was therefore invaluable.

Apart from needing to address the coaching and fitness side of things, we were woefully short of specialist equipment ranging from a modern scrummage machine right the way down to tackle bags, flags, training tops, balls, etc., along with effective flood lighting. Fortunately for us, the committee were very much behind the direction Roger and I wanted to take the club, and set about raising funds for the major items.

By the time the 1989/90 season came around you could feel positivity running through the place. Owing to an influx of Southern Hemisphere players, we were comfortably able to put out four teams with a few more on the bench. The club had, in my opinion, the right balance of players. Those that trained twice a week and played with the competitive edge required to move us up the leagues, and those that played for the 3rds and 4ths who were proud to be playing their part in the Old A's revival but at the same time enjoy the social side without having to crawl off the training paddock each week. The camaraderie that this created proved to be almost as important as the results.

As the season progressed the club found itself with a new problem – we had too many players! Not only had the pre-season recruitment campaign worked well but word of mouth, particularly amongst the Antipodean brigade, meant that a lot of new guys were turning up on a Saturday with their kit requesting a game. Many of the Kiwis were travelling around Europe and wanted a run out and a few beers. As the national league structure had just been established it was very restrictive in terms of selecting overseas players; in fact, you were only allowed to play one in a league match and, even then, only after a long qualification period. As a result, we were forced to play Kiwis, Aussies and Boks, many with senior grade experience, in the 3rds, 4ths and a newly formed 5th team. Some of the scores posted by these teams on the club blackboard on Saturday evenings made eye-watering viewing and with the 1sts and 2nds also running up winning sequences, chalking up the points added to the entertainment. A hush would spread around the clubhouse as the away teams arrived back, followed by loud cheering as another win was posted.

By the start of the 1990/91 season, the reality of what was actually happening at the club was made clear when, bowing to pressure from the Kiwi contingent, I set up a 6th team, the Acton Aardvarks. It was run on the basis that we would give it a go to arrange fixtures for guys who just turned up on the day, whether the squad had 11 or 20 players. Again, reassuringly, word got around and there was hardly ever a problem in getting out a full team. The main issue was finding kit for the lads who had literally stumbled into the club straight from crashing out at a party the night before. On the back of some good wins, the highlight for me, as their impromptu manager, came when we sent the Aardvarks off to play Ruislip 3rds. Being four leagues above us, I felt that it was probably a step too far, but it was all that was available in the fixture pool that weekend and the guys were chomping at the bit, so off they went. By the time they returned, via several of the local Kiwi haunts, the clubhouse was in full swing with the blackboard already showing five wins. The Aardvarks' skipper, playing to the baying crowd, first chalked up '15' against 'Ruislip III' which drew a few groans. When he inserted a '6' into the Aardvarks square, there were even more and several lads turned back towards the bar, only to be dragged back into the revelry as a '2' was added to the right of the first digit. Yes, it was true, our 6ths had beaten a more senior club's 3rds by 62-15. Euphoria abounded and a spontaneous delivery of 'Sunshine Mountain' broke out. Apart from two lines, the lyrics seemed nonsensical to me. As the years together mounted up, we would all come to understand their simple message:

> *Climb, climb up Sunshine Mountain,*
> *Where the Little Breezes blow,*
> *Climb, climb up Sunshine Mountain,*
> *Faces all aglow-oh-oh-oh*
> *Turn, turn your back on sorrow,*
> *Reach up to the sky*
> *Climb, climb up Sunshine Mountain,*
> *You and I, you and I, you and I*

As for the 1st XV, we easily extricated ourselves from Middlesex's basement tier in 1989/90 which was followed a year later by a 'double' promotion from Middlesex 4 to Middlesex 2 during which time we remained unbeaten in League games. The club was absolutely buzzing now and league success had also been matched with good cup runs, firstly in the national Provincial Insurance Cup for junior clubs, where we reached the last eight. However, it was the Middlesex Cup of 1990 that really galvanised the club, not because of a glorious cup run, but the fact that we were pitted against the once mighty London Welsh. Even with our stellar rise up the leagues, it was perfectly understand-able that a collective deep intake of breath was detected around the club when the draw was announced. London Welsh were not the force of old but they were still playing in the senior national leagues, way above Middlesex 4, so the Actonians would not be expected to pose any great test, even with home advantage. We were, though, a close-knit group growing in belief and, by the time of the fixture, for four months we had been under the coaching regime of Andy Keast, Dick Best's understudy at the

Harlequins. An ex-Metropolitan police officer and friend of future club captain, Dave Duff, Andy's style was blunt and uncompromising but brought us a level of coaching far above anything that Roger or I could deliver.

Tuesday night training fundamentally changed when Keasty arrived at Pope's Lane. His experience with the Quins not only meant that we were brought up to speed both technically and tactically but the level of intensity during training went off the scale. I recall one session when we were practising line-out drills that he dismissed three hookers for lacking the necessary pinpoint accuracy. At times his methods were sledgehammer-like and guys from the lower teams started switching to Thursday nights where John and I continued coaching in a more relaxed way. Mind you, even as 1st XV skipper, I got off to an inauspicious start with Keasty on his very first session. Having taken on the coaching duties for the previous season, I had got into the habit of warming up and going for a run around the ground before the guys pitched up. Unknown to me, Keasty had turned up early to the club and was sitting in his car planning the session. As the arrangements for his position were yet to be finalised, we had not been introduced so he didn't know me from Adam. After the players came together for his initial briefing, he set everything up for the first set of drills using tackle bags and told the guys to line up behind the try line.

"Not you," he said, pointing at me. "Since you like running so much, fuck off around the posts!"

Despite the sniggers, I said nothing and set off towards the posts expecting to be recalled to the main group after a couple of lengths of the pitch. Ten minutes later I heard the shrill rasping sound of Keasty's whistle.

"Oi, Seb Coe, rejoin the main group and don't insult me by training before one of my sessions ever again!"

I lined up next to Duff who, like a school kid trying to control himself in class, giggled and snorted his way through the next set of drills.

"Told you he was good, didn't I, me anzum?" he mumbled between large gulps of air.

By the time of the London Welsh game, Keasty's influence on the

1st and 2nd XVs was clear for all to see, both unbeaten and full of confidence. I arrived at the ground early to get the changing room prepared; shirts on pegs for once, avoiding the need for the guys having to rummage through the kit bag, plus liniment, strapping, Vaseline, etc., all laid out. I also took the opportunity to run through my pre-match team talk, having visualised the various scenarios we would face on the pitch. One by one the team appeared, excited by the sight of a large crowd building up, but there was a distinct air of apprehension. Dave Rutter, our inside centre, was a great bloke in the changing room, a real jack-in-the-box always full of confidence and wise cracks to raise the spirits. That day he was rather muted and fidgety. Sensing his newly found introversion, I made the point of sitting next to him as we got kitted out.

"Rutz, what's up mate? Something eating away at you?"

"Hammers, I've got loads of experience of playing footie in front of crowds back in Dinas Powys but this is different. I'm not sure what I'm doing in such a big game."

"You're here on merit, Rutz, have no doubt about that. You've had a great season so lots of the same please. Straight running, big hits, close down the oppo's space – you know our style. Just be yourself mate, you'll love it once we get going."

"Alright, Hamms, there's only one thing I can say about that," Rutz said, smiling.

I knew what was coming, given that it was his usual rallying cry, although, to be honest, I had no idea what it meant.

"Steamboats!" he bellowed.

All was back on an even keel with Rutz; now for my clarion call.

"Robbo, can you do the warm-up whilst I do the team talk? Nice and quiet for now and then we'll build it up."

Just one look across at him was all that was needed. Straight onto his feet as if ready for manoeuvres, Andy went into his familiar routine of stretches, shoulder rolls, squats, face slapping, pounding his chest, stomach and thighs, gradually increasing the rapidity under hushed commands until sweat ran freely from our brows. By that time, I'm walking around the room, looking each of the guys in the eyes, bringing their aggression to the surface until I could feel that the moment was right. I glanced and nodded to Andy. The room went eerily quiet.

Our wedding day, July 1992, at the Alverton Manor, Truro. Proudly wearing the Cornish tartan.

With our parents.

My best man, Verm and myself.

Father and myself.

Leading the team off after promotion from Middlesex 2, 1992.

Middlesex Division 1, first XV squad, 1992.

Northern v Southern Hemisphere squads, 1993.

Fletch's 40th celebratory match, 1997.
(My old mate Bob Snook popping up in the Cornish colours!)

Doting first time
dad to Ellie, 1994.

Father meets Ellie for the
first time.

Bruv's 40th at
Truro Rugby Club,
1997.

Typical family
outing to
Porthtowan
beach.
Summer 2002.

The X-man and
family, 2002.

Me and the girls, 2004.

The girls buy into the beauty
of St. Michael's Mount, 2006.

Family holiday, Menorca,
2006.

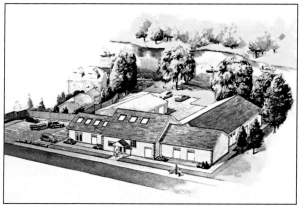

The vision of the Samson Centre, 2003.

Anthea gives

Local personality, Anthea Turner is the latest celebrity to lend her support to the hardworking Guildford-based Multiple Sclerosis Therapy Group (MSTG), currently forging ahead with their plans for a dedicated resource and therapy centre for MS sufferers and their families in West Surrey.

Anthea's support comes just as planning permission has been received to go ahead with the work on the Guildford Waterside Centre — in which the MSTG's new Samson Centre will be incorporated. Whilst the project is now out to tender and over £68,000 has been raised so far, the group still has a long way to go and fundraising activities are at the top of their agenda.

If you would like more information about the Samson Centre Project, log onto www.samsoncentre.org.uk or e-mail info@samsoncentre.org.uk.

PHOTO: Anthea Turner with members of the Multiple Sclerosis therapy Group (Guildford), outside the existing Waterside Centre (courtesy of the Surrey Advertiser)

Anthea Turner supports the fundraising initiative, 2004.

Demolition of the Waterside Centre, early 2005.

The Centre begins to emerge, April 2005.

John Hambly, Fleur Crowther Smith, Bill Bellerby, and Sue and John Steelspening at the opening of phase one of the Samson Centre, Bellfields, Guildford.

Samson Centre hopes to go from strength to strength

MEMBERS and supporters of the Guildford Multiple Sclerosis (MS) Therapy Group celebrated the opening of the first phase of a purpose-built centre on Saturday.

The official opening phase one of the Samson Centre in Stoughton was marked with a ribbon-cutting ceremony by Bill Bellerby.

During the last two years the charity has been working hard to raise £250,000 to build the dedicated MS resource and therapy centre.

The centre is now up and running but fundraising continues at pace with a view to the construction of the phase two gymnasium block during the early summer of 2006.

The charity is now asking residents from the area who are planning to enter next year's London Marathon to consider raising funds for the centre.

In previous years, the charity has obtained Golden Bond places, assuring it of sponsored runners.

However, due to the popularity of the marathon, these are now much more difficult to acquire.

If you (or someone you know) are looking to run for a local charity and wish to support the Samson Centre project, contact chairman, John Hambly, on 01483 429220 or e-mail info@samsoncentre.org.uk

Opening phase one of the Samson Centre, October 2005.

The new Centre, 2005.

The Samson Trophy programme, 2006.

Me with Zinzan, Enzo, Jason Leonard, Tugger, Duff and Big Gerry after the Samson Trophy 2007.

Me with New Zealand rugby legend Zinzan Brooke at the first Samson Trophy match, 2006.

2007 Samson Trophy with nephews Ian and Owen either side, plus Jamie Hutchinson.

The Samson Trophy return match v McGee XV – Old Actonians' Jolly Boys Squad, 2007.

Glenn's epic bike ride from Truro
to Guildford, 2006.

GlaxoSmithKline
Awards 2006.

Cerys fronting
the 'Surrey
Stumble',
March 2009.

"Fellas, let's get out there today and give these bastards downstairs a good old fashioned Acton welcome. If they think they're here to thump one of Middlesex's minnows, then they've got a nasty shock coming. We're well up for this and you all know how to use this pitch to our advantage. Yeah, OK, they've got a few big boys, but let's stick to what we're good at. Anything in red, you fucking deck it! Keith, Snoidy, get the ball in and away quickly at the scrums and let's move them around the park. Matt, if you've got good quick ball, try and bring John into the game from full back. Robbo, Glenn or myself will be on your shoulder if you need to offload, otherwise play the territory game and kick long. Right, time to give these Welsh boys an Actonian welcome."

Pulling the guys in closer, I stood in the middle. Drawing on the memory of the Cornish warm-ups with Curt at the helm, I began breathing more deeply, exhaling through the mouth.

"Suck it in fellas. Nice and steady, let me hear your studs in time. Just a gentle jog. Let 'em think that's all we've got."

Rhythmically, the mesmerising march began. The sound of metal studs on plywood boarding resonating around the room. You could feel the electricity building but the squad held it together, all the studs still hitting the deck as one.

"OK, all in sync, knees to hands and give me a quiet five."

"ONE, TWO, THREE, FOUR, FIVE."

Looking around the circle, I could see that everyone was in the zone and it was time.

"This is your day, boys. Get out there and give this crowd something to shout about. Let's build to a ten on my NOW!"

The synchronised clatter of studs was now full of menace.

"Ready. . . ready. . . building. . . building. . . come on! More fire!" I was now growling. "Ready. . . ready. . . ready. . . get ready. . . on my call. . . readyyy. . . readyyyyy. . . NOW!"

As the warm-up reached its climax, the sound must have been deafening London Welsh sitting directly beneath us. They could have been in no doubt that we would not be a walkover.

Being an avid rugby fan, I had occasionally read accounts of players saying that they had competed in matches and yet they had only a vague recollection of what had gone on over the previous eighty or so minutes. It seemed that this had nothing to do with any bangs on the head but more to do with the pace of the game and burning lungs blurring the memory. This match was to be like that for most of us as the bigger, faster outfit of the Welsh moved the ball around the pitch at a tempo that we were unaccustomed to. However, unsurprisingly, at least to me, the lads held firm throughout the opening salvo, growing in self-belief as each drive was repelled. The home crowd were packed in around the perimeter of the pitch, cheering us on at every tackle, every line break, every penalty awarded. Their heckling of our visitors was relentless and partisan but generally very good mannered. Probably the worst that it got was when Hugh Duffy, an injured 1st team winger, brazenly bawled out in his broadest Scottish brogue, "London Welsh, nine divisions higher and you're still shite!"

By half-time we were still well in it. Despite having conceded a try to a smart midfield move, if Matt's kicking boots hadn't deserted him (in fairness, he had played most of the game on one good leg after being nobbled by their open-side flanker early on), amazingly we could have been in front. The second half brought much of the same. They were rattled and we were inspired, but as is often said in boxing circles, 'a good big 'un will usually beat a good little 'un'. By the end we were beaten 15-3, succumbing only to their fly half's long range penalties (I found out later that he was Michael Dawes, the son of the Welsh and British Lion's legend, John Dawes). Clapping the Welsh boys and the ref off the pitch, I felt immense pride in what the club had achieved. This was not just for the match day squad, it was also for all the players who had pushed us in training, for Keasty and, of course, our wonderful supporters. Needless to say it was a great night!

Losing is not normally lauded but the *Ealing Gazette* the following week had a full page spread, headlined 'On a Day of History Actonians are Heroes' and snippets even made the national press. The real plus was that at the end of the season *Rugby World & Post* ran an article on the Old Actonians, nominating us as Southern Team of the Year. Around the same time another bolt out of the blue came from the Old A's football club who invited me to their end of season dinner in acknowledgement and celebration of their rugby counterparts' success. I gladly accepted and was utterly gobsmacked to find myself sitting next to Sir Geoff Hurst!

The 1991/92 season saw us playing in Middlesex 2 and with the momentum built up over the previous two seasons, we were still able to hold our own in this tougher division. With the top two teams eligible for promotion to Middlesex 1, it soon became apparent that we were in the mix, with Old Hamptonians, Belsize Park and Roxeth Manor providing the main impediments to our further rise up the leagues. Of those clubs, Old Hamptonians were the most formidable, having a huge front five and a good back division. We were aware that we would need to match them up front when we played them at their ground early in 1992. Going into the selection meeting on Tuesday evening after training, Keasty, Duff (now Club Captain) and I decided to bolster our front row with Darcy Lentle, who weighed in around 20 stone and would also bring an 'edge' to our forward game. Like Hamptonians, we were unbeaten and therefore we felt no need to make wholesale changes. So much for fine tuning. On the Friday night Darcy pulled out through illness and Duff was unavailable to stand in, so I was forced to go with Grant Paynter, a newly qualified Kiwi tight head prop who had been 'tearing up trees' for the 2nds.

On the day of the game I had an uneasy feeling, which was unusual. I had got well beyond the point of having match day nerves so just put it down to adrenaline in anticipation of a difficult game. Maybe I had developed a sixth sense because it became just that. Unfortunately, after only one scrum, Grant tore a calf muscle and hobbled off. We had travelled with three reserves but no substitute prop (as top flight rugby requires these days) so it was left to me to move from No.8 and lock horns with one of the biggest guys I had ever propped against. I guessed that I was 6 or 7 stone lighter and even slightly shorter. Foolishly I thought I stood a better chance against him if I got low enough to drive up underneath him. It was wishful thinking as the bloke was just monstrously strong. I expended every ounce of strength I had over the next 75 minutes trying to anchor the scrum whilst also contributing in open play. I can seldom recall leaving a rugby pitch so utterly drained. We were well beaten in almost every area and went down 27-6. For the moment, the bubble had burst.

Testament to the attitude running through the team, the result was nothing more than a blip and the 1st team racked up another sequence of wins, so that by the time we were due to meet Hamptonians at home we were comfortably second in the league and needing one more win from our three remaining fixtures to secure promotion to Middlesex 1. The unfortunate part was that I had broken my collarbone three weeks earlier and would be unable to play so I handed over the reins to Robbo, confident that he would get the best out of the guys. Reverting to our tried and tested tactic of moving heavier sides about the park, we selected a light pack and a quick, elusive back line as well as opting to play the game on Gunnersbury Park where the pitches were much larger than the Field of Dreams in front of the clubhouse. It proved to be a masterstroke as apparently Hamptonians turned up with an even heavier pack of forwards than the one that had squashed us earlier in the year.

I say apparently only because I had had to shoot home to Cornwall late on the Thursday as my father had been rushed into hospital with a severe lung infection and related heart problems. It was touch and go for 24 hours, so much so that Bruv and I slept in the hospital waiting room on the Friday night. Rugby was the last thing on my mind as the ward sister woke us with the dawn sunlight filtering through the thin nylon curtains.

"Good news, boys, we've managed to stabilise your father. The next few days will be crucial, but after what he's just been through he must be very tough and we're optimistic that he will get through this episode."

The rest of the Saturday was a bit of a blur, mainly through tiredness and having to ferry my mother and Marianne up and down to Treliske Hospital. It was only around 7 o'clock that I came up for air and stole five minutes to ring the clubhouse. It rang and rang for a couple of minutes without answer so I assumed the worse and rung off. Never mind, there were two games to go and we were still well placed. I told myself that there was no need to panic.

The following morning things were looking much more settled as far as the old man's condition was concerned, so after chatting with my mother and Bruv, I made the decision to head back to London. I was really busy at work so needed to knuckle down for a few days. On returning home I called Robbo straight away.

"Hi Robbo, it's Hammers. I'm back from Kernow."

"Alright, John. How's your Dad doing?"

"Thanks for asking mate. He's out of danger and slowly improving, which is a huge relief."

"Thank God for that. Me and the guys were really worried when we heard that you'd had to drop tools and rush off like that."

"Yeah, we all were, but he's a tough old boy and could even be back home by next weekend."

"Just like you then, is he? Doesn't know when to give in!"

"Nah, he's far more resilient than I'll ever be."

I quickly dismissed the compliment which I probably shouldn't have done, as coming from Robbo it was something of a collector's item!

"Andy, now stop buttering me up. What happened yesterday? I tried calling the club around 7 o'clock last night and there was no one there to answer the blower. Was it that bad?"

"7 o'clock? Now let me think, what were we doing about that time? Hmmm, I think we were '*Climbing Up Sunshine Mountain*'. . . for the third time!"

I immediately knew that that could only mean one thing.

"You won? We're going up!"

"Yep and yep. Good call to play them on the Park pitch. Our tactics were spot on. Congratulations mate, you've got us into Middlesex 1. See you on Tuesday for a beer with Keasty. He's pretty chuffed."

I put down the receiver and, for the first time in four days, allowed myself a wry smile.

It was only when Duff called me later that evening that the full extent of Saturday's emotions were revealed.

"We did it for you, John. Simple as that."

Unknown to all of us, that sentiment would be used by the rugby lads time and time again over the next 25 years.

Chapter 18

Brown Willy
April 1990

THERE can be little doubt that touring is an essential ingredient in the rugby mix. Become a good tourist and you're 'in'. Do something absolutely outrageous and you're a legend. Quite what makes an eclectic group of different professions, nationalities and cultures gather together then migrate vast distances for just a matter of days in order to engage in all manner of excess and hedonistic ritual has confounded non-rugby folk for decades. A well-planned tour sets off exuding unity, order, pride, ambition, sporting prowess – even sartorial splendour! A well-executed tour limps back home, totally dishevelled, exhausted, disordered and largely disinterested in returning to the real world.

As with most clubs, whether senior or junior, the Actonians were dedicated tourists as well as hosts when the opportunities arose. In previous years preference had been for foreign tours during the Easter recess and, indeed, that was the intention in 1990, at least until the whole thing was scrapped when the tour operator proved to be nothing of the sort. Faced with no end-of-season jamboree in my first full season as skipper and with precious little time to organise anything too complicated, I opted for a familiar route. As a teenager, I used to love the atmosphere at Truro RFC when coach-loads of touring teams would descend on the club. The Cornish weather usually deigned to offer an early taste of summer so there would be a wonderful festival atmosphere with two or three games played each day right through from Good Friday to Easter Monday.

In the event, the hurriedly thrown together 'Brown Willy' Tour of mid April 1990 proved surprisingly popular as we set off down the A303 on Good Friday with a squad of about thirty plus a few socialites and Reginald Bradford, the Mayor of Acton. Each tourist was presented with a personalised pewter tankard complete with a lanyard made of baler twine, Brown Willy T-shirt (brilliantly designed by Jane with caricatures of the club's various characters) and the obligatory slab of cheap beer. Two and a half hours into a painfully slow journey, the coach driver was forced by Big Gerry and Warren, one of our Maoris, to do a 360° turn at Sparkford roundabout after they'd spotted a pub sign proclaiming 'Carvery – Eat All You Can'. Given that the pair were cursed with gargantuan appetites and had been barred from several West London restaurants offering similar deals, they were simply unable to let such challenges pass them by. Much to everyone's amusement, the newly opened Mongolian Brasserie in South Ealing, just down the road from the club, had been lucky to survive its first month after Gerry and Warren had accepted their introductory offer of an all-day buffet and virtually moved in!

For most of us lunch at the Sparkford Inn lasted just over the hour, so we were back on the coach bracing ourselves for the next leg of the nose-to-tail grind through the West Country. It was wishful thinking! We were soon drawn back to the bar as our gastro-giants demolished the pub's carvery. The tour eventually got back on the road two hours later. By late afternoon, in bright sunshine, we hit Bodmin Moor, with Brown Willy, at 1378ft, looming to the west. Those who hadn't consumed all of their tour ale and were still awake remained completely underwhelmed by the sight of Cornwall's premier hillock!

Mrs Trebilcock had seemed so positive when I had booked the Fistral Heights Hotel in Newquay six weeks before. My broadest Cornish accent may have helped get a foot in the door, but it was the introduction of the words 'sports association' (which, in truth, we were part of) in place of 'rugby club' which had appeared to seal the deal. As the guys staggered off the coach, tankards swaying in front of their Brown Willy emblazoned shirts, Mrs T's welcome was not quite as warm as I'd hoped for. Realising that we might not actually get past the front door, I grabbed Roger and The Mayor who were both still sober and more suitably attired and headed up the steps.

"Good evening Mrs Trebilcock, I'm John Hambly. Very pleased to meet you at last," I rattled off quickly, offering her a handshake. "May I introduce our Mayor, Reginald Bradford, along with Roger Lee, our Club Captain."

"Umm, nice to meet you all. . . errr. . . gentlemen."

The poor lady looked equally confused and distracted as one of our party emerged from the coach festooned with all manner of puppets – Gordon the Gopher around his neck, Colin the Crocodile under his arm and Roger the Rottweiler carrying his case.

"Oh, I'm sorry Mrs Trebilcock, I should also introduce Keith Ewart, the Association's Merchandising and Kit Officer." As if that explanation could possibly have helped!

Against all the odds, with an air of resignation, Mrs T turned and strode back to the hotel reception. Within the hour though, things were definitely looking up as the guys, now settled into the bar area, began to relieve her of most of her draught beer. It soon became clear that we formed a large part of the hotel's clientele for the weekend and that our patronage would be much appreciated. With Mrs T beginning to relax, Roger sealed the deal.

"Gentlemen, may I have your attention." And when silence had fallen: "Please be upstanding for The Mayor of Acton."

With grace befitting his standing, he slowly made his way to the bar for his customary tour tipple of whiskey and water whilst the lads raised their glasses and toasted our dignitary. The masterstroke was in leaving The Mayor perched on a bar stool chatting away to Mrs T. Within no time Thelma and Reginald were on first name terms.

Around midday on a sopping wet Easter Saturday, our coach breasted the brow of St Clements Hill. With Trelander estate to the left and the road down to the estuary off to the right, I was back in familiar territory albeit with a few butterflies. I desperately wanted to beat my old Truronian teammates but the weather had turned in favour of their heavyweight pack and several of our squad were feeling the effects of clearing Thelma's top shelf!

I had made the short trek from the estate to the rugby club hundreds of times, whether it be as a child climbing trees to watch the games or as a player proudly donning the blue and yellow jersey. In all that time the metal 'TRFC' gate had never been shut at noon on a match day. As the coach drew alongside the entrance to the club, I almost did a double-take. Not only was the gate shut but it was crudely shrouded in woodchip paper upon which various confrontational messages had been posted; the general thrust of which was that, with the club AGM looming, my captaincy credentials were under fire.

As we departed the coach and approached the clubhouse, the full extent of the smear campaign became clear. Yard after yard of wallpaper, daubed with further electioneering rhetoric, obliterated the front windows. This caused no end of amusement amongst the touring party, only for it to be elevated still further as we stepped into bar. Fred Flintstone and Barney Rubble, to the best of my knowledge, had never put in an appearance at Truro RFC before but there they were, appearing on many of the walls. And at the bar, already lining up the pints, stood the culprits, the tour gatecrashers – Duff, an officer of the law and his loyal deputies, Tugger and Snoid. Who else would get up at the crack of dawn, drive 250 miles to Cornwall, break into a property and redecorate it with Bedrock's finest!

With the Old Dunstonians from Kent also in town and the Colts playing later on, by kick-off time the place was buzzing. Aside from the locals who'd turned up baying for some 'foreign' blood, non-playing tourists from the various clubs were already indulging in the hair of the dog, aided and abetted by Truro's club stalwarts. Running out from the changing rooms after an excusably lacklustre warm-up, I recall getting a fair bit of good-natured stick from the home crowd.

"Hambly, you bleddy turncoat!"; "Judas!"; "Grockle!"; "Clear off, back over the border with yer posh city boys!" were just a few of the more polite jibes directed my way.

Early on, the game bore all the hallmarks of touring rugby.

Players walking from breakdown to breakdown, others throwing up, some just too inebriated to be allowed to stay on. All very amusing if you weren't the one retching or gasping. Truro, with a front five averaging 18 stone a man, took full advantage of a boggy pitch by pinning us on our line for long periods of a game that felt like an eternity. Like a kid on a long journey continually asking 'Are we there yet?' I made sure the ref was aware of the time with regular checks of his watch. The number of scrummages soared as my old mates kept to their one dimensional, tried and tested game plan. Keith, shorn of his soft toy accompaniments, and Greg at his uncompromising South African best, were immense on the flanks in repelling everything that their pack and scrum half threw at us. From No.8, I was also in the firing line and copped Knocker Kneebone's bald bonce on the side of my head in one desperate attempt to prevent the whitewash being crossed. Being clocked by Knocker was tantamount to heading a granite boulder and a sure fire way to scramble cognitive function.

As with so many games when a team is in the box seat but fails to nail their opponent, late on we got our lucky break as the ball squirted out of yet another scrum and our winger, who must have been close to hypothermic, scooted the length of the pitch to touch down under the posts and seal an unlikely win. Relieved, we dragged our mud-caked bodies back to the changing rooms through the disgruntled home support. Whilst it was nice to get one over the natives, I knew that retribution would swiftly follow!

Half an hour later, Phil Rowe, the Truro XV captain and one of Bruv's closest friends, hauled me up in front of the club to a mixture of cheers and good-natured boos.

"You lucky git, Vertical. How the hell your boys won that is beyond me but now it's time to take your medicine." Phil announced with a mischievous glint. "Dickie, pass it over please."

Just by bringing a touring team home, I had half-expected to be collared into having to complete some dastardly deed, but with my head still ringing from its close encounter with Knocker's noggin, a yard of ale (almost certainly with 'bonus' spirits) was an unwelcome sight. I had mastered the challenge only once before and not in front of a screaming mob. Still, as a matter of pride and honour, I had to give it my best. Drinking a yard is a strange thing. It's not the two and a half pints that's the main problem. You think you're getting there, gradually raising this curious glass blunderbuss near to the horizontal, gently turning it as the ale within the straight stem disappears, only for the bulbous vessel at the end to deposit its contents all over your face! As pathetic as the attempt was, at least it created the sort of hilarity that served to kick-start the proper drinking and singing. The Old A's might have thought that they could hold their own on the latter but when the Truro boys hit the harmonies in 'Trelawny', it was time to sit back and soak up something very special. 'Going up Camborne Hill, Coming Down' and 'Little Eyes' swiftly followed.

Six hours post match, accompanied by Knocker and a dozen ladies from Truro's fish filleting factory, we were back at the Fistral Heights swelling Thelma's bar takings to an all-time high. Without doubt we were irritating the hell out of her, but the presence of The Mayor presiding over the Players' Court and liberally dishing out all manner of punishments and forfeits seemed to take the heat out of the situation.

"Oh Reginald, I have to say I am very impressed. Thank God you've got these lads under control."

"Not a problem, all part of my civic role, Thelma. Sometimes they just need reminding that they're representing the London Borough of Ealing," the Mayor asserted somewhat smugly. "Would you please excuse me for a moment. I'm just going to freshen up."

"Of course not Reginald. I'll have your favourite tipple waiting upon your return." I sensed a twinkle in our landlady's eye.

With the court no longer in session, Roger and I gathered the guys together and took the calculated gamble of delivering our finest rendition of 'Sloop John B'. Despite the general level of inebriation, it proved to be a smart call as Thelma was a Beach Boys fan and dropped tools to listen and admire. After a couple of verses she even joined us in the chorus.

"I want to go home. I want to go ho. . .ho. . .home. Well I feel so broke up, I want to go. . . oh my god! What are you doing Reginald?"

To Thelma's absolute horror, there in the middle of the lounge, bandy legged and pot bellied, stood The Mayor in nothing but a pink thong!

Regrettably there would be no more mayoral or judicial duties conducted on the premises, no more cosy chats at the bar, as Reginald's true colours were revealed to a distraught Thelma. Reg Bradford, a widower in his late 60s and one of the Association's full-time stewards, with his deadpan sense of humour had acquired cult status within the rugby club and toured with us for years, revelling in his quasi-municipal standing.

The Sunday match against St Agnes RFC proved comparatively uneventful until, with Knocker making a guest appearance for us, a few of the Truro lads arrived to liven things up. Optimistically, we were planning to go to Falmouth on a boat fishing trip the next day so unless you wanted four hours with your head down in the bilges puking into the fish guts and diesel, then a heavy drinking session was to be avoided at all costs. Everyone was made aware of this after the game but it made not a jot of difference as the men of St Agnes, many of whom were ex-Truro players, upped the ante. We may have comfortably won the match but there was no way that our hosts were going to let us off the hook! The ingenuity of the bar games and extraordinary stunts provided a couple of hours of riotous entertainment but we came off second best by some distance. By the time we had arrived at the Loft night club in Truro around 11 o'clock several of our touring party were in an awful mess. For some being unable to stand made queueing rather difficult. Roger and I faced the prospect of loading the lads back onto the coach and heading straight back to Thelma's until a large hand came down on my shoulder.

"Wot's she like 'en, John?"

Steve Ivey, one of Truro's supersized props and fellow Trelander resident, greeted me in his capacity as head bouncer.

"Hiya Steve, I'm good thanks mate. Just trying to keep it all together after a few of the lads came off worse in the bar at St. Agnes. Not looking good for our sea fishing trip down Falmouth tomorrow!"

"Yeah, that could be fun as it's meant to get quite blowy along the south coast."

"Is that right, Steve? Best we find something else to do then I reckon."

"You haven't heard then? Our game is off tomorrow. The Welsh touring side we were meant to play have headed home early because of a serious injury to one of their players."

"Bloody hell, that doesn't sound good, Steve. Must've been a bad one if they've called off their tour."

"Tell you what, the guys would jump at the chance for a return match after your lucky win on Saturday. Why don't we get it on again around 2 o'clock?"

"You're on mate, but I've no idea how many of my lot will be in a fit state to make up a team."

"Good, I like the sound of that!" Big Steve said, laughing out loud. "Do your boys want a couple more beers just to make sure you're all well and truly pickled?"

"Fat chance of that with this queue, Steve," I said, more in the hope that we wouldn't get into the night club!

"Don't worry about that John, just get 'em all together and follow me!"

As we pulled into Truro rugby club less than 12 hours after leaving the Loft I knew that I'd made a mistake in agreeing to the game. Getting the squad up and out of the Fistral Heights had been a logistical nightmare. Six of us at breakfast was a fair indication of how much had been downed the previous night and to make matters worse an even larger cohort of fish factory ladies had made the trip back to Newquay. Thelma, having spent the early hours patrolling the corridors apprehending bed-hoppers, was in a foul mood and virtually slammed the door as the last of the group, found in an understairs cupboard, staggered out to the coach on Easter Monday. Without question we were close to meeting all the 'right' criteria for a successful tour. Exhausted – tick, dishevelled – tick, disordered – tick. Just one problem – we still had a fixture to honour!

A look around the changing room confirmed my worst fears as

the majority of the XV I had selected on the coach either had pale sweaty faces cradled in their hands or were sat rocking and talking gibberish. As usual the forwards were in more of a state than the backs and that's where the main problem lay. We didn't have enough of them to take on Truro's heavyweight scrum. Even Greg, our iron man Springbok, who'd been 'filleting fish' through to dawn, looked decidedly green at the gills.

"Roger, the boys are in a mess and we're gonna get absolutely mullered up front. I'm going to speak with the Truro guys and see if they'll lend us 3 or 4 forwards. Are you OK with that?" my tone was bordering on desperation.

"Hurts me to say it but I think you're right, skipper," Roger conceded, looking none too sharp himself.

I knew that I would take some stick but ventured along to the home changing room, tapped on the door and strode on in.

"Here Vertical, wrong team, me anzum. You're playing for the grockles today!" Muscles fired off in a flash.

"Very good Muscles but we might not be having a game at this rate. Who's captain today?"

"It's Phil, but he's in chatting up the ref at the moment! Have a chat with Stevie Ivey."

At mention of his name Steve piped up.

"Hi John. Everything alright with your boys?"

"If I didn't know you better Steve, I'd say you stitched us up good and proper last night."

"No idea what you're talking about," he said with a mischievous grin.

"Listen mate, I've barely got fifteen that can stand upright but, even worse, I'm four light in the pack. Any chance we can have Knocker and three others?"

"Can't do that John. Several of the guys heard yesterday that we didn't have a fixture so they've gone down to watch Redruth play."

"That's a shame, mate. Unless you've got any other ideas, it'll have to be a game of touch rugby then."

I wasn't being entirely serious, but given the size of some of the Truro boys, including Steve, I knew that would get him thinking laterally!

A decent-sized crowd had turned up to watch the ritual slaughter of a touring party in the final throes of its now discombobulated existence. Having bumped into loads of old mates at the Loft the night before, there was a fair smattering of friendly faces on the sidelines, so as we staggered our way out onto the pitch the tone of the banter was largely good natured. Five minutes into the match, judging by the howls of laughter, it was also abundantly clear that Steve and I had managed to come up with a novel format that would win over the Bank Holiday support. Simple really – the backs would play as forwards and the few fit forwards we had as backs. Not quite rugby's version of 'It's A Knockout' but entertaining all the same. The sight of 20 stone Stevie selling a ludicrous dummy to 16 stone Simon Taylor from scrum half and then bouncing off five tacklers during the ensuing thirty yard trundle rather set the tone.

Over the years of playing the oval ball game I had witnessed and heard of some hilarious moments on the field, usually at the expense of others. Apparently David, my brother, had once induced uncontrollable laughter when, in trying to charge down a clearance kick, he had caught the point of the ball flush on the crown jewels. By all accounts, he lay in the foetal position groaning for ten minutes whilst the magic sponge was tentatively applied, before eventually being helped off the pitch on his Bambi legs. That was very much a case of the unfortunate. Then there could be the ever recurring case of the incompetent; invariably a serial offender. Big Gerry was one such player. A man mountain at 6' 5" and 22 stone, at the kick-off he would strike fear into the minds of the opposition with his 50" chest, size 16 boots and trademark leather scrum cap, but that's pretty much as far as it went. Don't get me wrong, Gerry could put it about in short spurts but in between he'd go through fallow periods, particularly at line-out time where he had acquired the moniker of 'Rizla', which aptly reflected how far he was prepared to leave the ground. "Sort it out Gerry, he's a fucking circus dwarf!" in broad Scouse was one memorable rallying cry from our 2nd team skipper, Dave Henshall, that caused players and spectators to corpse.

And then there were the surreal incidences that just defied belief. This day was to be my moment. Midway through the second half, having spotted what I thought were several slow boats in Truro's back line, I set off on a wildly ambitious arcing run towards the touchline where predictably, with my lack of pace, I got brought to ground right in front of the clubhouse. Cue raucous baying for blood from the partisan crowd as I was pinned face down, delaying release of the ball on Truro's side of the ruck. Home bred or not, there was an inevitability to the thorough shoeing that ensued. At times like that you simply bite down hard on your gum shield, block out the pain and wait for the free-for-all stampede to end. Except on this occasion, accompanied by a mixture of laughter from the crowd and a lone high pitched screechy voice, it was over rather more quickly than I'd anticipated. The commotion continued whilst the bodies pealed away from the ruck, at which point I was grabbed by two Truro boys and hauled to my feet.

"Sort her out for God's sake, Vert!"

If the ground could have opened up I would willingly have dived in. There on the pitch, gesticulating wildly and spitting all manner of Maltese-Cornish vitriol, was my dear mother. Never in all the years that I had played rugby in Cornwall had she been able to conquer her maternal fears and get along to watch either David or me. It got worse.

"Steven Ivey, Dickie Vinson, Anthony Caruana, get off him you bleddy sods! Wait till I speak to your parents!" she screamed in one last finger-pointing outpouring.

"Mother! Mother!" I repeated to bring her back to her senses. "It's OK, it's part of the game. Please leave the pitch and stop frightening the players!"

"Game? Game? You could've fooled me son!"

With that my mother rejoined the ranks of the spectators, chuntering away as she went, to leave me facing thirty grinning faces (including the referee!).

At the final whistle, the 39-39 scoreline told you all you needed to know about the spirit the match had been played in, in spite of my mother's jaw-dropping intervention! I can seldom recall a warmer players' 'tunnel' as we filed off the pitch arm in arm, and that camaraderie continued in the clubhouse during the end-of-tour drinking, singing and bar games which included the bizarre ritual of Stevie Ivey wet shaving all tourists with facial hair. . . using a cut-throat razor and liberally applied Brut!

The coach rolled into West London around 00:30 on Tuesday, fulfilling the final component of a successful tour. Everyone was totally disinterested in returning to the real world. At least for some they smelt nice and wouldn't be needing to reach for their razors before work!

Chapter 19

Together
May 1990 – March 1994

I pondered and agonised over the writing of this chapter for months, not because of the sadness and raw emotion I would have to retrieve from the back of my mind, but for the pain and grief it would resurrect within the loved ones so devastatingly affected by a series of tragic events that occurred over a four year period at the club. The continued success of all the sides and the social scene were key ingredients in our development but it was to be ill-fortune that brought the entire club together, reinforcing incredibly strong bonds in overcoming major adversity.

With a large proportion of the club being made up of guys aged between 25-35, it was only a matter of time before we would experience a cluster of weddings and new additions to the Old A's brood. As with everything we did on and off the pitch, each event was embraced and celebrated with no lack of relish. Stag do's had their obligatory mischief and mayhem. The wetting of babys' heads was comparatively restrained albeit still involving copious amounts of alcohol.

In Dave Duff we had the ideal man to take over club captaincy from Roger. Comfortable as the frontman, the ambassador, the fixer, the jester, in fact with almost everything thrown at him, 'Duff' would deal with it in his own inimitable fashion. My respect and love for the man has always been immense. Yes, we had great success in moving the club forward, but this pales way into the background when I reflect on the dignity, poise and resolve Dave showed all of us in dealing with the most heart-breaking of scenarios.

These are Dave's words:

We lost Benjamin on 5th May 1990 – normal pregnancy, born without any issues. After a few hours, the docs said that they were concerned about his temperature and wanted to put him in an incubator but they were down in the special care unit. I went with him and Jeanette rested. I went home, showered and brought back stuff for Jeanette. I've always trusted my instincts and something in me was saying get back to the hospital. I returned and saw Jeanette who was getting changed and would follow me down to the care unit.

I walked into the unit and saw the doc and three nurses around the incubator. When they saw me the faces told me all I needed to know. They had tried to feed him through a tube into the stomach, but somehow he had choked and by the time they realised, he was dead, they had ventilated him and he was now on a life support machine. The doc tried to explain, but for me it didn't make sense. I knew Jeanette was following me down and didn't want her walking in and seeing all the tubes and the ventilator. I asked the doc to come with me to tell her what was going on but for some reason the bastard refused.

I went back to get Jeanette but she was already coming towards me along the corridor to the special care unit. I had to tell her the terrible news there and then. The scream she let out still haunts me today. From then on we were in a world of shock. Over the next day we had to consent to the machines being turned off and Benjamin was handed to Jeanette where he died in her arms. The cause of death was shown as choking on the milk and asphyxiation.

The reason I've outlined this is that the period of shock just seemed to be endless; having to bury him, the endless visits to the grave, I got back to work, but there were constant reminders of death, so my only escape and return to some

139

normality was returning to rugby; back with the club and the guys, from all walks of life, who felt for you and were there for you.

Having another child became an obsession for Jeanette, almost immediately, and I could understand why. Having had a baby with you for nine months then just walk away with nothing must have been the end of the world for her. I was reluctant to try so soon, but it seemed that this was her way of getting through it and soon enough young Sam was expected.

Again, a normal pregnancy and Sam arrived 3rd September 1991. Normal birth, great celebrations, everyone happy. Then 10 hours after he was born he began to get weak, and within 6 hours of this he had died. We had gone from being so overjoyed, with family and friends visiting within that first 24 hour period, to the devastation of losing another baby. The weight of the world just descended and crushed us so much. I have never known grief like it. Everything felt like a dream. You wanted to run, to escape, but there was nowhere you could go.

I think that most of us have experienced situations where every day is a battle just finding the emotional strength to get through. Getting up the next day and going again can be so hard on your own. We all need support and for me, when Sam died, I needed to draw that support from outside the world of grief, and I found that in a little wooden clubhouse. It wasn't the building, it was what was in the building, it was what made us all want to be there.

And what made us all want be there? Well, that's the easiest bit. It was all of us being strong together. Rugby teaches you a lot of life skills, friendship, respect, team work, support and, for me, never giving up, but what we as group of young guys did was that we built on all those skills and developed a love for each other that is still there to this day. Some guys don't like the 'love' word, but deep down it's in there and it's evident in the way we care about each other. We aren't together every day anymore, but we are in the shadows of each other's lives, in our memories, in support and can be counted on when anyone needs us.

So that is what was there for me. The day of Sam's funeral was one of the hardest days of my life; walking with Jeanette, carrying a coffin with a broken heart. By being there with us at that time, or just a look or pat on the back when I went back to training showed me the depth of support from everyone. You all felt our pain but were determined not to let us stand alone and be beside us when we fell. And that's a commitment we have always had for each other.

That feeling is still with me. When my mum and dad died over these last few years, I had the wake for them at the club. At both funerals, the guys were there, to support you in person, in messages. I wasn't alone.

Saturday 10th October 1992 – a bright autumnal day signalled the start of another league campaign. Enfield Ignations RFC had always provided us with stiff opposition, so we set off around the North Circular with our strongest XV anticipating a stern test given that we had been promoted to the upper reaches of the Middlesex Divisions. We had a good balance of youth, experience, brain and brawn so we considered ourselves well prepared for most things that would come our way that afternoon. At least, that is what we thought.

Piers Forsyth, the 'Tower of Acton' at 6' 5", had become one of the first names on my team sheet and an ever-present in the second row, providing a reliable source of quality line-out ball and great mobility around the park. He was also a thoroughly decent man and epitomised the old adage of 'rugby being a game for thugs played by gentlemen' [football being described as 'a game for gentlemen played by thugs'].

This is Piers's recollection of that day:

We arrived at the Ignations ground in good time (despite there being no sat-nav in 1992!) and were shown to the changing room; away teams always seemed to get the smallest ones. We got ready and then it was time for the Captain's pre-match team talk prior to Andy's warm-up routine. A rap on the changing room door interrupted John in full flow.

141

'There's a phone call, an urgent phone call for Piers Forsyth. The phone is on the bar in the clubhouse.'

I scooted from the changing room through to the bar in a flash, my studs clip-clopping across the floor. My wife, Mary, sounded strained and came straight to the point. Our 12 week old baby boy Hanley, had stopped breathing and she was at Ealing General Hospital. The gravity of the situation hit me hard as I rushed back to the changing room and tried to put my jeans on over my boots. I realised that I had to slow down and get my head straight. I was normally the calm one in the changing room, but it must have been obvious to the team that I was in a blind panic.

"What's happened Piers?"

"It's Hanley, he's stopped breathing. They're at the hospital."

John piped up immediately: "Piers, it's OK, I'll take you. Robbo, you're skipper. Can you go through and grab a couple of forwards from the 3rds?"

He was the complete Captain and would do anything for his team. Quickly we were away and off back round the North Circular. The devastating news made small talk somewhat difficult. After just a few minutes on the road, we realised that the petrol light had come on and that we weren't going to make it back to Ealing without finding a filling station. Whilst it added a bit of time to the journey, strangely it came as a welcome distraction as we worked out our detour, then once we'd refilled, we managed to get chatting about the club, our jobs and just about anything other than the purpose of the journey. However, it helped to eat up the time and soon we were driving up the ramp to the A&E entrance. John offered to wait, but deep down I knew that it was not going to be a short visit.

"Thank you, John, but I think I'm going to be here for a long time."

Our eyes met, unspoken words were exchanged and I went on my way to seek out the reception. As soon as they had my name, it was a simple: "Come this way please," to a private area. The Sister came and I confirmed who I was. I don't remember her exact words, but they were something like:

142

"I'm so very sorry to tell you that your baby boy stopped breathing and he has died."

I couldn't keep it together any longer and started to cry. Sister showed me to the room where Mary was holding Hanley. For some time we just held each other and cried. The staff there were really good and comforted us. It may sound odd but we requested that a member of staff take some photos of the three of us. It was our last time together and we would cherish them forever.

Old Actonians was a strong and close knit club. The tragic news got around quickly and then came phone calls from team mates and offers to help in any way possible. We felt the warm blanket of care from the rugby community. There was a generous whip round if we wanted to get away some time later. In fact, we donated it to the Foundation for the Study of Infant Deaths (now called the Lullaby Trust). Hanley's post mortem and histology eventually showed that he had died from a streptococcal infection in his lungs. Many from Old Actonians came to Hanley's funeral a week later.

It must be the nature of the game, all committed to frequent collisions, the element of personal injury, the knowledge that alone you are vulnerable but together feel invincible, that means rugby players bond quickly and strongly. In spite of all the larking about, banter and quirky nicknames, there was always immense respect for each other. As a family, we felt that strength and togetherness from the Old Actonians. The weeks ahead were a roller-coaster of calm and grief but there was no awkwardness on my return to training. It was 'welcome back Piers', 'good to see you mate' and 'so sorry for yours and Mary's loss'.

It was our tragedy but the club made it theirs too. Thank you guys.

Thursday 17th December 1992 – Robbo and I had organised a charity race night for the following evening to raise funds for new shirts. With so many teams being fielded each week, we were, literally, threadbare in the kit department. Held in the clubhouse, it promised to be a great evening. I commissioned Beneficial Arts, who specialised in these type of events, to bring the occasion to the boil. As Honest John, I would run the Tote table with Robbo.

A combination of the end of the working week, no league game the following day and something different on the entertainment front, meant that the evening was a rip-roaring success with a tidy sum raised and very healthy bar takings for the Association. Just one thing ate away at me all night – Robbo hadn't shown. I resolved to call him in the morning, once my head had cleared.

Robbo and his wife, Lucy, had become great friends and not just because of the rugby connection. Even though we trained together a lot and there was rarely time for small talk once Robbo was in the 'zone', socially the shackles were off. Both were from country stock, loved their jumps racing and were pursuing careers in the construction industry. We had a lot in common. They even helped rekindle my lapsed faith by introducing me to Nick the Vic and the good folk of All Saints Church on Ealing Common.

By late morning, with my grey matter slightly less befuddled following two cups of coffee, I picked up the handset.

"Robbo, you missed a cracking night with the lads. We raised well over a grand. Where the hell were you mate?" I jauntily chirped.

My stomach tightened the moment I sensed the timbre of his first word.

"John. . . can I stop you there. . . Chloe. . . died on Thursday."

"Oh my god, Andy!" several seconds passed as I struggled to find the right words and then said next to nothing, "I feel so devastated for you and Lucy."

"Thanks John. We appreciate that."

"Is there anything that I can do, Andy? Anything at all?"

"Actually John, why don't you come on over. I think Lucy needs some time with the family and I could do with some fresh air."

Saturday lunchtime trade was brisk at the Rose & Crown in South Ealing. Only a stone's throw from their house, we were close by if Lucy needed Andy. We managed to find a quiet spot in the back room and set down our beers. Robbo was as stoical as ever although bloodshot eyes set against his drained face told you all you needed to know as to the depth of emotional turmoil he was going through. Chloe, their first child, who was only four months old, had died in her sleep whilst being looked after by a childminder. We talked a little about Chloe and the past 48 hours but, with hindsight, it was far too soon to be contemplating how and why such a tragedy happened. Robbo could be a closed book and incredibly stubborn at times but, mercifully, his iron will began to yield.

"It's alright, Andy. Let it go mate."

Silently we sat, supped and wept together.

Saturday 19th of March 1994 – Five Nations days were always special at the club but none more so than when the England/Wales clashes were on at Twickenham. Traditionally our fixtures would be brought forward to mid-morning so that those lucky enough to have tickets could shoot off to nearby Twickers and the rest of the guys would settle down in the clubhouse for a long day of beer, banter and rugby on the box. On this particular day I was not down to play as our physio had told me that a shoulder injury needed a couple more weeks recovery time, but given that we had an important league match a week later and I was going onto the big game, I took the opportunity to watch the 1st XV who conveniently were playing at home.

On that bright spring morning the game was quite brisk so I was not surprised to see a few of the forwards struggling to keep up with play. As half-time approached I noticed that Andy Hickman, one of our second rows, had slowed to a walk near the touchline and was being attended to by our first-aider. Initially, hunched over with Ann's 'magic sponge' on the back of his neck, I simply assumed that he had taken a bang on the head, but it was only when he straightened up to his full 6' 4" that I noticed the pallor of his face.

"I feel pretty rough, John. I'm sorry, I know we haven't got a forwards sub but I'm going to come off," Andy uttered quietly, in between deep breaths.

"Don't worry about it, Andy. You're not looking so sharp. Let's get back to the changing room and sort you out," I said, putting an arm across his broad back.

145

After ten minutes rest and some water, despite still sweating heavily and regaining very little of his colour, Andy insisted that he felt much better and stripped off for a shower. I had never been a very good spectator when there was a chance that I could don the cherished blue and white jersey so, after checking that he was OK, I changed into Andy's kit and ran out to play the last half hour of the game. I couldn't help but notice that every single piece of the kit was absolutely drenched in cold sweat.

On returning to the clubhouse, I was glad to learn that Andy had recovered well enough to cadge a lift down to the Queen Victoria in Isleworth which was the usual watering hole for the guys on International days. Nestled in a quiet residential area without direct vehicle access to the main Twickenham Road, this little gem of a pub was an ideal venue for a few beers and the customary pre-match analysis before a 30 minute trek across to HQ.

"Hey, fellas, over here. There's a few beers lined up." Andy's head appeared above the crowd, gesturing for our car-load to make the steady shuffle across to the bar. With Duff and his partner in crime, Martin 'Tugger' Hull, holding court whilst baiting the Welsh boys, there was a 'business as usual' feel to the place.

"Cheers, Andy. Pleased to see you've got a bit of your colour back. How are you feeling, mate?" I enquired on finally getting through to the bar.

"Yeah, I'm good, John. A bit knackered but OK, thanks. Think I'm just struggling with a virus or something," Andy replied in his typically understated way.

Andy and I had always got on very well, at least, that is, until it came to 1st team selection. He had been at the club a lot longer than I had and, in previous years, had been a regular pick for the 1st's. Given that he trained most Tuesdays and was a good scrummager and line-out jumper, I could understand his frustrations when I would call the next day only to say that he was in the 2nd's. For a quiet, kind-hearted bloke, he could really make me squirm with his 'cross examination'. Unfortunately, due to the fluid style of rugby we wanted to play and with Andy nearing his mid-30s and carrying a few extra pounds, it meant that he was probably our third or fourth choice lock. Having said that, I played him as often as I could outside the league games. Perhaps that was my mistake, but it was all forgotten by the time Saturday evenings came around and we had had a few beers. That relationship had been extended in 1992 when Andy asked me to carry out surveys on a couple of properties in Ealing.

As if it were possible, the Queen Vic seemed to fill up even more, becoming uncomfortably warm and smoke-filled, at which point Robbo and I decided to get the hell out of there.

"Why 'e goin' so early, me anzums?" Duff cried out across the bar as we made a move for the door.

"Not up for lung cancer today, Dave!" chirped Robbo.

And with that we were off, closely followed by a few more of the lads. A beautiful sunny afternoon greeted us as we emerged from the blue haze, turned left into Worple Road and then right into 'Dog Shit Alley', the unofficial name for the long straight footpath down to Twickenham Road that would once again lead us to rugby mecca. As we shimmied our way through the metal bars at the entrance to the alley, about 200 metres ahead we could see the back of a large figure, bent over as if stretching his hamstrings.

"Hey, Hammers, that's Andy, isn't it?" commented Robbo, squinting his eyes.

"Yeah, I think you're right mate, although I didn't spot him go before us."

Instinctively we quickened our stride. Moments later Andy slowly slumped to the ground.

"Oh, shit! Andy!" Robbo and I screamed in unison, as we broke into a sprint.

We were with him in seconds. Robbo was medically trained and did not panic even though Andy's facial colour looked alarming, much worse than the episode during the morning, plus he was unresponsive and not breathing.

"Right John, quickly. Andy's vomited so let's get him out of the brambles and onto the path so I can check his airways."

Andy had nosedived and was below the level of the path so, even for two fit blokes, it was a struggle to haul up his prone body. Thankfully Duff and the crew magically appeared at our shoulders and it was done. The ensuing ten minutes felt like a lifetime as we stood over Andy with Robbo performing mouth to mouth and CPR. Someone had the sense to run to the pub and call for an ambulance. Despite Robbo's best efforts, the only signs of movement from Andy came as his lungs deflated and his throat gurgled. The seriousness of the situation was obvious to everyone but the group stayed composed throughout, each taking turns to quietly reassure Andy that we were there with him. To a man, we believed he'd be all right.

With the ambulance station just a stone's throw away, the paramedics soon arrived. Completely unflustered by the situation, their professionalism settled our nerves a little. It was decided that Duff and I would go with Andy to the hospital whilst one of the guys would get word to Gea, Andy's wife of just one year. Even during such a difficult situation, there was still time for a moment of surreality. As Andy was being rolled up to the ambulance, an insensitive prat sidled up to Duff and asked whether he could have Andy's ticket! It goes without saying that he got short shrift.

Fifteen minutes later we were sat together in an emergency bay at the West Middlesex Hospital as a team of nurses and doctors worked tirelessly to bring Andy around. The cadence of his treatment had urgency but was totally controlled with not a semblance of panic. The soft hushed voices and the busyness of the rustling from behind the curtains were initially heartening. Then came the snap of the defibrillator pads and the unmistakable sound of Andy thumping back down onto the hospital bed.

'How are we looking?'

'Nothing.'

'Get set, we go again.'

Dave and I tried to remain calm, chatting away even though we were listening more intently to the activity a few feet away. The subject matter must have been total rubbish as I cannot remember what was said. We needed to avoid silence and our innermost thoughts getting the better of us but that single word, 'nothing', burst our protective bubble. There was now a more routine feel to the efforts within the bay. Twice we heard the same sequence of words, until there was no more '. . .we go again'. Everything was still.

'Time of death, 3:47.'

Dave held himself together but his eyes said it all. Cruelly, gut-wrenchingly, all too recently, he had been here before. I had not. As Dave's tears flowed, the stark realisation that Andy was not going to sit up and smile hit me like an express train. Helplessness overwhelmed me. Dave slung his arm across my shoulders, gripping and squeezing as we sat there for several minutes with our heads bowed as the nurses bustled around us.

"Come on John, let's stretch our legs."

Dave moved to get me to my feet as Gea, clearly stunned and disorientated, rounded the corner. She had been told the news on arriving at the hospital but, understandably, had not really taken it in. Unavoidably, the state of the two of us reaffirmed to Gea that dear Andy had indeed passed away (from a massive aortic aneurysm).

We stayed with a distraught Gea whilst she regained some clarity of thought and a little composure. Eventually she looked up.

"I told him not to go today. He's been feeling unwell for the last six weeks but still he carried on working and playing rugby," her voice clogged with emotion and frustration. "Only this week, he'd been on a treadmill and had an ECG. It showed nothing. Nothing! How could that be? They'd just asked him to go back for more tests."

We did our best to console her. The fact that Andy had not suffered and we were all with him at the end seemed to be of real comfort. Once one of her friends had arrived, Dave and I stumbled out into the warm sunshine. It had become the most horrible of beautiful days.

The traffic was light so the big game had not yet finished but we could not have cared less about rugby at that very moment. I cannot remember how we found our way back to the Old A's. Call it a homing instinct. We had done it often enough whilst half cut after long trips to away games. The anticipation of the buzz of the clubhouse had always been too strong to resist. That afternoon the hollowness and need to nestle back into the bosom of the club was what drew us home. As we made our way to the bar, I recall guys being on the tables performing 'Sunshine Mountain'. Amongst a throng of grinning faces, the Welsh boys were shouting jibes and playfully ruffling our hair. Dave, for once stony-faced, had always been the catalyst for the after-match revelry so very quickly the lads detected that something was desperately wrong. Word of Andy's passing spread rapidly around the packed room until a hush fell. Somehow Dave found it within himself to climb up onto the pool table and address the club.

"Fellas, today we have tragically lost one of our own, a true gent and an Old Actonian to the core. Will you please raise your glasses and join me in honouring a great friend."

As every glass went up, a collective roar of "Andy Hickman" boomed through the clubhouse and out across the Field of Dreams.

Chapter 20

Hitting the Wall
April 1991

SINCE 1990 I had been feeling a bit odd during exercise but it was only during the closing stages of the London Marathon a year later that the symptoms became more acute. No great surprise there, I had thought at the time, as the demands of 26.2 miles on a hot day had brought many fit looking folk to a grinding halt well before halfway. I was enthusiastic and keen to achieve a good time even though long working hours and rugby left little time for lengthy training runs. I had managed to fit in a couple of half marathons and one 18 mile slog around West London but beyond this I was into unknown territory. Four weeks before the Marathon, suspecting that all was not well, I had made a rare visit to my GP. She had clearly had a hard week and quickly dismissed my concerns, putting the fatigue and tingling down to the stress and strain of everyday life. Given that I was only 28, I questioned her diagnosis straight away.

"I'm sorry Doctor, but it can't be as simple as that. Work is fine, I'm physically fit and lead a healthy lifestyle. Something just isn't right."

"Well, the effects of hard work and physical training can show themselves in strange ways."

"You may be right, but bearing in mind that I'm running the London Marathon in a month's time, would you mind taking a blood test just to discount anything untoward?"

"Very well, if that's what you want, roll up your sleeve."

I left the surgery feeling rather stupid for having bothered her. Even if the blood test revealed something, there was no way I was going to miss the run. This was the first time in five years that I'd got through the public ballot and having already raised substantial sponsorship money for the Queen Elizabeth Children's Hospital I was determined to press on. Defiantly, I went home, got kitted out and ran around Gunnersbury Park for two hours.

By the time of the race, I was actually feeling in much better shape than that of the previous six months. Perhaps it was the fact that I'd eased off training in the final two weeks and felt quite fresh. Or maybe I was just so pumped up with adrenalin. I had heard nothing regarding the blood test so pressed on anyway as so many people had told me that the Marathon was an exhilarating experience. I hadn't really doubted them, but the scale of the event was totally staggering, making it very easy to get dragged into the bunfight signalled by the starting hooter. Instead, I made a point of going right to the back of the mass of humanity. As a result the first 15 minutes were a gentle mix of jogging and walking. . . just getting up to the starting line!

As there were thousands of charity runners in all manner of costumes, by starting from the back the first five miles was very comfortable as I was overtaking without having to put in a huge effort. Between 8 and 12 miles was even more satisfying as I was passing runners who had just gone off too quick and were slowing in the heat. I had got into a good rhythm and was able to take in the intoxicating party atmosphere created by the crowds. Going over Tower Bridge I felt in great shape and, glancing at my watch, realised that I been averaging a 7.5 minute mile pace. As a client had offered to make an additional £250 donation if I finished under 3 hours and 10 minutes, his best time, I worked out that 7 minutes per mile for the remaining 14 miles would just about do it. For the first time I began to push myself to shave 30 seconds off each mile. At 18 miles I was tanking along and, using horse racing parlance, needed to 'take a pull'. The problem was that I was now way out in newly emerging Canary Wharf with sparse support, less cover from the blistering sunshine and, perhaps most importantly, fewer groups

152

of runners to latch onto for cover and help with settling into a pace. There had been a lot of banter and laughter between the runners and crowds during the first half of the race which had reached something of a crescendo as we hit the bottleneck on Tower Bridge Road leading up to the iconic landmark. Now it was eerily quiet amongst the hoardings that shrouded the construction sites. However, I still felt strong and ploughed on at the same pace thinking that I would get in front of my target time and then coast the last few miles.

As I passed under the balloon arch signalling the 21 mile mark, I started to think in terms of there being less than an hour's running time left.

'Come on! This is no different, in fact easier, than the St. Clements run down in Truro.' I said to myself.

Within 400 metres of concluding my own team talk, things had changed. I wasn't breathing any more heavily nor did I feel that the petrol gauge was nearing 'empty' but something was definitely different. I had taken three or four false steps in the last mile but just put it down to manhole covers and an uneven road surface. Now it was happening every 10-15 paces, most alarmingly only with my left leg. Another 200 metres and it was down to every other stride. This was not the infamous 'Wall', more like trying to run with one training shoe magnetically attracted to the tarmac. My running gait became very lopsided as the right leg continued to move through smoothly followed by an increasingly reluctant left that I was now having to hitch up and swing around. Picturing the end of a gruelling rugby training session with Robbo screaming obscenities, I refocused and pressed on to the 22 mile marker. A quick glance at my watch showed '2:30'. Forty minutes to finish inside 3:10. Just less than 10 minutes per mile.

'You dickhead! You've pushed it too hard since Canary Wharf.' I muttered under my breath, annoyed that I'd not been more restrained, then contemplated further; *'Well, that being the case, why am I not feeling tired and my right side is perfectly fine?'*

This brief loss of concentration was all that was needed for me to take one too many false steps and, stubbing my left foot, down I went just as I met the cobbles adjacent to the Tower of London.

Within a matter of seconds, a medic was there beside me as I tried to get back to my feet.

"Hey, big fella, just give yourself a moment. There's no rush, a couple of minutes won't make a difference. Now, let me look you over."

"I'm fine, thanks. Really, I just tripped."

"I'm not surprised. I watched you hobbling along as you came into view. When did you pull your calf muscle?" enquired my Good Samaritan.

"I don't think I have, to be honest. Feels more like I've trapped a nerve or tweaked something in my hip, as my left peg has tightened right up. Is there anything you can do about that in a couple of minutes?"

"Well, I'm not sure about that self-diagnosis, so why not shuffle off the cobbles and let me have a good look at you? What's your name, my friend?"

"It's John."

Sensing that I was about to be pulled from the 'field of play', I righted myself and leant against the crowd barrier, stretching my hamstrings and calves.

"Wooah, hang on a second! Let me give you a rub down, then you can try that."

Still the nagging feeling that I was blowing £250 of sponsorship bugged the hell out of me but I could not deny the fact that I was seriously in trouble. A few seconds became a few minutes as this kind man did his best to patch me up.

"How does that feel, John? I'm pretty sure that you've pulled your calf muscle as it's as tight as a drum, but if you take it easy, you should get there."

"Thank you so much. . . errr. I'm so sorry, I haven't even asked your name."

"It's Bob. Think nothing of it. This is why we're here."

And with that I was away again, to rousing shouts of encouragement from the spectators lined three deep behind the barriers. If that couldn't spur me on for another 4 miles, then nothing could. My watch showed '2:42'. I had been stationary for just over 10 minutes but, clearly, Bob had been right as I now moved a little more fluently than the previous mile. I accepted that the £250 bonus was out of the question so just concentrated on holding myself together. Reaching the 23 mile mark in '2:52' gave me much needed confidence and I began to relax into my running again.

'Pah, wall? What wall?' I smiled inwardly.

On turning off the Victoria Embankment 20 minutes later, there was a small incline up Northumberland Avenue and that's where the full extent of my problems re-emerged with a vengeance. The bad leg/good leg combo was embarrassingly evident for all to see. Not only did my left leg fail to fully obey the message to leave the tarmac, I was now experiencing tingling in the toes and a feeling akin to a knife blade in the calf. Slowing markedly, I staggered on into the Mall with Buckingham Palace in the distance. The effort of hitching and swinging the leg through was taking its toll and for the first time I felt tired, nauseous and sensed the toxicity of self doubt.

'It's only pain, you woose, get your arse in gear and finish the effing job.' Robbo's weekly mantra thudded around my head.

Avoiding several well-meaning attempts to pull me over for attention from the first aiders, I knuckled down, imagining that the feeling was no worse than one of the lung bursting speed circuits at the rugby club. Buckingham Palace became like a mirage as the trudge down The Mall seemed to go on forever. Finally the left turn into Birdcage Walk meant that I was in the home straight but never had half a mile felt so long. I was stopping frequently to stretch and nurse my leg, almost oblivious to the shouts of encouragement from the crowds. It was now definitely a case of mind over matter. It may have looked heroic but I felt deeply embarrassed, almost sickened, and just wanted the whole ordeal to end.

After 4 hours and 9 minutes, I crossed the finishing line on Westminster Bridge and, with a massive outpouring of relief, found myself unable to take another stride. It had taken over an hour to cover the last three miles. I could probably have hopped it quicker!

Two days later I was back on more familiar territory, stretching off before training at the club. Whilst I was stiff and jarred up, despite Sunday's exertions, my energy levels felt OK so there was no logical reason why I shouldn't get back in the groove. Unfortunately (or, perhaps, it was fortunately), Keasty was unable to coach that night so it was left to me to organise the session. Apart from setting out the equipment and barking out the drills, I would be able to have an easier night than I'd anticipated. Even then I was really tired at the end, made my excuses for Saturday's game and shot off home to get my head down as I had an early site meeting. Almost as if I'd aroused the demon that had terrorised me two days previously, I had a wretched night's sleep, twitching, tingling, tossing and turning. How could I be so knackered yet unable to relax?

By the morning, the strange sensations had subsided but I was pretty jaded after nothing more than a series of catnaps. Nonetheless, I dusted myself off and by 8am I was up scaffolding inspecting a new roof in North Kensington. After the meeting I had 30 minutes to spare before shooting around to a renovation scheme for a new client in Willesden so sat in the car and flicked through the job file to refresh my memory. The next thing I remembered was being awoken with a real start as Tony, the foreman from my last site, slapped his paddle-sized palms on the car roof.

"Have you and those rugger boys had a night on the sauce again, John-boy?" shouted the highly amused Galway man.

I raised a hand in acknowledgment, slapped myself around the chops and started the car. It wasn't until I glanced at the dashboard upon reaching Harrow Road that I realised I had been asleep for nearly an hour.

'Right, that's it, you're going to the quack again tonight.' I vowed to myself.

I managed to pick up a late appointment and, as was the way with overcrowded surgeries, sat there for what seemed like an age with the inevitable slumber engulfing me.

"Mr Hambly? Follow me, please."

Abruptly I was brought back to the land of the living. Bleary-eyed for the second time that day, I stumbled after a locum GP, seemingly intent on sprinting out of sight.

"Yes, how can I help?" enquired a young lady doctor as I sat down opposite her.

"Well, I ran in the Marathon on Sunday and haven't been right since."

"That doesn't surprise me. It's not for the faint-hearted and, without wishing to sound rude, you're not an ideal size for running extreme distances!"

"Yes, you're probably right, but I've always enjoyed running so it was only the tiredness and strange sensations over the last few months during rugby games and training which made me ask Dr Smith to do a blood test when I came to see her five weeks ago."

"Oh, OK, let me have a look at your notes and see what's going on here."

After a couple of minutes sifting through a pile of loose papers, she finally settled on one page.

"Well, that's interesting. Did you not follow this up after the blood test?"

"No, I assumed that the surgery would contact me. Why? Is there something wrong?" I hesitantly asked.

"Yes, the test revealed that you are post-viral."

"Alright," I said very slowly, pondering whether I really wanted to know more. "That might explain why I've been so tired then. Dare I ask, what sort of virus, doctor?"

"Of course you should. You have had a bout of glandular fever but thankfully it looks like it's behind you now," she said with a smile. "However, I have to say, I am surprised that you have been able to play rugby with the virus and, frankly, amazed that you actually ran in the Marathon. How far did you get?"

"Errr, well, I managed to finish but it wasn't pretty," I offered, still feeling embarrassed for the state I had finished the run.

"Wow, I was not expecting you to say that! No wonder you are feeling out of sorts. I suspect it'll take you a while to get over this fatigue now, so you must take it very easy on the sporting front for the next 2-3 months."

'Great,' I thought, *'I'll only miss two games this season and be back for pre-season training in late July!'*

157

Chapter 21

Out of the Frying Pan
1988-92

L ASTING five years in your first full-time job and the majority of that time being within an uncomfortable working environment was, I felt, fairly admirable, but two years after gaining my professional status, I decided that it was time to spread my wings and look for a position with another surveying practice. Whilst I wanted a fresh start, it was still a difficult decision to break up the great working relationship I had developed with Marc. It therefore came as a pleasant surprise that, on announcing my departure, he confided in me that he intended setting up his own practice and asked me to consider joining him in a year or two. We had often talked about such a move when in the D.A's Office following a difficult day, but to actually be looking at putting a long-term plan in place was even more exciting than my immediate career move.

My choice of career enhancement with Cyril Silver & Partners on Tower Bridge Road, SE1, whilst living with Jane's parents in Chorleywood, was not perhaps one of my wisest decisions in terms of commuting, but the salary was substantially higher and Tony Barnes, the Senior Partner, offered quite a few other incentives. The practice was a similar size to Philip Andrews and dealt primarily with private and public sector residential projects, but it was most definitely not the West End. Tower Bridge Road may have had a grandiose ring to it but in reality it was Bermondsey. Swap the deli in Selfridges for Manze's Pie & Mash shop; swap private garage parking in Montague Mews for the pavement on Leroy Street; swap salubrious stucco-fronted premises for ramshackle offices over a laundrette; swap structured workload for organised chaos.

Tony was an astute, charismatic businessman of Italian descent, a qualified pilot and a doppelganger for American actor Stacy Keach. Socially he was charming and good fun, but when it came to work Tony expected his pound of flesh, and more. My first week at 'CSP' was rather misleading as he paraded me around the practice's ongoing building projects and various clients' offices. Mixed in with daily lunches in trendy restaurants across the breadth of the capital it was enjoyable and, to be honest, quite flattering. Such was his aura in a business environment, he had been able to develop a very strong rapport with the development and maintenance teams amongst a plethora of Housing Association clientele and, as a result, was able to swan in and out of their offices almost unannounced. Throw in the fact that he was impeccably groomed, smartly dressed and cologne infused, Tony was captivating and persuasive. Finally, add in the new Volvo 760GLE with state of the art car phone and a private property portfolio, and he was the antithesis of Marcus.

The second week could not have been more different. The honeymoon period was most definitely over as I arrived in the office at 8am on the Monday to find a Manhattan skyline of files obstructing the approach to my desk. I wondered whether Tony had had an archiving purge over the weekend. Eventually I got through and pulled out my chair, revealing four pages of handwritten notes neatly fanned across the seat. In total they amounted to a dozen projects, some already on site, others still requiring working drawings and specifications, but most were running behind programme and required urgent attention. Neither were they all small jobs, some were major schemes that would take months to get ready for site. It appeared as though my predecessor had left under something of a cloud and I was the one about to get drenched! However, one great attribute Marc had instilled in me was how to graft, so I rolled up my sleeves and did just that. Up at 5:30am and in the office for 7:30am each day, after a month, I felt as though I was beginning to get some order and control over the workload. It was just as well as Jane and I were in the process of gearing up to refurbish the flat in Hanwell, so at the end of that hectic four week spell I needed to get on with stripping out the property. Imagine my despair therefore that, upon arriving at the office the following week, I found another one of Tony's 'fantailed' memos waiting for me on my chair. Owing to the resignation of another senior surveyor I would be inheriting ten more schemes!

I heard Tony rock up during the mid-morning, so immediately gathered up the collection of memos and pounded my way upstairs to his office. As if knowing what was coming, Tony looked up and drew heavily on a Gauloise.

"Morning John. Good weekend? How'd the rugby go?" he rattled off with a smile, whilst wafting away a thick cloud of smoke.

Rarely one to spoil for a fight (unless there was a rugby ball involved!), I could not contain my irritation at what was being asked of me.

"Tony, this is mission impossible as far as I'm concerned," I exclaimed, holding up the wadge of instructions. "There's more than enough work here for two surveyors and probably an assistant as well!"

"I'm aware of that, John, but Chris has really dropped me in it by handing in his notice. Can't you hold it all together for the moment whilst I do the interviews and get us two new surveyors?" For the first time I was seeing Tony on the back foot. "A few of your current schemes need less attention than you're giving them and you can cut a few corners on Chris's projects."

"Well, I'm sorry, Tony, but having spent six years of my life becoming a qualified surveyor, I am not prepared to lower my standard of work, potentially drop a ricket and risk being pulled in before the RICS on the grounds of professional misconduct!"

Tony took another long drag then held his hand out.

"OK, I get your point, John. Give me back the latest memo. I'll review the priority jobs, speak to the clients and see if I can buy us a bit of time."

One thing I could say about Tony was that, despite constantly pushing his staff to their limits, he was a man of his word. No doubt after numerous business lunches and much client schmoozing, somehow he managed to get the most crucial deadlines moved back and, sure enough, a new surveyor arrived a few weeks later with the promise of another within the month.

Roy Singleton was unlike anyone I'd ever met before. Not in his appearance – cheap brown Crimplene suits with flares and cream nylon shirts would have been all the rage when he started out in his career in the early 1970s. I had also played a lot of rugby with similar looking 6' 3" hunchbacks, sporting broken hooters, grossly receding hairlines and missing front teeth. It was his persona that was so different. Painfully shy, Roy's 'warming' to his co-workers generally involved making crass, unfunny observations about any unfortunate news items and individuals that happened to catch his attention. Completely and utterly in his own zone, Roy was oblivious to offence caused by his mutterings and would simply shrug his sizeable shoulders, return to his desk and light up. All that said, he was a specification-writing and drawing machine and seemed entirely happy sat there hour after hour with pen and fag in hand. My misfortune was that I had to endure forty Marlboro a day when I wasn't on site as Tony had decided to shoehorn Roy into my office. As far as Tony was concerned, Roy was his saviour, churning out all that work and earning quick fees in the process. Seldom did he take Roy to clients' project meetings and he was relieved of building site work so that he could concentrate on the written word. His site visits and contract administration roles duly fell to me. At that point, Roy would make it perfectly clear that he wanted nothing more to do with them. Even the most polite enquiry about a particular aspect of a scheme would be met with what was to become his trademark response: "Uh, uh, uh. . . don't know, that's not my job," after which he would take a long drag, curl his tongue to savour every last particle of nicotine, chuckle and turn back to his desk.

No sooner had Roy become part of the furniture, than Tony (and me come to that) faced another period of upheaval when his most experienced surveyor announced that he was leaving to set up on his own. In his desperation to fill the position quickly, Tony seemed to operate a revolving door system of hiring and firing a succession of semi-retired elder statesmen from the property sector. Unfortunately, none of them could handle the frenetic pace and Tony's demands. This provided Roy with hours of fun as each one came and went. One particularly proud gentleman, Jack Gearon-West, decided to throw in the towel and walk out after just two weeks of mayhem and in the process deliver a well articulated verbal volley at Tony. Roy (who else?) happened to be in earshot at the time and found great hilarity in this scenario. Day after day, repeating the same line:

"He just jacked it in, put his gear on and headed west."

The only time I found it remotely funny was when Tony eventually cracked and unloaded an expletive-laden rebuke. Once he'd finished and walked out of our office, Roy lit up yet another fag, shrugged his shoulders and picked up his trusty biro.

"Uhh? What's up with him?"

Despite being the golden goose, at least as far as Tony's fee book was concerned, Roy was still capable of laying rotten eggs. It was then down to Tony to smooth things over with the clients and my task to tidy up the mess when the jobs got to site. This trait may well have led to Tony's outburst but the cumulative effect of Roy's detached lackadaisical attitude must also have had something to do with it.

On one occasion, Roy's company BMW got broken into whilst parked in Leroy Street. The inside of the car got trashed and the hi-fi was stolen. Roy was totally unfazed and showed no interest in lodging the insurance claim. Infuriated, Tony ended up dealing with the insurers and got the car repaired for Roy, after which he issued him with specific instructions to remove the radio/cassette every time he parked up on Leroy Street. For once, he listened. So, for a few weeks, each day upon arriving at the office, he would remove it, put it in his briefcase and then place it in the drawer of his desk, alongside his daughter's dismembered dolly (Roy had been promising her that he would repair it ever since he'd arrived at CSP). All good we thought; that is, until the office got burgled one night and, yes, Roy's hi-fi went missing again!

"For God's sake, Roy, how the hell am I going to claim for a £300 car hi-fi on the office contents insurance?" Tony shouted. "What was it doing in your desk anyway?"

162

"Uhh?" Roy looked on with his customary vacant expression. "I just forgot to take it back to the car that night. Anyway, I've never turned it on!"

"You are fucking unbelievable, Roy! I'm minded to take the cost of it off your wages." As exasperated as he was, turning away Tony almost chortled at Roy's logic.

Thankfully Tony's raised blood pressure and memo-writing affliction were about to go through a spell of remission. Antony 'Two Shirts' Iannaccone arrived at CSP completely unannounced in late 1989. I wondered if Roy's incessant jibes about Tony employing a succession of washed up surveyors got to him so much that when he finally found a good one he chose to say nothing. By this time, I had managed to secure my own office at the top of the building far away from Roy's smoke-filled world so it was something of a surprise to find Antony sitting there at 7:45am on his first day. Even though he was Italian, Antony was as far from being a Mafioso type as you could find, but after a few weeks I couldn't get away from the sense that Tony now considered he had his own team of '*Goodfellas*'; Tony could play Robert De Niro (really!), perhaps with me as Ray Liotta, but Antony, whilst similar in stature, would not quite match up as the psychopath played by Joe Pesci.

Antony and I got on well from the moment we met. Maybe it was our shared love of sport, a similar sense of humour or a desire to do our jobs properly no matter how much was heaped on our chairs, but we just hit it off. After twelve months stuck in a room with Roy, it was perhaps understandable that I sought bromance! However, one thing we didn't share was dress sense. Even though we would spend a good proportion of a working week on filthy building sites, Antony was still a very snappy dresser. I was just not interested in risking a shiny £200 suit on a rusty nail. And then there were his Italian designer shirts with their two-tone collars. It took me ages to work out that he was actually only wearing one shirt!

Within twelve months of being in harness, Antony, Roy and I were generating a high level of fee income for the practice and the job book for 1991 looked very healthy. I was therefore concerned one morning to find Antony in a right lather. His usual mild-mannered, jovial outlook replaced by a distinct air of desperation.

"Blimey, you look really fed up, Tone. What's happened?"

"I'm sure you've got a similar letter so you'll find out in a minute, mate."

As if it were contaminated, pinched at one of the corners between his thumb and forefinger, Antony held up a letter written on CSP headed paper.

Sure enough, concealed below the top piece of correspondence placed on my chair was an envelope with my name in Tony's unmistakable scrawl. I opened it and slowly digested the contents. I was probably as astonished as Antony, but perhaps not quite as exasperated given that he had just taken out a large mortgage on a property in preparation for his marriage to Lucy the following summer. Essentially, Tony was cutting our salaries by 20% on the basis that the country was officially in recession after many years of prosperity under Maggie Thatcher. However, the gut wrenching bit was that his decision was being made at a time when we were absolutely busting our balls and working long days.

"What do you think of that? And after all that we've done to dig this place out of the shit." Antony, who was surprisingly more agitated even with the problem shared, screwed up the letter and tossed it in the bin. "I'm gonna tell him where he can stick his job!"

"Wait a minute mate, don't be so hasty. I need to tell you something."

I retrieved the ball of paper, flattened it as best I could and slid it back across to Antony.

"Look, I should've said something a while ago, but I'm not going to be here for much longer. As you know, the old man's not too sharp, so I'm going to get back to Kernow for a while and then the plan is to come back to the smog and join up with Marc again. If you bite your lip and knuckle down here, I reckon there's a real opportunity for you at CSP."

When the time came to move on from CSP, handing my notice to Tony proved more difficult than I had envisaged. For all the melodrama, pressure and frustration, I had quite enjoyed my three and a half year spell in SE1 and left feeling as though I had learnt a great deal and matured as a professional. In Tony I had run into a very savvy businessman with an extraordinary ability to secure a plentiful flow of instructions and coerce the best out of those who were able to withstand his relentlessness and focus. In Antony I met a great guy with a tremendous determination to succeed in business and life in general. He did indeed 'knuckle down'. Twenty-seven years on from my brief attempt at anger management counselling, Antony is Group Director of Silver, a large London surveying practice. We remain close friends but, professionally, this would not be our last project together.

As for me, I did head south for a few months of sea and sunshine whilst spending invaluable time with the folks. It was a refreshing interlude, but inwardly I sensed that my long term career prospects lay with Marc and the new surveying practice he had established in Wimbledon. Inevitably, in following my instincts, I would end up breaking the hearts of those I loved most.

[A sad postscript to this part of my life was that Roy, Tony's rather unwilling but very productive workhorse, unfortunately suffered a massive stroke and died shortly after I left the practice. The words 'mould' and 'broke' regularly spring to mind when his name is mentioned.]

Chapter 22

Mazzarati
October 1991

OVER the years, I have been very fortunate to have met many wonderful people who have been influential in shaping my life and the choices I have made. From such meagre beginnings, my mother and father created a stable loving home environment and instilled the simple values of honesty, gratitude and integrity. Some, like Bert and Derrick, were probably oblivious to their 'bit parts'. Marcus, my mentor, soulmate and business partner would, without doubt, be too modest (and embarrassed!) to acknowledge the huge role that he has played. Alongside all the personal influences, rugby, with its core essentials of teamwork, discipline and respect became the cement that bound everything together.

The 5th of October 1991 seemed like any other ordinary Saturday when it came to playing rugby, getting lubricated at the club and then going off into Ealing to finish off the evening. It was just that this particular Saturday turned out to be rather pivotal. It had nothing to do with Rutz's birthday which we celebrated with typical gusto after the game. He was never one to miss out on creating an occasion and was really going for it on that day. Such was his boisterous nature, inevitably he dragged several others with him. Crispins wine bar on the Uxbridge Road was to be the final watering hole before we'd stumble over to Monty's curry house, except we got distracted and never did treat Rutz to his birthday 'ruby'.

Whilst quite a few of us had made the walk across Ealing Common from the club, it was left to Rutz, myself and Glenn 'The Carpet Fitter' Karpeta to prop up the bar. The others were more intent on sitting down to chat and sup away, but our position gave us a decent vantage point to people watch. Well, at least Rutz and I could. Glenn had had a skinful on top of a concussion so was present but not on effective observational duty. At 5' 9" Glenn was small for a flanker but, pound for pound, one of the most durable guys I had played rugby with. Unfortunately he chose to use his head as a weapon so his forehead and face were a patchwork of scar tissue, making it difficult for him to open his eyes! At this stage of an evening he was merely good for grinning and grunting.

"Here, Hamms, check out those three birds sitting by the window," Rutz piped up with his customary air of assurance. "I like the blonde one in the middle. You and Glenn can fight for the other two!"

"Get away, Rutz, I'm not looking. Anyway, even in his state, would you want a fight with Glenn?" I tried to make light of Rutz's suggestion.

"Oi, Hamms, I'm not asking you to get married! How about helping out a birthday boy and at least taking a butcher's?"

Away with the fairies, Glenn simply maintained his grin.

"Alright Rutz, just to help you get some attention!"

Capitulating, I turned and looked towards the window. Notwithstanding his beer goggles, I had to admit that Rutz's judgement had not been skewed. The 'blonde one' was very attractive.

"See, told you Hamms, didn't I?"

Perhaps a tad smug as no semblance of acknowledgement of his interest had even been registered, Rutz puffed out his chest as he peered over my shoulder. It deflated almost as swiftly.

"Oh shhhhit, she's your's Hamms. It's Godzilla!"

Glenn even managed a snort.

Given Rutz's covert operation, I probably turned around a little too quickly. In hindsight, I'm rather glad I did. His 'blonde' and her two friends were making their way to the bar for another round. She was tall, very tall with heels, but definitely not Godzilla and, wow, what a figure to go with amazing looks.

167

"Mine? You're off your head, Rutz, she's way out of my league!"

Somehow, three hours later, in spite of Rutz's live-wire antics and Glenn's zombie-like state, the six of us parted company outside the Broadway Boulevard nightclub. Even more remarkable, Marion Reeves, 'the blonde one', had divulged her contact details to me.

I stewed over ringing Marion for quite a few weeks. Being crazily hectic at work and worrying about the old man's health did little to help sort out my head, but the main reason for my hesitancy related to Jane. A knot in my stomach tightened each time I thought about Jane and how badly I had treated her. After one particularly boozy night at the club I had bumped into an old flame whilst staggering around Ealing and, as they say, one thing led to another. I loved Jane and there was no reason to have treated her that way but, once the guilt had set in, I began to seek absolution through a beer glass and my behaviour became more irrational. In periods of clarity the disgust just chewed me up. Eventually I came to the realisation that my betrayal had wrecked everything and we broke up shortly afterwards.

We hadn't been apart for that long, so I felt bad for not throwing away the crumpled piece of paper with Marion's number on it. That feeling would have ended there and then if I had, but something stopped me. Eventually my resolve gave way and I picked up the phone.

"Hello. Is that Marion?"

My uneasiness may have been obvious.

"Yessss. . . who is that?" came the hesitant reply.

"Hi Marion, it's John. We met at Crispins in Ealing a few weeks ago," I announced, only marginally more confident.

"Uh, sorry I don't remember meeting a 'John' recently," she said dismissively.

'Oh no, this could be really embarrassing, just hang up you idiot.' I thought momentarily.

"Yes, sorry, it's been a while but I've been rather busy at work," I offered as a limp excuse. "You might recall meeting three rugby

Ian McLaughlin and friends take the Samson Centre to the world stage; Kilimanjaro, 2008.

Fletch and Andy pedal to Paris for the Samson Centre, 2009.

The rugby boys join Marion and myself on the Deal Or No Deal set, 2007.

Receiving a Service to the Community Award in April 2010 with Mayor Pauline Searle.

John Dunbar and I crack open the champagne after Samson Quest's first run at Lingfield, 2004.

Collecting at Lingfield Races with Fleur and Mary, 2010.

Fletch and myself at Twickers, 2013.

Put in my place by Mother, 2005.

Renewing our wedding
vows, 2008.

Bruv and myself enjoying
the sun at Marazion, 2007.

Marianne and Justin's wedding,
2011. I'm about to do the father
of the bride speech.

The girls at Marianne and
Justin's wedding.

Newspaper coverage of the Michael Owen charity event for the Samson Centre.

Martin Dent and myself with Michael Owen, 2015.

Rugby legend Jason Leonard presents me, Stumble and Mac with a plaque following the 16 Idiots extraordinary fundraising efforts, 2016.

Frankie Dettori joins the party at another Samson fundraiser at Ascot, 2016.

Greeting the Countess of Wessex to open our new treatment rooms, July 2015.

Receiving a cheque from the Inner Wheel of Godalming (Woolsack), 2016.

Receiving the Local Heroes Award, 2014

The Centre gym, 2017.

The Centre gym in use, 2017.

'Always the cart horse' – RebelX Sports Day fundraising for Samson, 2017

Samson Centre class activity. June 2018.

Marion and myself with the
girls at a Samson Centre
photo-shoot in Feb. 2017.

Our 25th wedding anniversary,
2017 – Me with Bruv and
Marianne.

Honour for MS centre founder

THE founder of the Samson Centre for Multiple Sclerosis (MS) in Guildford has been awarded the Order of Mercy by the League of Mercy, for his voluntary service over many years to charities and non-profit organisations in the UK and overseas.

John Hambly, who is from Milford and is an MS sufferer himself, has worked tirelessly in pursuit of the health and well-being of those living with MS in Surrey and surrounding areas. MS is the most common neurological disease affecting young adults in the UK today. It is a lifelong and debilitating disease of the central nervous system for which there is currently no known cure.

Many years ago, Mr Hambly had a vision to build a centre where people with MS could receive therapies that would assist them to remain as active as possible for as long as possible, within the community. He also realised that those with MS and their families and carers need emotional support and somewhere to be able to talk to others in a similar position as themselves.

After much hard work, fundraising, leadership skills and the determination of Mr Hambly the Samson Centre for MS was born and opened its doors in 2005 at the Riverside, near Bellfields in Guildford.

Today, it remains a centre of excellence, providing more than 10,000 much needed therapies each year for those living with MS. Mr Hambly works as vice-chairman, a trustee and a volunteer for the centre. His vision continues as he wants to be able to extend the services currently available at the centre as well as to be able to substantially increase the number of MS sufferers that the centre can assist.

Despite his own ill health Mr Hambly remains committed to "Making Samson Stronger" and as such for the greater good of all those living with MS in Surrey and surrounding areas.

The awards ceremony took place on July 11 at Mansion House, in the City of London, before Princess Katerina of Yugoslavia, the Lady Mayoress of London and many other areas.

Lord Lingfield, president of the League of Mercy said: "Mr Hambly has done extraordinary work for those most in need. He is a marvellous example of someone whose longstanding and voluntary dedication to the service and welfare of others is noteworthy and remarkable and we were delighted to be able to make this well-deserved award to him."

The League of Mercy, originally created in 1896 for the encouragement and recognition of voluntary work in hospitals and the community, was refounded in 1999 and continues the work of the original founder, the then Prince of Wales, later King Edward VII. Visit www.leagueofmercy.co.uk

For information about the Samson Centre for MS visit www.samsoncentre.org.uk.

Receiving the Order of Mercy from Lord Lingfield
at Mansion House in 2017.

Sir A.P. McCoy joins us for a Samson Centre fundraising event at Newbury Races, 2018.

Ellie, Meg and myself meeting ex-England Captain, Chris Robshaw, at a Harlequins game in 2018.

Marion and the girls after running the British 10K in 2018.

players on a birthday booze-up. We ended up at the Broadway Boulevard."

"Oh, yes, I remember now. You and your friends were very drunk."

A week later, early one evening after work, I headed for The Globe on Baker Street. For some reason I was as twitchy as I had been in years. Very few exams, interviews, work scenarios or big match warm-ups I'd ever been involved with had quite produced that degree of nervousness in me. Much of it would have been down to the fact that part of me still felt like I was being untrue to Jane and the rest, I guess, was just the anticipation of meeting up with a stunningly attractive woman. I may have had a few beers the night we first met but I trusted that my instincts had not been impaired. As the heads turned and followed Marion from the pub door across to me at the bar, it appeared as though my judgement had indeed been very sound.

The date went pleasantly enough but, by our own admission some months later, it was a little stymied. Marion, PA to one of the head honchos at a leading insurance company, had recently broken off her engagement to a police detective and may have had similar reservations in respect of entering into another relationship quite so soon. However, we must have felt that there was some potential as we agreed to meet up for a meal the following week. That date could not have been more different. The conversation flowed freely in a more pleasant environment and we got to know each other much better. Marion admitted that she disliked trains, pubs and London so had seriously considered blowing me out when I'd suggested The Globe. Knowing her idiosyncrasies as I do now, I should have been flattered that she had agreed to travel from Watford to the Metropolis on a rainy November evening.

As we began to see a little more of each other, I realised what a lovely person Marion was; always keen to talk about others before revealing much about herself and any issues in her life. Without being nosy or overly opinionated, chatting came easily to her. I once read that the art of good conversation came from 'polite giving and taking of subject matter'. Between my helter-skelter working life and the light-hearted banter of the clubhouse, I had not quite mastered the skill. Unbeknownst to me though, Marion's ability to make others feel at ease in her presence began to wear off on me. Networking probably wasn't such a buzz word then as it is now, but it would serve me well in the years to come.

Yet, with her looks and people skills, one thing confounded me. Marion still had a lack of confidence in herself. As much as I showered her with compliments, she would flatly dismiss the contention that she was attractive. In hindsight, and as strange as it may sound, her 'negativity' was a positive. Whilst we maintained our separate social lives for a few months, I trusted her implicitly. This could be considered a major sea change in attitude for me. Jane was lovely, honest and very loyal and, socially, we had tended to do most things together so trust was never an issue. However, I had been badly hurt by Tasmin when she went off with the guy from the polytechnic rugby club and then several years later, having been in a great relationship for 18 months, inexplicably we began to irritate the hell out of each other and tearfully agreed to go our separate ways. I never quite got to grips with why that happened, as at times we had been inseparable and I was so happy to be part of her wonderful family. Perhaps we were just too young and impulsive. Whatever the reasons, both episodes were massive emotional jolts that had left their scars.

With Christmas approaching, as much as I wanted to spend time with Marion, it was more important that I headed home. My father's condition had worsened significantly since the onset of winter, so I needed to be with the folks. Before setting off, Marion and I tentatively agreed that if matters were reasonably settled in Cornwall, we could try and get away for a few days around the New Year.

My father, with impeccable timing, shook off the worst of yet another chest infection, perked up during the festivities and, sensing that my mind might be elsewhere, gave his blessing for me to hit the road. Three hours after leaving Truro, I stood on the southbound platform at Bristol's imposing Temple Meads station. The butterflies were back.

'What if her train phobia had got the better of her and she was still in Watford?'

Half an hour late, the 13:05 from Paddington came slowly into view, manfully pulling its eight carriages. As it screeched to a halt and the doors swung open, I moved closer to the platform exit. There were a lot of festive travellers so it would be easy to miss each other. As the bustling mass began to clear, I could see Marion in her black leather jacket and jeans serenely making her way along the platform from the end carriage. When she eventually got to me, smiling broadly, we hugged and kissed. By no stretch of the imagination was it a re-enactment of *A Brief Encounter* but, just in the week that we had been apart, our dynamic had changed.

From Bristol we made our way to Stratford-upon-Avon. I had booked a room at the very cosy looking White Swan Hotel a couple of days after Christmas. It turned out to be even better than that. Bedecked stylishly and festively, with a roaring open fire in the bar, we were enchanted from the moment we stepped over the threshold. So much so, rather than venture out into the wintry weather and explore the town, we opted for an evening meal in the hotel restaurant followed by a few drinks in front of the glowing coals. As always we talked for hours about anything and anyone but it felt different. The emotional armour was off and, able to relax into each other, we found ourselves lingering over every glance, smile and touch.

After two nights we moved on to Stow, a beautiful little market town high up in the Cotswolds. A seasonal dusting of snow made for a picture-postcard setting. If Stratford had been enchanting, Stow was even more alluring. Normally quick to shy away from gift shops, tea rooms and the like, I almost found myself taking the lead role. What on earth was happening to me? With Keasty away I hadn't even thought about, let alone planned, the club training session ahead of the first fixture of the New Year. For once my obsession with all things rugby-related had receded way into the background and the reason for this was growing stronger day by day. I wanted to be with Marion. Not just for the romantic nights out and weekends away, but forever. I proposed early in the new year and we set about organising our nuptials with unbridled energy and joy.

11th July 1992
The feeling of nausea was overpowering but I pressed on. Down on my haunches I threw up for a third time near the in-goal area.

'Suck it in and go again, you bloody waster.'

I straightened up, looked skywards and breathed deeply as the sweat ran down my back. I mustered one last lap of the pitch before hitting the pads of the scrummage machine. I tried to throw up again but there was nothing left in me. Even though I felt wretched, the best of a bad job had been done. I glanced at my watch. It was 6:34am. Time to get home and face the music.

"Well, you're a right one, aren't you?" my father, an early riser, once of habit now of necessity, was already sitting in his armchair in the kitchen with the teapot on the stove, "Bleddy 'ell boy, look at the state of 'ee!"

"Yeah, you're right there, Father. I'm feeling as rough as rats but at least I've got some of it out of my system."

"Thought that you 'n' David were only goin' for a couple of quiet pints down the Barley last night?"

"We were. . . errr. . . we did. Well, that is, until we bumped into a few of the rugby boys and ended up at Secrets nightclub, but I swear, we only had a couple of beers in there."

I stripped off the soaking wet T-shirt, leant on the worktop and squinted out of the window across a murky, sleepy looking Truro.

"Christ boy, you're as white as a sheet. Reckon some beggar must have slipped 'ee a Mickey last night." My father summed up the scenario fairly accurately. "Get a couple of glasses of water down 'ee. Then Mother'll sort you out a fried breakfast."

"Ugh, my stomach is still up at the club. I can't even think of food at the moment, Father."

"Better get 'un back pretty quick boy, you're gettin' married in five hours!"

Strolling through the back streets of Truro on a Saturday morning had a familiar feel but add in the Cornish kilt, jacket, sporran and it was most definitely new territory. The head had cleared a little but my colour, not unlike the yellow hue of the tartan, combined with a cold sweat, were a total giveaway as I greeted Marion with a smile at the doors to the Registry Office.

"Good morning darling, you look amazing. Before you say

172

anything, I didn't get smashed last night. Someone spiked my pint. Just ask Dave."

Perhaps it was not the best preamble to the most sacred of vows, particularly as 'Verm', my Best Man, looked even more rough than me. We both knew that we were on thin ice. Thanks to Bob Taylor (Simon's big brother), my stag day at Sandown races whilst shackled to two concrete filled rugby balls turned into a long weekend, with us rolling back home at 3am on Monday, for which I received my first 'public warning'! However, if Marion felt let down, she didn't show it. She may have been more concerned about her dress and hairdo as, true to form, Cornish mizzle had set in for the day.

In an ideal world we would have gone for a church wedding in Cornwall. However, the requirement to attend a service once a month for six months was impractical given that we had only decided to get married in January. With my father's health being such a concern, time was of the essence and there was never a thought that we would tie the knot anywhere other than Truro. The next dilemma was the invitations. Our chosen venue, the Great Hall at the Alverton Manor, a converted 1830s convent, could cater for 120 at the afternoon reception, which just about covered our families and a few close friends. However, somehow we also needed to accommodate our other friends, including those from both rugby clubs which, after no small amount of deliberation, we decided we would do with a buffet style evening reception mainly for the Old A's, and a Sunday barbecue with the Truro boys up at the club. Ah, the best laid plans of mice and men. . !

The afternoon was a wonderful occasion as generations of our respective families came together for the first time. Watching my mother and father enjoying themselves in a social environment after all the years of ill health was especially uplifting. It reminded me of my childhood when the whole Trelander arm of the family would descend upon the British Legion to celebrate Christmas. Verm and I had agreed that when it got to the speeches we would observe the usual protocols and then muck around. For me, amongst other stunts, that involved revealing what a Cornishman wore under his kilt (fortunately Speedos!) and kept in his sporran (a pasty, of

173

course) as well as presenting Marion with a few gifts which included an honorary Cornish rugby shirt as recognition of her acceptance into the clan, some Celtic jewellery and somewhat unsurprisingly, to tumultuous laughter, a cook book entitled *The Last Time I Looked It Was On Fire!* Marion's reputation for 'burning water' appeared to be well known! Verm's unconventional approach in addressing the wedding party began with a minute of flapping and muttering from underneath the top table before emerging to conduct the formalities and then dish the dirt on me. Given all the shenanigans we had got up to on various rugby tours and the time we had lived together after Poly, I was fortunate that he kept it relatively clean.

By the time we began the process of bidding goodnight to our young and elderly relatives a situation had developed outside the Great Hall. As if in commemoration of the first time Marion and I had met, Rutz was completely blotto having been on the sauce all day. The rest of the Welsh lads, who had also had a lively afternoon, had done their best to contain his enthusiasm to join in the main reception, but Rutz in full flow could be a real force of nature. It was only when Knocker and Co rolled up (a day early!) that matters were contained. Rutz was swiftly bundled into a van by three heavies and whisked off to his hotel to sleep it off. The floodgates were now well and truly open as the Truro boys rumbled through into the evening reception. So close was the rapport between the two clubs, within an hour you could have been mistaken for thinking the bar area was the clubhouse following a tour game. A moment of decorum descended as Marion and I got up to dance to Bryan Adams's *(Everything I Do) I Do It For You* after which 'normal' service was resumed.

I proudly fulfilled the bridegroom's role, meeting and greeting our evening guests with Marion by my side, before obtaining special dispensation to retire to the lounge bar for a quiet beer with Verm. We were soon joined by a few of the Welsh and Kiwi lads. As if playing out the last vestiges of being single, half an hour of going down Memory Lane turned into an hour, then, with a few rugby anthems and hakas thrown in for good measure, several hours passed. It was only when Verm tapped me on the shoulder and nodded towards the stairs that I emerged into the 'new world'.

"John, it's 12:30, don't you think you ought to come to bed now?" Marion's polite but fully merited enquiry was met with a few coughs and sniggers so, just to qualify the terms of the demand, she swiftly added, "We've got another busy day tomorrow and need to get some sleep!"

I glanced across at Verm for some support. He simply smiled and raised an eyebrow. My bachelorhood may have been well and truly over but in marrying 'Mazza', I was ecstatic and looking forward to our life together.

Chapter 23

X-Man!
June 1994

B Y getting married in our early thirties there was an expectancy that we would press on with the matter of adding a few more branches to an already broad family tree. For a fit and healthy young couple this might have been viewed as relative plain sailing, but it actually worked out very difficult for us to get our feet on the first rung of the ladder. Marion suffered two miscarriages early on, the second of which occurred whilst we were celebrating our first wedding anniversary at the Land's End Hotel. Immersed in emotion and worry, the long drive back to West London was difficult and bereft of meaningful conversation. Neither Marion nor I have ever been prone to dwell on sadness and we were desperate to produce a grandchild for the folks before my father's illness got the better of him, but even after successful surgical intervention, it would still take many months before the air of anxiety and hollowness would begin to lift.

It was therefore with huge relief that on 16th June 1994, at Queen Charlotte's Hospital in Chiswick, Ellie safely appeared on Planet Earth with her beautiful dark brown eyes and shock of black hair. After 24 hours in labour an exhausted Marion was whisked away for a well deserved bath so I was left 'in charge'. Never had I felt such an overwhelming mixture of love, wonderment and fear(!) as I sat cradling our bundle of joy, quietly singing Simon & Garfunkel's

'Baby Driver'. So totally captivated was I by Ellie, thoughts that I should have been at Lord's for the 1st Test between England and New Zealand were quickly dispelled! In fact, I would have to get used to this type of interruption to my sporting indulgences as it would become something of a trend.

Once Marion had recovered her strength and we had become accustomed to life as a trio, we hurriedly made plans to shoot down to the West Country. Walking through the back door of my childhood home with Marion and Ellie in her baby seat had a surreal feel. In that moment I sensed my mother and father realise that their chubby little child, their smelly scruffy fisher boy, their wild intoxicated student and their occasional lodger from the Big Smoke, had finally become a man. The tears of happiness were tinged with those of sadness as it was abundantly clear that my father was entering his final furlong. For someone so proud of his appearance and always impeccably turned out, it was hard to take in how poorly he looked. My mother had managed to get him down into the sitting room and spruce him up but the pyjamas and dressing gown told me all I needed to know. Brave man that he was, he perked up for the camera as he proudly held Ellie.

"Our little bit of London Pride," he whispered between painfully short breaths.

Almost four months later in the autumnal drizzle, as I peered into the river at Kirby Lonsdale in Cumbria, I had an overwhelming sense that my father's spirit was there with me. It was the eve of his 70th birthday. Four days earlier I had left Treliske Hospital with the feeling that I would not see him alive again. On that visit, for the first time that I could remember, my father had shown no interest in picking out his Saturday horses.

"Just give me a shave and then make your way off on holiday, boy."

He had not been his usual fussy self, as so often he would have asked me to lather him up for a second shave.

When we arrived back at the cottage that evening, instinctively I knew why a handwritten note had been pushed under the front door asking me to call Dave.

"Hi Bruv, he's gone hasn't he?" the tears had begun to flow even before I'd finished speaking.

"Yeah. . . he's gone. . ." There was a long pause as Dave regathered his composure, ". . .early this afternoon, Bruv. Mother was with him. . . right up 'til the end."

Heartbroken and only able to utter truncated sentences we were relieved that my father's suffering was over. It was a merciful release for him and, in truth, for my mother too. Her love and devotion had kept him alive way beyond all the timescales given by the respiratory and cardio consultants but she was emotionally and physically wrecked.

Sunday 22nd September 1996 promised to be a cracking day at the rugby club as we were holding an early season barbecue, plus a live band, with the aim of getting the new players together with the old guard. Indeed, it was such a successful afternoon/evening that I gathered quite a few sickies were thrown on the Monday morning. I went into the office late that day, not because of a thumping hangover, but because Megan's stubborn arrival (around the time that the hog roast got fired up the day before!) had left Marion in a right pickle, once again requiring surgery and a hospital stay. Astonishingly tough and matter-of-fact about her latest ordeal, mother and child were back home within a couple of days and straight into an extended family regime. With me working long hours, Marion needed to be regimented in the way she organised our home affairs and that included me – just take a look at the regularity of the birth dates as they mounted up!

After Meg had joined the party, I started to get a few jibes from the guys at the club playfully questioning whether I possessed a predominance of female genes! Big Gerry, especially, used the emergence of the Hambly harem not only to reinforce his regular assertion that I had 'no shoulders' (compared to his gorilla sized ones!) but that I was more woman than man and should consider changing position from No.8 to hooker! I had not the slightest concern about my gender and did not bite, but eventually curiosity got the better of me. Could I one day coach a son to play the great game, perhaps even run out onto the Field of Dreams together? I eventually found a research paper about how men determine the sex of a baby dependent on whether their sperm carries an X or Y chromosome. An X chromosome combines with the mother's X chromosome to make a baby girl, but of course it's not quite that simple. Genes control whether a man's sperm contains more X or more Y chromosomes. The study suggested that I was an 'ff' man producing more X sperm. As much as I relished my chats with Big Gerry, this was not a subject we would ever be airing over a Guinness!

Tuesday 18th May 1999 – true to form, Grace chose to make her entrance on the day of a Cricket World Cup match involving England. However, our emotions were so different this time. The sporting interest became utterly incidental as the serenity of the midwives evaporated when a true knot in the umbilical cord was spotted as a very lethargic Grace emerged into the world. She was quickly taken off Marion for tests. It transpired that the distress of the birth had also resulted in her releasing and ingesting meconium. Basically, she had swallowed her own poo and there were concerns that some may have got into her lungs. We waited anxiously as they worked on her. Eventually quiet squeaks were followed by a volley of reassuringly full-blooded screeches which were to become Grace's trademark for the next six months. That said, we were still not out of the woods as during that period she was diagnosed with a heart murmur, so regular trips to the hospital followed. Her christening in the summer of 1999 gave us the opportunity to get the family and our close friends together in a show of love and togetherness. Thankfully Grace's health had stabilised but there were now some new black clouds massing overhead.

Late on Saturday 9th March 2002 I was sitting in front of the computer studying the *Racing Post* form in preparation for my final trip to the Cheltenham Festival on the Monday morning. Ever since I had organised the first 'Jolly Boys' trip to the National Hunt Olympics back in 1995, it had become an annual pilgrimage for six of us. However, the daily scrimmage with 60,000 racegoers and four days of excessive drinking and eating had begun to take their toll and meant that I was sluggish and out of sorts for at least a week beyond my return. The aftermath was not only unfair on Marion and the girls but also on Marcus, so the decision to pull down the shutters on one of the most enjoyable of social occasions would have to be made in future years.

Marion, who had just turned 40, was heavily pregnant again but not due for another three weeks, so there was plenty of time for this one last hurrah. That is until she started bleeding and was induced in the early hours. At six o'clock on the Sunday evening, a rudely awakened Cerys joined the Hambly party. There would be no rugby playing son after all, but at least I would have enough for a five-a-side ladies football team, provided Marion went in goal! The remarkable thing was that she turned to me an hour after giving birth and said, "Go on, off you go to Cheltenham. You'll be unbearable stuck at home this week if you don't." I had to agree!

Fast forward to Monday 16th August 2004:

The castle on St Michael's Mount looked imperiously across the vast expanse of Mount's Bay on a gloriously clear, warm summer's day. Since it was my birthday, I had been allowed to choose the venue for a family day out. My mother, Marianne and her first child, Kensa, had joined us along with Bruv, Nikki and their two daughters, Shelley and Holly. Marazion beach had been a favourite of mine ever since I had spent a couple of days sea kayaking as an eleven year old on school summer camp, followed by the long nights of sea fishing with Ken and Bert, and then lazy days lapping up the sunshine as a beach bum. It did it for me back then, and on that day its breathtaking vista and seaside charms were doing it for Marion and our girls. Reliving my childhood in the unbroken sunshine, we spent the afternoon rolling around in the surf, fashioning elaborate sand art creations, hunting for treasure, playing frisbee and boule, all punctuated by regular strolls to the beach cafe for drinks and ice creams. To the casual observer this family scene must have appeared close to perfect. How deceptive first impressions can be. The stark fact was that a great deal of uncertainty and turmoil was hovering over us.

Although on that day we had our problems, we were oblivious to the dire situation developing over Brown Willy, as unstable air was about to inflict the most devastating of flash floods onto idyllic Boscastle and Crackington Haven on the opposite side of the county.

Chapter 24

Something's Amiss
June 1997

Come the 1996/7 season, I have accepted that family life, work and health should come first, so begin winding down playing every week and concede that it will be 2nd, 3rd and Vets XV rugby for me from here on. Perhaps I was doing a typical bloke thing in refusing to visit the GP when feeling unwell. Episodes of illness would flare up and then recede after a week or so, meaning that I would rarely take time off work. The business was taking on a lot of new instructions which was exactly what we had striven for, so both Marc and I, no matter how we felt health-wise, would keep our noses to the grindstone and work through ailments. Determined to meet our clients' demanding deadlines, we would often work 14 hour days, sometimes 7 days a week, much to the annoyance of our better halves and the disappointment of the children. Even when I submitted to being home for supper and bedtime stories, invariably it would be followed by a few hours of dictation. I did occasionally succumb to back pain and take a couple of hours off to visit a chiropractor, which initially did the trick but became an exercise of diminishing returns with so many hours spent at the wheel driving between sites and the batterings on the rugby field every two or three weeks.

As my back problems became more and more persistent and debilitating, with pain often keeping me awake throughout the night, I was getting desperate for some respite, so booked to see an alternative therapist specialising in hypnotherapy and reiki. This practitioner had been recommended by Marion's father, John, who being equally reluctant to visit his GP, had grudgingly gone along to see his 'witch doctor' and been pleasantly surprised when his chronic sinusitis improved. What did I have to lose other than a few precious hours and £30 per session? Whilst I was familiar with some types of alternative medicine, I was quite apprehensive about hypnotherapy, particularly after Marion had quipped that John had come around from one session with his trousers on back to front! On pitching up at the practice in North London, so dilapidated were the premises that I actually wondered whether I should be offering them some professional advice!

'Hey ho, don't judge a book by its cover,' I thought, drew a deep breath and ventured on in.

Time had clearly stood still inside as well. The decor was tired, all the floors and door heads sloped and there was the unmistakable whiff of dry rot wafting amongst the incense from the joss sticks dotted liberally around the reception-cum-waiting room. It did not bode well.

The appearance of my practitioner ten minutes later also threw me. I am not quite sure what I was expecting, but a cross between a professor and an ageing rock star with a goatee was not one of them. After the preambles of filling in a medical form and multiple choice questionnaire, which I think had been devised to suss out your state of mind, I was asked to jump up onto the couch. Stifling the urge to burst into laughter proved almost impossible as I chuckled and snorted for the first few minutes. Apparently it was totally normal and something to do with nerves (and, completely unrelated to the misguided thought of having my trousers pulled down!). Eventually I got a hold of myself and, with the assistance of some mesmerising utterances from the hypnotherapist, began to relax. It was all very odd and not an experience I intended sharing with anyone at the rugby club, but it seemed to work as I found myself volunteering very personal information with just minimal prompting before falling asleep. I attended two or three more sessions before he revealed his findings and conclusion.

"Everything that you've indicated on the forms and from what you're showing me when you are relaxed, points to the fact that you are very stressed by your work but also troubled by many things from your past. In my opinion, if you carry on pushing yourself in the way you are at the moment, you are heading for a major anatomical breakdown."

I was totally stunned by the frankness of the last three words.

"I'm sorry, but what do you mean by that?"

"You are dwelling on too many things from years and years ago. People that you feel you have let down. Things that you have done badly or incorrectly. John, you need to stop beating yourself up and live in the now. What's more, when you do eventually settle, you keep talking, almost to the point of obsession, about lying down in the woods in warm summer sunshine. I am not sure if you're trying to relive something traumatic you have experienced or whether it is something you are hankering for, but what is clear to me is that, if you don't get some balance into your life, you are in danger of making yourself really ill."

"Well, how are you suggesting I go about remedying that then? I have a lot of responsibilities at work, a young family, financial commitments and we're looking to move to a new area in the next few months. Not exactly ideal circumstances for de-stressing!" I blurted out with an air of incredulity which, on reflection, could only have substantiated the practitioner's conclusions.

"John, calm down. There is no need to go into a tailspin. I can help you to move in the right direction and understand what your mind and body are telling you."

Over the course of the next two months I attended weekly sessions of hypnotherapy which were occasionally combined with either reiki or osteopathy. I desperately wanted them to work, but the three hour round trip and the treatment time meant that I was sacrificing half a day's work each week which in itself was stressful. When I decided to draw stumps at the end of this period, I felt that I had benefitted from the advice and gained a slightly different perspective on life without quite getting to grips in respect of where to go with it. Despite this, the hectic lifestyle continued virtually unabated and my health issues intensified.

As the rugby season drew to a close, our search for a new property took us from West London to West Surrey, and by late June we had moved into a small bungalow in Milford, near Godalming. It proved to be a masterstroke, as we found ourselves in the most beautiful area of countryside within a warm, welcoming community with good schools and local facilities. Perhaps as important, providing the infamous A3 behaved, my journey time to the office in Wimbledon was cut by half. The property was quite run-down but good enough for us to live in until the following spring when we intended to convert it into a 4-bed chalet bungalow.

For the first time in a while everything felt settled as we looked forward to exploring our new environment. In my case, I couldn't wait to put on my trainers and seek out the bridleways and footpaths. The long summer evenings lured me away from the office relatively early, so within an hour of leaving the outskirts of the metropolis I was on Milford Common warming up before setting off with no particular route plan in mind. I had had a good look at the OS map so knew roughly which direction I wanted to go. Ever since I had started running as a teenager, I simply loved the escapism of being out in the country. This had been difficult to recapture within the hustle and bustle of West London. Almost as soon as I had set off, I could sense my mojo rising. The spring in the step, the silent inward squeals of delight and the overall feeling of freedom, all came flooding back. The warm evening sunshine providing the last ingredient for a massive endorphin rush. Thirty minutes later I was bowling along at a fair old lick, taking in as much of the beautiful surroundings as possible without losing my bearings. On leaving the Common land near neighbouring Witley, I crossed the main road to Petworth and headed down a track close to the Waterloo to Portsmouth railway line knowing that I should eventually end up at Milford Station and then back to the village. I passed the local allotments, crossed a bubbling brook and then disappeared under the tree canopy which ran alongside the train tracks.

Perhaps it was the transition from the bright evening sunshine to the dimmed dusky light on entering the wooded area, but within only a few strides I had stubbed my left foot and fallen heavily. As I was going down, I managed to turn and roll so that I landed on my

185

back. Startled and aware of having twisted my ankle and skinned my elbows, I lay there for a few seconds re-gathering my thoughts.

'Had I caught my foot on a tree root or had I possibly taken a false step not unlike my experiences in Canary Wharf six years earlier?'

Even though there was no one else around, I felt embarrassed that my enthusiasm and spirit of adventure could have come to this. I would probably end up limping my way back through the village covered in pine needles. It was only then, as the sunlight glinted through the foliage overhead, that I realised I had been here before. The hypnotherapist had been right about one thing after all!

Chapter 25

Staring Down the Barrel
March 1999

I suppose it is only natural that people live in fear of the day that they might be diagnosed with something life-threatening or life-changing. The day that everything you take for granted comes to a shuddering halt and you have to address your own mortality. It is a simple fact of life. It will happen to most of us and, yet, when it arrives the chasm that opens up can be so broad and deep, you are swallowed up in a silent swirl of emotion. Any rationale you might have, even fleetingly, contemplated deploying at such a moment is swept away from you in a few words.

On so many occasions over the previous 18 months, I'd had the feeling of being on the precipice, only for the sense of foreboding to evaporate as quickly as it had arisen. I had almost got used to this ebb and flow punctuating my life. It was irritating and of concern but not debilitating enough to interrupt work. However it did play havoc with my fitness regime; but given that I had now grudgingly entered the world of vets' rugby it really didn't seem to matter if I played intermittently. Despite feeling absolutely fine when turning up with my kitbag, not even I could predict how I would perform from game to game. On one occasion in late 1997, I played for an Invitation XV as part of a good friend, Russell Fletcher's, 40th celebrations and finished the match as spritely as I had started it, even putting the birthday boy away for a glory try in the last 5 minutes. My next match could not have been more different, as I trudged around as if carrying Big Gerry on my shoulders!

Matters really came to a head in early December 1998 when, not feeling great, I played for the Vets away at Ruislip. I had phoned in the morning with the intention of crying off but when the captain said that they might be short, I agreed to play. It was a big mistake. I nearly threw up in the warm up and then, after 15 minutes, had the indignity of being removed from the field of play for looking ill. On driving back to Milford, a burning sensation down my left side and spasms in my back convinced me that the correct decision had been made for me.

By 5am on the Monday morning the symptoms had become so acute that I had to wake Marion and ask her for painkillers. I had been rolling around in agony for only about 10 minutes but the sensations were so weird and unlike anything I had ever felt. Even before I'd fully come out of my slumber, in the pitch black, panic hit me.

'Oh my God, there's something horribly wrong with me.'

Once a startled Marion had rushed back from the kitchen with the pills and put the bedside lamp on, I realised that I had also developed double vision. The pain in my back was excruciating, penetrating through to my stomach almost as if I had been impaled by a blunt lance. The medication had little effect so I resigned myself to the fact that I would have to visit the surgery. Marion called Marc and said that I wouldn't make it in to the office that day. Blurred eyesight aside, my discomfort was so intense I suspect that even I would not have been stupid enough to get in the car and soldier on up the A3.

However, stupidity did not stop me from insisting that I wanted some fresh air and would walk to see the doctor. From the moment I left the house and entered the alleyway at the top of our road, I recognised one of my symptoms all too well. Old 'glue foot' from the London Marathon was back, but now in both legs. By the time I emerged onto the main road and headed right towards the surgery, I was staggering like a punch drunk boxer. I felt very conspicuous as the school run and work traffic crept its way alongside me.

"What seems to be the problem?" enquired my doctor, looking a little surprised to see me first thing on a Monday morning.

"Well, I awoke early this morning with an awful pain in my back which sort of ran through to my stomach, and since getting up my vision has gone very blurry and I'm dizzy and struggling to walk properly."

"Hmm, doesn't sound much fun," smiled my GP. "One thing at a time. Hop up onto the couch, face down and let's have a look at your back pain."

I obliged, although just standing up and walking the few steps to the couch were a bit of a giveaway with regards to my state of imbalance and juddering gait. After the obligatory taps and prods around my ribcage and lumbar area, my doctor asked me to sit up straight, at which point, embarrassingly, I toppled over to one side.

"Woh, don't worry John, just relax and lie back down a moment. Clearly something is affecting your balance, so let's do this a different way."

I willingly complied.

Raising up the head of the couch, he pulled out a gadget with a torch on the end and had a good look in each eye, followed by testing my various reflexes with his trusty rubber hammer.

"OK, John, I can see that you're struggling, so very carefully make your way over to the seat."

Slowly I shuffled my way back to the chair, fully aware that the doctor's watchful eyes were scanning my every movement.

"Right, John. Have you got someone who can get you up to the Royal Surrey? There's nothing to worry about, but I would just like to have you checked over in A & E."

"Yes, I am sure I can get someone, but going to hospital sounds a bit drastic. What seems to be the problem?"

"Well, when you first described your pain I thought that maybe you were passing a kidney stone, but your sensory symptoms, dizziness and blurred vision, would suggest that there's something else going on. Possibly a virus. I would like that checked out today. I will ring through to the hospital, so they'll be expecting you."

Eleven days after stumbling into the Royal Surrey, I emerged into the weak winter sunlight having been introduced to the delights of a toe-curling lumbar puncture, an MRI scan and an armful of IV steroids. Marion, who was pregnant with Grace, was clearly relieved to be walking arm in arm with a seemingly recovered hubby. The diagnosis; a viral infection of the spinal cord.

"Take it easy for the next few weeks and then slowly return to your usual routines," were the neurologist's parting words.

I did just that. Marc was kind enough to bring paperwork down from the office, so I worked from home for a month. I felt pretty normal again but resisted the urge to train. By late January 1999, all seemed good, so I returned to the office and eventually some of my building sites. Perhaps it was the gentle build up of hours and the inevitable stress associated with contract work and party wall disputes, but my energy levels soon dipped and on one occasion I tripped over on broken ground whilst doing a site inspection. Perceptive and understanding as always, Marc just cut to the chase.

"Hammers, the practice pays a small fortune for private healthcare so just give the insurers a call and get yourself looked at by a specialist."

Within two weeks I had an appointment to see a neurologist at the Nuffield in Guildford. The consultant, Dr King, who I guessed was in his late 50s, and dressed in a stylish pinstripe suit, also worked at the Royal Surrey County Hospital, so there was no need for some of the tests to be done again. Thankfully another lumbar puncture was not required although the results were not available for this first consultation. After an examination involving the now familiar neurological tests and a very relaxed chat about surveying and rugby, I was given an appointment for another MRI scan on my neck and head together with a follow-up consultation date of 11th March. My symptoms had receded yet again, so I felt like some kind of fraud as I marched out through the reception where a couple of very poorly looking patients sat quietly.

Three weeks later I am sitting in their place on a bright spring morning.

"John, the doctor will see you now. Please would you follow me."

This soothingly delivered invitation drew my attention away from the rural retreats in February's edition of *Country Life* to an attractive young nurse, standing adjacent to the receptionist's station. How could I resist?

She ushered me into one of the immaculately presented consulting rooms where Dr King sat imperiously behind a large desk.

"Good morning, please take a seat, John."

He glanced across, smiled and then returned to reading the file laid in front of him.

A minute or so passed as he slowly turned and scoured the pages. Having absorbed the contents, he took a swift breath before looking up, smiling once more.

"How are you feeling today, John?"

"Good, really good, thank you. All those weird sensations have finally disappeared, so I am looking forward to getting back up to speed at work and doing some early morning training."

"I'm very pleased to hear that you're feeling better. That is good news, but don't let your eagerness scupper your recovery." commented Dr King with a look which hinted, almost imperceptibly, at something else going through his mind.

"Don't worry doctor, I'm not planning to play again this season. My wife is expecting our third child in the next couple of months so I had better behave myself!" I said with a chuckle.

"John, can I just stop you there? I'm afraid there'll be no more rugby." This time he drew a deep breath. "There's no easy way to say this, but I am very sorry to tell you that you have Multiple Sclerosis!"

In a split second just those two words caused the room to close in on me, leaving me looking at only Dr King's mouth which continued to open and shut but I heard nothing. I knew the potentially devastating effects of MS all too well having been involved in many aids and adaptation schemes for various local authorities. Quite how long I sat there 'staring down the barrel', I cannot be sure. It was only when Dr King stood up and walked around to the side of his desk that my peripheral vision returned. Perching himself on the corner, he pursed his lips.

'Oh shit, there's more!' I thought.

"John, I can see that you're struggling to take this in. I fully understand what a shock this must be, but I need you to be aware of something else that the scan has shown. Are you still with me or would you like the nurse to bring you a drink?"

"No, no, I'm fine. I just thought you were going to confirm that I had shaken off the virus they diagnosed when I was in the Royal Surrey."

"Unfortunately, it's not that simple. There are lots of things that we're looking for during all the tests and scans. Multiple Sclerosis, in essence, means 'many scars'. Scars to the myelin sheath around your brain and spinal cord which can affect your central nervous system. Also, you need more than one relapse for us to call your illness 'MS', so your first episode in December would not have led to that diagnosis."

"Bit of a bummer then, really," I said with an air of resignation.

"Yes, it can be a difficult illness depending on which course it takes. At this time you are experiencing good and bad periods which probably puts you in the remitting/relapsing MS bracket. It might not even flare up again, in which case we will class it as benign MS."

'Please, God, let that be the case,' I prayed.

"However, as I said, there is something else. The scan has shown that you may have a further complication. A condition we call a syrinx. We will need to scan you again to identify precisely what is going on in your neck area, but if it is that, potentially your symptoms could worsen quite quickly."

Once more the room was closing in on me. It felt like both 'barrels' were now firmly planted on the bridge of my nose. Dr King was still talking but only in muffled tones. My mind was elsewhere, whirring along at a million miles an hour.

'How on earth am I going to tell Marion and the girls? What about my mother? Will I end up in a wheelchair? What about earning a living? Will we be able to stay in our new house? Am I going to die?'

Would things have been any less traumatic had I been even half-expecting to be told that I had a chronic illness? Maybe not, but I probably wouldn't have had my guard quite so low. If I had one criticism of Dr King, it would have been to drop the initial small talk and put on his 'game face' from the moment I walked into his consulting room three weeks before. After all, I would hate to think that I'd have had a chatty ten minutes with some clients before telling them that their property had major subsidence or rampant dry rot!

As I pulled into our drive my emotions were red raw, but I had not cracked up and blubbed in the car, so when a very pregnant Marion met me at the front door with our two year old Megan, and a peck on the cheek, outwardly everything probably looked fine.

"How did it go? Has the virus gone?" enquired Marion, instinctively sensing that we had not reached closure.

"Umm, not exactly. Why don't you pop Megan into the playroom and then we can have a chat," was the best I could offer without giving too much away before I had sat Marion down.

I plonked myself on the edge of our bed as I waited for her to return.

"Right, she's happy in there for the moment. What did you mean by 'not exactly'?"

"You had better sit down," I said, offering her my hand.

"What is it? You're really worrying me now," Marion implored me for an answer, almost pulling back as if I'd been unfaithful.

I strengthened my handhold, pulled her next to me and put my arm around her shoulders. I felt awful for having to put her through this.

"I'm really sorry, Marion, but I've got Multiple Sclerosis. It's a disease of the central nervous system."

And with that the waterworks opened as we held each other tightly, rocking slowly from side to side. Telling her that I had another woman would probably have been easier.

Chapter 26

Black Hole
1999-2001

FOLLOWING the shock waves from my diagnosis, knowing how much pressure would be going on to his shoulders, I reluctantly agreed with Marc that I would again work from home for a few weeks to give Marion and I a chance to get our heads around the situation, which was made all the more acute as she was so heavily pregnant. I was hugely grateful to Marc for this, as mentally I was just not in the right place to preside over site meetings, carry out house surveys, nor deal with the minutia of design work or party wall disputes. On reflection it was absolutely the right way to approach the surreal situation I found myself in. I wasn't exactly sitting in a corner rocking back and forth with my head in my hands, but the portal to an all-consuming black hole of depression lurked very close. Not since my ordeals at school had I felt so helpless. From being someone who would happily run through the proverbial barn door, I was now incapable of setting my mind to do anything meaningful. It seemed as though almost every waking moment would be interrupted by the spectre of disability and all the repercussions that this might bring for me, Marion and our young family. The prospect of life with Multiple Sclerosis was bad enough, but the worry of not knowing what would happen to me if the additional diagnosis of a syrinx were to be confirmed ate away at me.

Whilst my mother, Dave and Marianne knew that I had been unwell, it took me a couple of weeks to summon up the emotional strength to tell them about the MS, without letting on that there was another potentially huge problem festering in the background. In particular, there seemed little sense in putting my mother through the mangle as she had been close to the edge ever since my father's passing. To my surprise, she took the news better than expected, but after a while I realised that she was confusing MS with ME which at that time was being unfairly labelled as 'yuppie flu'. I did not have the heart to correct her. It may have been a blessing as she was inadvertently being shielded from the seriousness of my diagnosis.

Three weeks after staring down the barrel, I was back in the line of fire waiting for Dr King's attractive nurse to beckon me to his consulting room. This time, however, it was different. I was totally preoccupied with what the rescan might reveal. I thought that there was no way I would be caught off guard as had happened before, but when the call came, the sensation in the pit of my stomach almost drained every bit of energy in me. I slowly rose and followed the nurse. By the time I had slumped into the chair my heart was pounding. Dr King was nowhere to be seen, which merely served to prolong my anxiety. All of a sudden he emerged from an interconnecting side door and moved toward me, offering a warm handshake. Was that a good or bad sign?

"Good morning, John. How are you feeling today?"

"Not great, if I'm honest, but that might have something to do with why I'm here!"

"I understand," Dr King attempted to settle me.

As seemed to be his manner, there were then a couple of minutes silence as he shuffled through the papers in my file, occasionally punctuated with a drawn out 'Hmm'. The difference this time was that he avoided eye contact and instead picked up his telephone. My heart rate quickened again.

"Joan, why aren't Mr Hambly's latest MRI scan results in the file?" he barked with an accusatory tone that surprised me.

There was then a brief interlude as Joan, no doubt flapping frantically in her office next door, rifled through Dr King's in-tray. Presumably, having got the response he was looking for, he offered a curt 'thank you' and hung up. Within seconds a put-upon Joan scuttled into the room and placed a new document on his desk before doing a neat pirouette and making a swift exit.

Upon examining the scan results, the 'Hmming' started again. Aware that beads of sweat had broken through to my brow, I surreptitiously stroked a finger across my forehead, making out that I was tidying up my fringe. As if having a sixth sense of someone else's inner turmoil, in that same moment Dr King looked up and smiled.

"You rugby boys take some beating. . . literally!" guffawed my learned consultant.

"Sorry? I'm not with you, Doctor."

"How long have you been experiencing neck problems?"

"Well, I don't think I have really. Maybe a bit of stiffness after a game. Perhaps some tingling down my arms for the last few years."

"And those symptoms didn't prompt you to get it looked at?"

"No, there was always just another game to get ready for."

"I rest my case. You lot must be slightly unhinged. What I was worried could be a syrinx turns out to be a bulging disc."

I closed my eyes, looked to the ceiling and let out a huge sigh of relief.

I had never considered myself capable of being psychosomatic, but with the massive release of pressure, I felt like a man walking away from the gallows and, with that, within two weeks my MS symptoms virtually abated. The weakness to my left side, the blurred vision and the fatigue were all gone. The only thing that remained was an altered sensation to the skin on my left leg and the same to a band of skin to my midriff. In fairly typical fashion I let the handbrake off and returned to work, looking to fire on all cylinders again. Shortly afterwards Grace arrived safely and brightened our outlook still further. For the first time in months, like so many of our friends, Marion and I felt as though we were able to plan for the future.

Dr King's parting words had been to respect the illness and reintroduce myself gradually to work, training and social environments. True to form, I did not. Treating the MS as an adversary I could demoralise and defeat, I threw my full weight into everything I did. It seemed to work as I was gradually able to re-establish my workload and take some of the burden from Marc. I did, however, decide to drop running around the local bridleways and footpaths, instead opting to join the gym at Charterhouse School which opened at 6:30am, thereby enabling me to train before shooting up the A3 to the office in Wimbledon. The gym was a fantastic air-conditioned facility with stunning views across the Surrey Hills and a great environment to release endorphins and re-inflate my spirit. Week by week, I managed to build up my cardio-vascular fitness and strength work which, for once, was not being constantly interrupted by rugby injuries. I found that the MS sensory symptoms almost acted as a gauge for the intensity of my training; self-restraint would leave them as they were, over exuberance would induce heightened levels of tingling and discomfort. By midsummer 1999, I reckoned that I was in my best physical shape for years and with that came mental strength and confidence. Work and home life were back on a steady footing, so our fears from earlier in the year that the MS would bring about wholesale changes to our livelihood had been allayed. Unfortunately, we had not factored in the indiscriminate nature of the disease.

With me feeling so well, Marion and I decided to take the family off to the fatherland in late July as soon as the schools had finished. For once we were spared the daily grind of traipsing around fun parks, zoos and ball pits with thousands of grockles, as the Cornish weather was glorious. Every day we were able to get to the beach where the children had the most wonderful time. Between Grace's clucking, Marion got to put her feet up and recharge her batteries whilst I relived my childhood, mucking around in the sea with the kids.

I could not have felt more refreshed and forward thinking on returning to the Big Smoke in early August. The warm spell continued to build, so the heat and humidity in SW19 was a lot more unpleasant than the Cornish Riviera with its cooling sea breezes. Our offices were on the top floor, smack bang underneath an asphalt flat roof and, in the case of my suite, I just had a perspex dome to indicate whether it was night or day. As a result, when the temperature outside hit 75°, it felt more like 90°+ inside. Both Marc and I tended to carry out our site inspections and meetings in the morning and then return to the office in the mid-afternoon, by which time the offices would be absolutely stifling.

I am not quite sure why the tradition of bounding up the stairs (as opposed to stepping one at a time) arose other than to give extravagant notice that you had safely made it back to HQ after tackling the demands of London's streets and the contracting fraternity, but it was mildly amusing for the staff and also served to give them warning to pack in whatever they shouldn't have been doing! On this occasion, as I lay in a heap on the reception floor at the base of the stairs, I merely thought that I had misjudged a tread through temporary sun blindness having just come in from the brightness outside. As it happened no one was in upstairs, so I felt a total idiot as it was left to Dawn, our trusty receptionist, and Margaret, the office manager, to flap around me like mother hens. I eventually convinced them that I was fine and made my way up to the first floor furnace. After unloading my files, I sat for a couple of minutes with my eyes closed before addressing the large pile of correspondence that Marc must have placed there earlier that day. It was only when I picked up the top letter that I realised my blurred vision had returned.

'Oh, bollocks,' I said to myself in exasperation, *'not YOU again!'*

In fact, if I had been a little more vigilant instead of rushing around, I would have picked up on the signs that there was something untoward. Although I had stumbled twice between site visits, I had simply cursed Kensington & Chelsea's appalling footpaths and given it no further thought. In addition, there was the burning sensation down my left side which had worsened as the day progressed, but I had just attributed that to the heat.

Never one to throw in the towel, for the next hour I did what work I could as the sweat trickled down my chest. My dictation was a little more laboured than normal, but it was only on getting up to grab a file from Marc's office that I realised things were going downhill very quickly. My left foot simply refused to move forward

198

without stubbing into the carpet. I knew this demoralising feeling all too well. There could be no doubt, a new bully had arrived on the scene!

Resigned to the punishment I might be about to receive, I left Marc a note saying that the heat in my office was unbearable and that I would achieve more at home, then hobbled my way out through reception, telling Dawn that I had twisted my knee during the staircase episode. Even with air-conditioning in the car, by the time I arrived home I was still struggling, so made no attempt to try and disguise the telltale signs from Marion.

"I might just have a bug but I'm going to call Dr King's office now and see if I can get an appointment with him in the next day or two," I said, giving her and little Grace a big hug, whilst Ellie and Meg played in the Wendy house.

Forty-eight hours later, thanks once again to the company health insurance cover, I was back at the Guildford Nuffield as an in-patient, plumbed into an IV drip of methylprednisolone. The surroundings, with all the trimmings and one-to-one attention, should have been comforting enough but the gravity of my predicament began to hit home as, courtesy of the high dose steroids, I lay wide awake each night. How could I be this fit and look so healthy but have to submit to a debilitating illness that by all accounts could rear its ugly face whenever and wherever in your body it chose to? Over the previous five months I had resisted the temptation to research what MS might bring to our door, and my consultant had only given me a broad brush overview of the disease without setting out the various possible scenarios that could evolve over the years. I found the vagueness bemusing as in my profession we were involved in assessing and resolving problems through practical measures. The term 'disease of the central nervous system' kept reverberating around my head. Here we were in an age when surgeons could give you a triple heart bypass, replace joints, transplant organs and yet, in simplistic terms, when it came to the body's electrical installation it could not be rewired.

As depressing as those long nights were, at least I sorted out in my head that for the sake of my young family, I would need to give some respect to the opponent I was about to pack down against.

Thankfully the course of steroids did the trick and I was back home in four days, determined that I would not make the same mistakes in terms of over extending myself again. I was certainly not the hyperactive type, but my tendency to want to please others maybe meant that I would often do more than could reasonably have been expected. The old adage of 'the customer is always right' was really not applicable to the construction industry and yet Marc and I would try and go the extra mile in order to satisfy the clients in the best way we could. Of course, there was just no pleasing some, particularly the private clients on residential refurbishment schemes, and that's where the stress levels went skyward. Marc was very resilient and outwardly appeared unfazed by these demands, whereas I was more liable to get het up. I therefore decided that I would have to do less of this sort of work and concentrate more on the public sector projects and party wall work in the hope that this would help me better manage my illness. Thankfully, Marc agreed and we set about reallocating the schemes.

No sooner had we set out on this path, than I received a call from a development manager who used to work for the Housing Association where I had pulled my Mars bar stunt 15 years earlier. I had clearly made a good impression as we had become great friends and even though he had since moved on and gone up the social housing ladder, he had been very loyal in offering us instructions whenever he could. The enquiry, albeit tentative, was to find out if we would be prepared to take on a large programme of house surveys and repair schemes along the South Coast. Whilst it was some way away from our usual area of work, I lived halfway between the office and the potential sites, so Marc and I agreed that I should take on the first phase with our graduate surveyor and two consultants sharing the workload. Given my recent relapse, it was something of a gamble, but over the next 12 months it proved to be a good decision as the project mushroomed and, perhaps as important, got me away from the London rat race for a couple of days a week. It also served to give me back a bit of confidence and an appetite for work. I was enjoying life again.

I'm not quite sure why people maintain that all good things have to come to an end, but for me it lasted about another 18 months before, without any semblance of notice, bully boy flattened me again. As if to make a statement of who was in charge, this attack was more acute; mobility problems in both legs and severe fatigue linking up with the usual sensory issues. However, the difference this time was that I didn't buckle and go into myself. Implausible, I know, but I could feel the emergence of a steely determination to defy this monster. Could it have been a reflection of my childhood defiance during Stephen's last failed assault?

Chapter 27

Faith
2002-3

LIFE challenges us in many different ways, and so often it would be easy to turn and walk the other way. Instinct, desire and stamina can be major factors in determining whether you are able to front up, but for me I found that it was faith and hope that held me together at such a difficult point in my life. I had had enough knock-backs to totally extinguish my faith and with that the hope might well have gone. I had been a lapsed Christian for many years, particularly during my headless drinking spells in the 80s, but the birth of Ellie in June 1994 and my father dying less than four months later, served to rekindle my faith. After MS appeared on the scene, almost inevitably there were dark periods. It was almost impossible not to ask myself, 'Why me?' 'What have I done to deserve this?' However, those long sleepless nights during treatment allowed me to sort out my head and I found myself thinking, 'Well, why not me?' 'Is there a reason I've been given this disease?'

In early 2002, I had been told by our healthcare insurers that the policy would no longer cover my treatments and hospital stays as Multiple Sclerosis was classed as a chronic illness. A simple case of three strikes (in this case, consultations) and you're out! As Dr King had been disillusioned with the NHS many years before and I could not afford to fund his private fees, we parted ways and I went back into the NHS system. It was a rude awakening, as I discovered that it was difficult to get an appointment with a neurologist in our area, nor was there a dedicated MS Nurse or a facility for regular physiotherapy. To say that I felt cast adrift without a paddle would be a massive understatement.

Undeterred, deviating from my usual modus operandi, I resorted to the Internet to see if there were any local support groups for MS sufferers offering hands-on assistance. The MS Society had branches in Guildford and nearby Woking but appeared to be more involved in disseminating information and fundraising for their head office. There was no harm in that, but what I really wanted was regular physiotherapy and exercises geared specifically towards maintaining mobility and suppleness. It took a while, but eventually I stumbled across a small charity, the MS Therapy Group (Guildford), who were operating out of a local village hall a couple of mornings a week, plus they held social events and talks on a Wednesday evening. It looked worth exploring, but I could not know what riches lay ahead.

Dear old Bert's saying that 'little fish taste sweet' was something that had consistently resonated with me, whether it be acting for a sweet old lady who needed help with a subsidence claim, taking the Old A's up the leagues or just raising a few quid for a children's charity. On walking into Shalford Village Hall I could be in no doubt that this was a little outfit, with a membership of only about thirty-five and the Thursday exercise classes numbering no more than eight MS-ers. Nevertheless, it was wonderfully uplifting to be amongst others who were in the same boat and to be able to compare notes and share concerns. The two part-time physios were extremely positive and vibrant despite the limitations of the hired facilities, and with the charity well shepherded by a close solicitous committee, the members were in good hands.

I really benefitted from such a positive ambience, but it was not very long before I started thinking about how much better it could be if the group had more control over their working environment. The Village Hall certainly had its drawbacks, being limited in terms of location, availability, storage facilities and basic creature comforts, to name just a few. Even though I was busy enough at work, something kept eating away at me. As the new kid on the block, dare I put forward an ambitious proposal to try and secure more appropriate premises? I was aware that the charity had had to move around quite a lot in previous years because the accommodation either was ultimately found to be unsuitable or the landlords hiked the rent up beyond what could be afforded. In my mind, there was little doubt that the group would thrive if we could just find more suitable premises, but was I wrong to think of suggesting something that could be unsettling and divisive? As a newbie I concluded that it probably was not the appropriate time for me to pipe up.

No sooner had I parked the notion to the back of my mind, putting it down to wishful thinking, than it would start popping up in the middle of a dream, in a quiet moment at work, at home watching the TV, relaxing on the beach; basically, anywhere, anytime that my guard was down. Like an irritating advert on the box nagging you to sign up to an irresistible offer, no matter how hard I tried, I was not being allowed to drop the idea. Very early one Saturday morning, after several weeks of being 'prodded', I gave in.

'OK Father, I get the message. I'll give it my best shot.'

That morning as I ran my thoughts past Marion, I half expected her to shoot them down in flames. Given everything we had been through over the last two years, she would have been fully justified in saying enough is enough. We had three young children and were gradually transforming the house when funds permitted, so even though I was having a good spell as far as my health was concerned, we could not afford to jeopardise everything with me overstretching myself.

"If you reckon you're up to it, I think you should try. I can see how frustrated you are with the way things are for MS sufferers within the NHS around here. Yes, definitely, I'll support you and I bet if you get it off the ground, loads of our friends will help too."

I should never have doubted Marion. She had been incredibly strong and resourceful throughout all the trials and tribulations that MS had brought to our door, whilst still managing to retain her wacky sense of humour. With her behind me, I knew I stood a chance of getting the project on its feet.

However, first things first, I needed to sound out the people that mattered – the physios and the committee. I had spoken to Julie Passmore who ran our Thursday classes about my idea and she had seemed very supportive but suggested that I meet with Helen Brodbin, the senior physio, who had been through thick and thin with the charity over many years. Helen was more apprehensive and concerned that this could be yet another false dawn. I fully understood her hesitancy but, fortunately through my work, I had chaired many residents' meetings where large refurbishment projects were planned and managed to allay their fears through careful planning and presentations to show the potential long term benefits. We agreed that there would be no harm in me preparing a feasibility study that I could put to the committee and members at a Wednesday evening meeting.

A month afterwards, I was pleasantly surprised to find the full committee and many members sitting in front of me at the village hall. I had prepared well, but was conscious that I could not afford to bamboozle everyone with property jargon and come across as patronising. On the other hand, I needed to enthuse as many people as possible and get across what a difference a dedicated facility could mean for the charity. In essence, I set out what I perceived to be viable options for premises which would enable us to expand in terms of the number of people treated each week, introduce one-to-one physiotherapy as well as group classes and accommodate more specialised equipment. Of course, the nub of the presentation was always going to be the likely funds that the charity would need to raise, whether it be for the purchase of land and the construction of a new building, the refurbishment of existing premises or just finding a more suitable property to let. At this point there was a perceptible collective intake of breath, although everyone stayed focused on me, without the meeting breaking down into murmuring cliques, so I swiftly moved onto 'any questions'. There were mainly low key concerns aired and even a few compliments thrown my way before Vic Worrall, the Chairman, got to his feet to wrap up the meeting. Simultaneously, with the timing of a late bidder foiling the auctioneer's hammer, a bearded bespectacled gentleman stood up at the rear of the room.

"I've never heard so much rubbish! You'll end up destroying this charity. How on earth do you expect us to raise half a million pounds?" he blasted, visibly shaking with rage.

No one turned around or seemed particularly surprised by the outburst. With the room having been so quiet and my audience apparently amenable to the thought of finding a better HQ, it was a nasty wake-up call. Fortunately, similar ambushes were quite frequent at residents' meetings so I was able to recompose myself quickly.

"I'm sorry you feel that way, but if the charity chooses to go down one of these routes, I am confident we can raise the necessary funds once we get the word out there." I announced with conviction which belied the fact that the sum total of my fundraising experience amounted to a few grand from the London Marathon, some fun runs and a couple of rugby club race nights!

"Do you really think that a small group of disabled people and their families should be put through all this when we're settled and doing very nicely here? You must be absolutely mad!" and with that he sat back down whilst continuing to chunter away.

With such unrest in the air, Vic promptly closed the meeting and most folk started to make their way out. Helen, on the other hand, sidled over as I tidied away my notes.

"Well done John, that was very good."

"Clearly it wasn't to everyone's liking though, Helen. Who was that chap?"

"That was our John – John Steeds. Don't worry about his dig at the end. Both he and Sue have been very involved with the group for many years and they're rightly proud of what we stand for. I'll have a chat with him in the next day or so. Give him time to get his head around what you've said."

Despite Helen's brief pep talk, I went home a little deflated and had a restless night's sleep wondering whether I had bitten off more than I could chew.

A number of weeks went by with me attending the Thursday physio sessions where Julie and the members would repeatedly urge me to push forward with the ideas I had presented. However, I was still worried that there might be other dissenting voices within the group and that I would just end up wasting my time and energy. After all, I was not even on the committee, so my chances of persuading trustees who were dead against the proposed changes were pretty slim.

I continued to ruminate over the matter until a chance conversation with Michael Marcel, my work practice's bookkeeper, replenished my desire to give it a go. Michael, who was a Lay Christian, usually popped in once a fortnight to keep our books in order and also try and badger me into attending his church in South London. In reality that was never going to happen, but he was a nice guy and we would quite often have brief chats about faith. On this particular day, Michael obviously sensed that something was eating away at me.

"Tell me to go away if you don't want to talk, but I've noticed that you've been very quiet in the last few weeks. Do you want to get it off your chest?"

"Blimey, your radar is working well today, Michael," I said, somewhat startled as I looked up from my drawing board.

"I'd like to think that I can pick up the vibes when someone is uneasy," he offered with a warm inviting smile.

I knew Michael well enough to offload without fear of it going beyond the four walls.

"Well, I think the main man upstairs has asked me to create a dedicated MS treatment centre, but at the first turn I've spun off the track. To be absolutely honest, I'm just not sure that I've got what it takes to pull it off."

"John, it's wonderful that you've understood the Lord is calling you. Keep strong in your faith and remember that he will walk with you all the way."

"I know you're right Michael, but I've been lapsed for so long and what I am being asked to do is quite daunting."

"Ask, and it shall be given you; seek, and ye shall find; knock, and it shall be opened unto you. Matthew 7:7-8. That's all I need to say to you my friend," Michael reassured me.

The following day when I arrived back from a meeting there was a book on my desk with a Post-it note from Michael which simply said: 'John, read this and be inspired.' The title was *George Muller of Bristol: His Life of Prayer & Faith*. Over the course of the next few days I learnt about this incredible man who, during the 1800s, established six orphanages which cared for over 10,000 destitute children as well as 117 schools where 120,000 children were educated. They were astonishing facts but, for me, the stand out thing was that Muller never made requests for financial support nor did he ever go into debt. In short, this remarkable Evangelist and Missionary, despite being in ill-health himself, put everything down to his faith in God and the power of Prayer. However, one of Muller's many quotes particularly grabbed me: "Be assured, if you walk with Him and look to Him, and expect help from Him, He will never fail you."

Michael was right. I had been inspired. I started praying as I drove up and down the A3, as I sat in the car between meetings, as I lay in bed at night, basically anywhere I could grab a quiet moment. Slowly but surely the clarity of thought and direction materialised. I knew that I needed to become a committee member in order to have a meaningful presence within the charity. Given Michael's quote from the book of Matthew and all the praying, I should not have been surprised when Helen called me to say that Vic was standing down and asked if I was prepared to put myself up for the position of Chairman.

"Wow, yes, errrr. . . absolutely, of course I will, Helen," I managed to splutter out.

"You sound unsure, John-boy," Helen enquired.

"No, sorry, you just caught me on the hop, Helen."

The truth was that I was a bit stunned, having pondered the same scenario just a few days before whilst sitting on the seafront at Worthing. There clearly was a lot to be said for this business of praying, as in October 2002 I was voted in as Chairman, unopposed. I was chuffed and terrified in equal measure. Ever since my grammar school days I'd had a fear of public speaking, but in my heart of hearts I knew that I would have to put myself out there in order to get the charity better known and, providing the committee agreed to it, raise awareness of the project for our new centre. Chairing meetings at work, bawling out instructions during rugby training and match day warm ups, even making the captain's annual speech at Twickenham stadium, all paled into insignificance when I considered the demands of addressing a room full of comparative strangers as the head of a charity. Fortunately, my first few engagements involved talking to Inner Wheel Clubs, one of which was presided over by Marion's Auntie Diana! The ladies were so welcoming and warm, I could not fail to relax and get across the message that we were a little charity with big plans. A week later a cheque arrived and I had got the fundraising bug.

In all the excitement, there was just one thing I had almost forgotten – my own illness and the repercussions of pushing too hard! Now able to recognise the signs of an MS dip, I managed to blag an appointment with a neurologist who agreed to stick me on another course of IV steroids early in 2003. I felt decidedly peeved as I lay in hospital plumbed in to a drip when I should have been at work, as well as drumming up more support for the charity in my spare time.

"How do, Hambers?" came as a very welcome distraction.

Pete Robinson, aka 'Stumble', stuck his head around the door. He was just the tonic I needed. A good friend and formidable front row forward, Pete was a brilliant raconteur and real team man. Between old tour stories and recent high jinks at the rugby club, we got around to talking about the plans I had for developing a therapy centre.

"Well, you've got the right skill set to construct it and you can count on me and the lads to be right with you when it comes to raising a few quid."

"Do you really think so, Pete?"

"I don't think so. I'd go as far as saying that I know so."

Whilst I was flattered and somewhat caught out by Pete's positive vibe, almost at once, my mind started to conjure all manner of fundraising initiatives; but even the eternal optimist in me could not have imagined the extraordinary sequence of events that were to unfold.

Chapter 28

Samson Rising
Summer 2003

O N recovering from my last relapse, I set about establishing a
Steering Group within the charity, which would be made up
of past and present trustees and some of the younger members who
I felt could bring some much needed energy and vision to the
discussions. The purpose of the group would be to settle upon the
type of therapy centre we would strive to create, as well as mapping
out our fundraising strategy and agreeing upon the all important
name for the project.

Through my profession and, to a lesser degree, with the rugby
club committee, I had experienced the corrosive effect of excluding
those with strong opinions. Even though at times they could
potentially upset the equilibrium, no matter how hard it would be to
reconcile everyone's desires, I felt it important to include anyone
prepared to contribute, particularly those with business acumen.
Despite his comments some months earlier, I was pleased that John
and Sue Steeds and their great friends, Chris and Annie Stevinson,
agreed to form part of the discussions. As a result the embryonic
Steering Group comprised about fifteen people, some of whom
were new to the cut and thrust of committee work.

We were seldom able to secure the village hall for our meetings,
so we ended up convening in pubs around the Godalming area. By
no stretch of the imagination was this ideal, but at least it got us up

and running. Whilst I would try and pre-book a room it was not always possible, so it was inevitable that wherever we gathered patrons would occasionally wander in with a pint, sit in a corner and light up a fag!

I had rather hoped that my attempt at a rousing Churchillian address at Shalford and the formation of the Steering Group would dispel any lingering doubts that the charity could pull off such an audacious plan for the greater good of our MS community. However, it soon transpired that the preliminary fundraising targets I was about to table simply dwarfed what the charity had raised year on year since its formation. Discussing our attendance at local events, producing Christmas cards and merchandise, talking to our communities, etc., were all relevant in elevating our profile, but from the standpoint of raising money we would be merely skimming the surface. Not only did I spot a few sideways glances and raised eyebrows at the meetings, but I sensed unease in the ranks from the moment that the full extent of the task ahead was laid out. Just as if I was eyeballing a gargantuan prop forward, I could not let the team detect any doubts that I may have had. I desperately needed to instil belief.

My prayers were answered in no uncertain terms within the space of a week. Firstly, one of Marc's clients, Bruce Kenyon, who we had worked with in the West End in the 1980s, called me completely out of the blue to say he had a friend whose husband had established the Previte Foundation and that they might just be interested in supporting our initiative. Apparently they held an annual charity race night at Wandsworth Civic Suite for about 200 people. It was an opportunity I just had to follow up, so I arranged to meet Antonia Previte a week later.

A couple of days after this Stumble called me.

"How do, Hambers?"

"I'm good thanks, Pete. Don't tell me you're moving again and want another survey!"

"Ha ha, nice one, but I'm not calling you about work this time. Remember our chat when I came to see you in hospital?"

"Yeah, of course I do. How could I not? My ribs have only just recovered from your laughter therapy!"

"Well there might be plenty more of that. Me and the guys down the club have been chatting about your little project and we'd like to put together a Charity Dinner around the time of the Rugby World Cup. What do you reckon?"

"Wow, that's great Pete. Sounds messy though."

"Yeah, that's true. We're trying to find a venue that knows and trusts the club!"

"I can't tell you what this'll do for the mindset of the charity's trustees. We need events like this to give them the confidence that we can pull it off."

"Oh, there's just one other thing, Hambers. What's the Centre going to be called, as we'll need that for the promo stuff?"

"Umm, not sure yet Pete, as the Steering Group are still chewing it over. I'll get back to you on that one shortly."

In truth we were struggling to come up with anything that really grabbed us.

When I met Antonia for a coffee in Wimbledon the following week, it was very cordial but much more businesslike. Her husband, Andrew, the driving force behind the Foundation, whilst having progressive MS, still worked full time, so it was fairly clear that she was on a fact-finding mission as well as sussing me out. Throughout the meeting I referred to the MS Therapy Group (Guildford) and passionately tried to get across our plans for the new centre. However, the same question arose again, that being the name of the project. I said that we would be voting on it within a week so the next time we spoke I would be able to confirm what the centre was going to be called. I left the meeting feeling like I'd rather fudged the whole thing and that we were probably not going to be in the picture for the charity race night.

It just so happened that we had a Steering Group meeting the day after, so I was able to bring the good news of two major fundraisers in the offing, but made it perfectly clear that we needed to address the matter of the project name as a matter of urgency. We decided to meet again the following week and in the intervening period each of us would go away and come up with two or three ideas, and we would then vote on what we felt was the most appropriate one for our cause.

The day before the meeting I arrived home from the office very late and extremely tired, so I agreed with Marion that I would sleep upstairs to give me a good night's kip. Cerys, our latest bundle of joy, was in the middle of teething, so sleep was at a premium, particularly as I had an early meeting in Kent the following day. I remember lying down and trying to think of names for the project but, having been so busy, I had little time to put my mind to it before I felt myself drifting off. Oh well, I would just have to rack my brains the next day or hope that someone within the Steering Group would pluck a rabbit out of the hat.

The sun began to make its very early midsummer appearance as it glinted around the edges of the blinds to the roof lights. I was not awake but restless in anticipation of my alarm going off at 6am. I turned away from the bright light and buried my head under the quilt in an attempt to grab another half an hour.

"SAMSON!"

There it was, as clear as the new day. Not my subconscious mind but a soft voice in the room. I lay there with my eyes closed, waiting for more, wanting more, wandering if I'd been mistaken but I had not, most definitely not. Eventually I turned and looked across to the corner where I sensed the words came from. There was nothing different about the room, except an air that I had experienced something very special. Up until that moment, I had strong faith and plenty of hope but also many doubts about what I was undertaking. In one divinely delivered six-letter word, I could be in no doubt. Michael had been right all along. The gentle nudges had been my calling and now, as if to reinforce that, I had heard it in all its glory. I lay there in wonderment for several minutes.

As I drove up the A3 and over the Hog's Back, with the sun already strong and warm, my mind was doing proverbial cartwheels.

'SAMSON – what a fantastic name,' I said to myself. *'Powerful but vulnerable, he lost his strength just like many of us with MS. And yet, in adversity, he regained it.'*

I continued my journey around the M25, still tossing the name around my head. By the time I had reached Orpington I'd had another 'light bulb' moment. Well, to be honest, it didn't take much spotting. There, smack bang in the middle of the name was 'MS'! It had to be a graphic designer's dream.

When I arrived home that evening, I had everything worked out in terms of the name and how I would present it to the Steering Group. There was just time for a quick bite to eat and the opportunity to run it all past my No.1 critic.

"Marion, what do you reckon about the name 'Samson' for the new Centre, with the 'MS' bit in capital letters?" I sprung on her as we tucked into our baked spuds.

She looked across at me with, what I perceived to be, a worryingly quizzical look, trying to take in what I had said.

"Do you know, that's just brilliant. It's a really powerful name and with the 'MS' highlighted in some way, it could be very eye-catching."

"Phew, I'm glad you've said that. I thought you might shoot it down in flames!' I said, smiling like the cat that had got the cream.

"You ought to run that by Bruce. I bet he'll be able to work his magic on a logo for the charity."

Bruce Duckworth, Marion's cousin, was one of London's up and coming stars in the world of graphic design and product branding.

"Yeah, you might be right there but it's not a done deal. First, I need to get approval from the Steering Group. Hey, let's face it, someone might have come up with something better." I finished my last mouthful and went to grab my paperwork and jacket.

"Talking about coming up with names, where did Samson appear from?" enquired Marion, following me to the front door.

"The main man upstairs."

Grinning, I pecked her on the cheek and left.

As I pulled into the Kings Arms car park in Godalming, I bumped into Helen. We both knew it was a key meeting.

"Evening, John-boy. I hope you've had your thinking cap on. I've got nothing inspirational and I know that Fleur has drawn a blank."

"Oh dear, Helen. I couldn't think of a decent name either," I said. Which was, of course, mostly true!

Ten minutes later, with eleven members of the Steering Group (four of which were husband and wife) sat down in the snug, glasses charged and anticipation in the air, I kicked off the proceedings.

"OK folks, thank you very much for coming tonight. We've got a little bit of business to get through relating to some potential fundraising leads, but our main reason for being here this evening is to agree a name for the project. So, without further ado, I'd like to go around the table and if you have a suggestion please shout it out. Right, away we go."

I looked left to Helen and nodded.

"Nothing that I'm happy with. Sorry."

"The same, nothing."

"The Enigma Project."

"Nothing."

"The Nerve Centre."

"Nothing, sorry."

"The Guildford MS Centre."

"Nothing suitable, sorry."

Hmm, the group had hardly set the room alight and the collective feeling of disappointment was tangible. I'm not really sure whether the paltry offerings were down to a lack of confidence or apathy, but the situation seemed perfectly set up for me to play my hand with what I considered a royal flush.

"Mr Chairman, what have you got then?" Helen prompted me, reversing the roles.

Given that I had been chewing it over and over all day, there was no point in beating around the bush. I would deliver the whole package.

"OK, I propose 'The Samson Centre' with a strapline of 'Building strength from adversity'. Also, within the name, I see the 'ms' in capitals to emphasise that it will be an MS centre. And the last thing, where appropriate, the name be used as an acronym saying 'Strength Against Multiple Sclerosis & Optic Neuritis'."

There was complete silence for a few seconds until Helen spoke, dropping the formalities.

"You're full of surprises, John-boy. A quarter of an hour ago, you told me you hadn't thought of a name."

"One day I'll tell you why I said that, but I wasn't lying, Helen!"

215

It was totally amazing to see how one word, a name, could so effectively galvanise a small group, then friends, families, communities and, ultimately, garner support nationally and internationally. Clearly momentum would be important in getting the project up and running from a fundraising angle, but the rate at which enquiries about the cause arose was at times difficult to believe. It seemed like hardly a day went by without an approach from an individual or a philanthropic organisation offering to assist us or put on an event in our name. Even though our venture was small in comparison, I began to get a sense of what George Müller might have felt all those years before.

Throughout this spell I continued to be busy at work, but with my MS behaving itself I was able to throw myself into following up all the general charity correspondence and fundraising leads after supper each evening. The girls would still get read a book, although I have to admit that I may have skipped a few pages when only Grace and Cerys were involved! Settled into my office around 8:30pm, rarely would I get off the computer before midnight. John and I persisted with our spats via email whilst Helen played mediator.

As Marion had thought, her cousin Bruce came up trumps with the Samson logo and an introductory gatefolded leaflet. The logo, in particular, was very effective even though it was simple. As suggested, his team had picked out the 'MS' in a different colour but the clever bit was the inclusion of an *accent circonflexe* (an upturned 'V') above the two letters to give the appearance of a roof providing shelter. With a strong identity our cause was quickly becoming known, but what was not as clear was how we proposed to form the new Centre. Would it be the purchase of land and construction of a new building, the purchase and conversion of existing premises, or locating a suitable property to lease? Even though I had worked out costings for these various options, at that stage we had set out to raise money for a 'centre' which, in hindsight, without a definitive vision was at best fanciful.

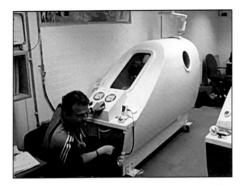

Me at the controls
of chamber 1 in
the old oxygen
room, 2010

Hoisting in the new oxygen
multichamber, 2018.

Oxygen multichamber
ready for action, 2019.

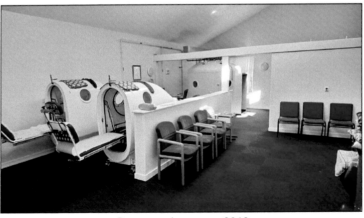

Oxygen suite set up, 2019.

Jim Fardell and myself with the Lord Lieutenant
of Surrey opening the new oxygen annex,
September 2019.

Ariel view of the completed Samson Centre, 2019.

Presenting Jackie with gifts marking her 10th anniversary with us in 2019

Receiving a large cheque from West Surrey Golf Club, January 2020.

Jackie and myself with Dave Kitching and Tony Iannaccone, at the entrance to the new oxygen suite.

Guy Williams and Jackie unveiling a plaque in the new oxygen treatment room. Jan. 2020.

Actonians reunion at the Samson Centre – presenting Stumble and Simon with a plaque commemorating the Club's support.

Actonians Reunion
September 2019

Andy, Rodders, Fletch, Symmo and Tugger.

Guy and Jim watching over proceedings.

I join Nev, Claire and the choir for a rendition of *'American Pie'*.

Kev M caught with a drink in the wrong hand by Meg and Rover.

Jonesey shares his strange dress sense!

Bob and the London Welsh Rugby Choir.

Me being interviewed by Ian Darke. (Carer Bobie pulls my strings!)

Duff and Glenn in great form.

The naughty boys take the Purple Nasty challenge.

Phil, Dave and Bruce enjoy the Actonians 'wall of fame'.

Mum and myself at Hayling
Island. Summer 2019.

Proud mum and dad at Megan's
graduation 2019.

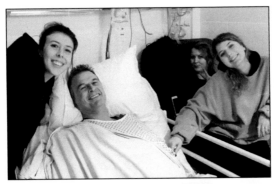

One of many
trips to hospital
in 2019.

The girls at
Meg's
fundraising
event, 'Only
Girls Allowed
Disco',
October 2019.

Sport Gives Back Awards, March 2020.

Simon Shaw and Andy Gomarsall present me with the Actonians Field of Dreams Award.

Me and my girls at the Royal Institute

Gommars joins the lads after the ceremony.

Mazzarati and myself, July 2019.

Cornish and proud of it,
May 2020.

Doorstep portrait during Covid-19, June 2020.
Ellie is social distancing because of her
invaluable work as a nurse.
(The yellow heart is in memory of Gaga.)

*   *   *   *

Remarkably our vision and the direction of the project became crystal clear in just one afternoon in late July 2003. At the time I was working from home quite a lot, so asked the Steering Group if they would be prepared to meet at St John's church centre at the bottom of my road during the day, as opposed to our usual evening sessions. The prime reason for calling the meeting was so that I could invite a leading regional fundraiser to address the group, cast her eye over our proposals and offer advice as to our best way forward.

A couple of days before we were due to meet Helen phoned to say that she had received a call from the Guildford Lions who were interested in finding out more about the Samson Centre project and could one of their committee members join us after the session with the fundraiser. I was aware that in the 1990s the MS Therapy Group (Guildford) had been in discussion with the Guildford Waterside Centre regarding the possibility of a new shared facility. The Lions had also been involved back then as they were regular users of the Centre. However, I gathered that there had been funding and planning issues which led to the proposals being shelved. As Helen sounded so positive I could see no harm in listening to what the Lions had to say.

To a sports commentator the meeting would have drawn the overused 'game of two halves' cliché, but in truth there could be no denying that it was an appropriate phrase on that afternoon. The first part with the fundraiser bordered on humiliating, as she told us in no uncertain terms that our plans were preposterous for such a small charity, let alone one with so many disabled trustees. However, we got to hear how great her own achievements were and what she could have charged for her time in gracing us with her presence. Having booked her in the first place, I felt particularly awkward, but in fairness there were no adverse comments directed at me from the attendees. Perhaps they were as affronted as I was by this lady's arrogance and negativity towards our dreams.

A little deflated, we decided to adjourn and regroup over sandwiches and beverages. Thirty minutes later, Dave Kitching from the Guildford Lions strode into our midst. The contrast in

217

attitudes between our two guests could not have been more strikingly different. Bristling with energy and positivity, Dave was a breath of fresh air at a time when the Steering Group may just have faltered in their commitment to the project. Essentially, the Guildford Waterside Centre had heard about our campaign and were interested in talking to us again about joining forces to construct a new building to accommodate the Wey Kayak Club, the Guildford branch of the British Sub Aqua Club and us. Dave's involvement was twofold, apart from his position within the Lions (who would also be users of the new centre), he was also Commodore of the kayak club. If we were interested, we would need to raise around £250,000 within the next 18 months. For me the most tantalising aspect of the approach was that this would be a fairly unique marriage of health, sport and community, with the three groups sharing the capital build costs as well as the annual running costs.

After Dave's pitch, he promptly departed leaving us to ponder the proposal on the proviso that we revert to him within the week. There could be little doubt that the vibe in the room had completely changed. Dare I suggest that we had just experienced another 'Mulleresque' moment? Instead, I reined myself back.

"Well, everybody, that was a pleasant surprise after our earlier dressing down! I wonder whether some of you may feel that you've been here before in terms of the Guildford Waterside Centre's proposal but, with the Group's agreement, I would like to look further into this and go up to meet their Chairman and look around the site."

As always Helen was positive, as were two or three other trustees, but the surprise package was John Steeds.

"To me it sounds like a much more realistic way forward for us. There's less risk in terms of the cost of maintaining the building, and even if we can't raise all the money for our share of the capital, I'd go as far as saying it would be worth considering a loan for any shortfall."

I was thrilled to hear John throwing his support behind the project. At the time, to have one of the 'old guard' saying that felt like a huge shot in the arm, not only for me but also I imagine for the committee too. Being determined to make a difference would be vital but being together would be crucial.

A week or so later I pulled up outside the Guildford Waterside Centre for an evening meeting with Jim Rossiter, the Chairman, together with Dave and a few of their members. The collection of dilapidated cabins and boat sheds were an eyesore, but fortunately my construction background enabled me to visualise the potential for the site which was right alongside a picturesque part of the River Wey. The opening minutes of our discussions were, at best, lukewarm as I sensed an air of déjà vu. Jim was undeniably passionate about developing their existing facilities but at the same time, perhaps because there had been aborted attempts before, he also came across as being quite guarded. It was only when the proposed drawings were placed across the table and we were able to talk openly about how the scheme could be moulded to work for each potential member group, that the enthusiasm and creative juices began to flow. Bolstered by my undeviating confidence that the MS Therapy Group would be able to raise their share of the build cost, we agreed to seek approval from our respective committees so that the project could be further developed. The prospect of bringing our dreams to fruition set my mind racing as I drove home, but once the adrenaline had stopped coursing through me, the stark reality of having to raise a quarter of a million pounds brought me back to my senses. The first of many sleepless nights was about to kick in.

Chapter 29

A[u]ction Heroes
September to December 2003

GIVEN all that we had been through together on and off the field,
I should never have had a moment's doubt that the rugby lads
would collectively put their arms under my shoulders and haul me
back on my feet. From the point I broke the news about my MS, I
had lost count of the kind offers of help and the goodwill messages,
so Pete's assertion that the club would not hesitate to fully embrace
the fundraising effort for the new therapy centre should not have
come as a surprise. Even so, on the 21st Sept 2003, as I sat down
having posted the opening address to 200 guests at the inaugural
Actonian's Samson Centre reunion dinner, I just could not have
imagined the warm rush of emotion and support that would hit me
during the standing ovation. It proved so strong, and instilled such
belief, that it would sustain me through the years to come.

As uplifting as that moment was, over the next 3 hours the
generosity and kindness of the lads simply blew me away. During
the preceding months, the club, led by Pete and Jimmy Bradley, the
2nd team's Welsh wizard at fly half, had compiled an amazing array
of auction items and ingenious ways of raising funds. On the night,
with the alcohol intake on the rise, the process became increasingly
bizarre and hilarious as everyone joined in the philanthropic frenzy.
The first sign of this came towards the end of the meal when Simon
Church, an excellent flanker who I had played with many times,

could be spotted walking around between the tables parading a large meat platter piled high with leftover food (savoury and sweet), fag ends, corks, cigars and all manner of detritus. Hot on the heels of this grotesque offering came Duff, champagne bucket underarm, urging diners to donate cash. But for what?

All was revealed five minutes later, as the mess was ceremoniously placed under the chin of Paul Neate who was poised with a large serving spoon and the table cloth tucked into his collar. Another 1st team regular and best mate of Simon, Paul was well known for his post match revelry and excesses but this bordered on insanity, particularly as he had already eaten a three course dinner! Urged on by a baying audience, manfully he demolished around half of the mound before making a rapid exit to the gents. Emerging after ten minutes to huge cheers, a perspiring Neaty looked decidedly worse for wear. Duff, with impeccable timing, took to the mic to triumphantly announce that £355 had been raised. The tone for the evening had been well and truly set (Neaty's efforts even appeared in the charity's end of year accounts, described simply as 'Silly Stunt'!).

Our guest speaker for the evening was Jeff Probyn, one of England's finest props during the 1980/90s. Wonderfully witty and wickedly cutting in his slating of various teammates throughout his playing career, Jeff merely added to the air of over-indulgence by consecutively downing three pints of lager in reaching the punchline of his final joke. The stage was now set for the main event, at least as far as the fundraising element was concerned; the charity auction.

In addition to booking Jeff, I had been tasked with finding an auctioneer. Whilst I had connections in the property sector, I did not really know an auctioneer who was willing to stand in front of a rugby crowd, so it was very fortunate that one of our past players, Wilf Grove-White, who was now at Hertford RFC, had mentioned to me about an old boy who did quite a few charity auctions at their club. By the time John Creasey (JC) and his gavel took to the rostrum, he had already sunk quite a few large whiskies so I had my reservations as to whether I had made a grave error. I need not have worried though, this man had clearly worked an audience before and from the outset had the room in the palm of his hand with a mix of rugby anecdotes and jokes. He could easily have passed for England's version of Sir Les Patterson!

As soon as the auction got underway I could see precisely why Wilf had suggested JC. No longer the rugby club entertainer, this guy knew the time to put on his 'game face'. With no real time constraints, this particular auctioneer's art of extracting the best possible bid for each lot was something special. Granted, all the guys knew why they were there and, come the hour, they were very well-oiled and susceptible to his well honed powers of persuasion, but his orchestration of the proceedings was a delight to behold. Three heavy raps of the gavel brought the room to a hush.

"Right, good men of the Old Actonians, it's time for the real business of the night. Lot 1, four tickets for a hospitality box at the opening game of the Rugby World Cup, all food and booze included. Who will start me at £500?"

Immediately three hands went up from chaps that I didn't recognise. I surmised that they were probably business contacts of one or two of the players.

"Thank you gentlemen, 500. . . 550. . . 600. . . 650. . . 700. . ." JC rattled up the pounds, tilting the gavel to and fro, until only one hand remained up, "750, sir? Yes? Yes, £750 I have. Any more, gents?"

I was chuffed to bits. What a great start.

"£800, for Hammers!" Rutz thrust up an arm.

"New bidder, thank you sir," JC nodded in Rutz's direction. "I'm looking for 850 now."

The previous bidder came back in and kept his hand up, clearly signifying that he intended to see out the bidding.

"Thank you sir. We have £850. Surely it's worth at least £250 a ticket?" JC glanced across to Rutz, eyebrows raised.

Now Rutz had an incredibly competitive streak on the pitch, but this was a different game and he was rocking and rolling around on his chair, egged on by his fellow Welshmen.

"Go on then. A grand for Hammers," Rutz slurred, punching the air.

Unflinching, the other bidder kept his hand up and nodded.

"Thank you sir, £1,100 we have."

"Who the fuck does he think he is?" muttered Rutz, glaring murderously across at his rival. "£1,250 for Hammers."

The hand disappeared.

"Any further bids?" JC enquired politely as he scanned his audience. "No? Thank you very much sir. The tickets are yours."

Rutz rose to a rousing round of applause and promptly fell over! The Welsh contingent were beside themselves.

"Wot have I won?" mumbled Rutz, clambering back up to table level with a huge smile.

"Four tickets. . . for Australia. . . v Argentina, Rutz. . . in Sydney. . . flights not included!" Jimmy spluttered, barely able to talk through the tears of laughter.

There was a brief pause as Rutz assimilated the cold hard facts.

"For Hammers!" he exclaimed before collapsing across his dessert.

As the auction moved along it was all too apparent that the guys were so wholeheartedly behind the cause that at times things bordered on madness. JC skilfully identified the most determined bidders and, interspersed with quick-fire quips, managed to extract results well in excess of the catalogue estimates. I say the word 'determined' only because at one point JC called a temporary halt to proceedings and came down from the rostrum for a word.

"Do you know that irritating little fella over there?" he muttered in a hushed voice.

"Yes, sure, that's Pagey, one of our New Zealand contingent. Why do you ask, John?"

"No real problem. He's as pissed as a fart, bids first for everything, then drops out. If it's alright with you, I'm going to have him!"

"Sounds fun. I'll leave it in your capable hands, John."

And with that, JC tottered on back to the rostrum and tapped his gavel.

"Sorry about that gents, just a bit of housekeeping. Right, we press on. Lot 12, we have a tandem skydive. Who will bid me £300?"

Amongst others, but as predicted, Pagey's hand shot up. Quick as a flash, JC's apparatus came down with a rare old clatter.

"Sold for £300 to the Kiwi!" JC announced, pointing unerringly at poor dumbstruck Pagey.

The room promptly erupted.

As the official auction drew to a close after 18 very lucrative lots, JC took a well-deserved round of applause and gave way to Duff who arrived on the stage with a carrier bag and his usual devilish grin. Naturally very funny and a gifted mimic, Dave was the perfect guy to round off the evening by telling a few jokes, tour stories and get the singing underway. The contents of the bag were intriguing though.

"Thank you very much for your generosity chaps. It's a great cause we're supporting tonight. Good on ya Hammers. As you can see, we're all with you mate."

That was Duff with his Met Police brain in gear.

"Roit, me anzums, 'ere's a couple more bits of bonus bootie, for 'ee," he announced with the bag held aloft, engaging his Cornish smuggler guise.

"Wot, oi got 'ere iz a 150 yer ol' bottle of Cote du Pizzpot. . . aaaaaarrrrrrr! Tis verrrry, verrrry rare, oi hav 'ee knowz."

It certainly looked old, being covered in dust, cobwebs, candle wax and having general discolouration to the labels. Duff's chief partner in crime, Tugger, unable to control his laughter, was already hunched over with his shoulders heaving up and down. A tell-tale sign that he had been well and truly embroiled in some sort of skulduggery.

"Comez on, who'll gimme a hundred guineas to get uzz goin' 'en? Aaaaarrrrrrr!"

Amazingly, four hands went up. Quick as a flash, Duff dropped the Cornish drawl and, with the precision of a crack gunfighter, indiscriminately picked off all of them, holding the pose on the fourth victim.

"100, 150, 200, 250! £250, thank you very much."

As Tugger was unable to fully re-establish control of his diaphragm in the immediate aftermath of the sting, it took some moments for him to reveal that the rarely seen Cote Du Pizzpot, turned out to be a cheap bottle of red wine bought from Sainsbury's which they'd doctored in Duff's old man's shed that very morning!

Meanwhile, up on the stage, Duff seamlessly rolled on, performing some form of hybrid Pacific Island war dance. As many of us had witnessed his semi-naked version of the haka far too often at the club, it was something of a relief to see him remain fully clad.

"Friends, sadly, this is the last lot of the night, but what a special one it is. On Thursday I had the great honour and privilege to spend some time with the Fijian Rugby squad just before they departed for Australia. And what lovely chaps they were too, signing this official Rugby World Cup ball for Samson. Here's your chance, there's not another one like it." He announced, holding up the lot, still in the carrier bag, "Who will start me at £100?"

After his antics of a few minutes earlier, the bidding was understandably hesitant. In fact, just one hand went up, that of Dave Poole, a former 1st team hooker and now ex-pat; maybe out of curiosity, possibly out of sympathy (for Duff!) but most probably out of generosity.

Never one to be daunted by a crisis, Duff slapped his ample chest; signifying that he, as the auctioneer, was bidding against the room.

"I've got a bid on the book of £150. Can I see £200, sir?" he enquired with a mischievous glint in his eye.

"Go on then. I'm game," Pooler shouted back, only for Duff to slap his chest again, much to everyone's amusement.

"I've got a commission bid of £250 here. Looking for £300, sir?" Duff's brazen assurance was clearly very persuasive.

"Yeah, OK Duff, I'll have a bit of that," Pooler submitted.

"I'm out. No more bids? It's yours for £300! Please give a big hand for Mr Poole," our apprentice auctioneer announced with aplomb whilst simultaneously revealing a large water melon covered with indecipherable 'signatures' scrawled in black marker pen. Mssrs Duff and Tugger clearly had no great regard for the Trade Descriptions Act 1968!

A rousing rendition of the club's adopted anthem, 'Sloop John B', rounded off the evening and sent shivers down the spine.

*　　*　　*　　*

One of the things I used to love about rugby tours, even with the obligatory thumping hangover, were the breakfasts. Tales of the previous night's high jinks would be told and retold as each participant emerged, head bowed, bleary-eyed, smirking, shuffling into the dining area. The volume of the cheering and laughter generally indicating the level of puerile behaviour or depravity involved. As I hadn't toured with the club for quite a few years, the 'morning after the night before' feeling following the charity dinner was a welcome reminder of the unique camaraderie within the oval ball brotherhood. Breakfast extended to brunch; brunch almost extended to lunch. Some of the guys just seemed reluctant to let the reunion end there that day. There was already talk of organising a charity rugby match as well as another dinner. Albeit alcohol induced, several were keen to get themselves fit (for some, to use the word 'again' in this sentence would be wholly inaccurate!) and enter sponsored events. Altruism was alive and kicking in Acton and any lingering doubts I may have had about being able to get Samson off the ground were dispelled during the course of that 24 hour period.

Five weeks later, buoyed by the confidence gained from the rugby dinner, I managed to suppress my inner demons and speak at the Wandsworth Civic Suite in front of 250 city traders and their partners. The Previte Foundation Race Night was an extraordinary affair. If I had thought that the rugby boys were well versed in the art of brinkmanship when it came to an auction, perhaps not unexpectedly, the city boys were in a different league. Given that the auction involved bidding for fictitious horses with highly dubious names, you could easily be forgiven for thinking that the lots would be knocked down for £50 or so. Not a bit of it. The first one sold for £300 and that would prove to be, by some distance, the cheapest of the night. Coupled with the frenzied 'betting' market and a raffle with tickets priced at £10, it soon became clear that the Foundation would be having a lucrative evening.

As Samson appeared to be on the rise, in early December 2003 the charity pulled together and put on our first Christmas Fayre, so it seemed like an opportune moment to offer some seasonal cheer. Pete and Jimmy had confirmed the total proceeds from the dinner earlier in the week and then, on the morning of the fayre, I received a cheque from the Previte Foundation. As the fayre drew to a close, standing on a chair at the front of the hall, I thanked everyone involved and asked for a round of applause for Helen who had masterminded the whole thing. And then added. . .

"Oh, yes, I almost forgot. I've got a couple of presents for our Samson Christmas stocking. The rugby club have this week confirmed that the charity dinner made almost £25,000 for us and. . ." pausing for effect, ". . .this morning a cheque for £45,000 arrived from the Previte Foundation."

There was a slight delay whilst everyone looked at each other and then back at me.

"Yes, folks, that's a total of £70,000 plus the proceeds from today's wonderful team effort. I think it is now safe to say that we appear to be on our way."

As Helen recounted some years later, that was the day when belief in the Samson Centre dream flooded in.

Chapter 30

Shoulder to Shoulder
2003-6

ONCE word about the Samson Centre project got out into the wider community, with the help of families and friends, the fundraising campaign rapidly gained momentum. For me, and many others, raising money became an adrenaline rush. Just like fitness training, the feel good factor rose sharply after exerting ourselves on a successful fundraiser. The donations and offers of assistance from organisations and individuals came so thick and fast, and with such diversity, that it felt like I was running another business alongside the surveying practice. Quite often I would return from meetings to find a larger than usual pile of telephone messages which included many enquiries about the charity. Unless they were ultra urgent, I'd put them to one side to deal with at home. Unquestionably, Marc was very supportive of the Samson cause, but I could not afford to allow it to get in the way of our work.

Throughout the early months of Samson's development there was little time to come up for air, so I knew that I was pushing myself close to the limit of what the MS would tolerate before it hit back hard. Helen was forever telling me to ease off before I regretted it. I'm not quite sure whether it was a case of 'fortune favours the brave' or 'fools rush in where angels fear to tread' or a combination of both, but I got lucky, remained well and was able to follow up and nurture most opportunities that came our way. Saying that, even throughout the emergence of Samson, the charity still had to stay focussed on generating income for our existing physiotherapy operation, much of which came from street collections, affectionately known as tin rattles (even though, conforming with Council regulations, nobody rattled anything!). Conducted within the many town centres in our locality, tin rattles proved very lucrative and a good way of spreading word about the charity's ambitions should the opportunity arrive. A surprisingly large proportion of donors would stop and chat about MS, mainly because a relative or friend had the illness, and that would be the moment to hand them a Samson leaflet.

Once I had realised the effectiveness of tin rattling, I requested the Steering Group's approval to explore other potential collecting venues. Their consent was very important given our limited numbers and the simple fact that some members just would not stand on a High Street and, in their eyes, be viewed as begging. Fortunately the approval was forthcoming, so I set about writing to out of town supermarkets, garden centres and sporting venues, as well as Councils for towns a little further afield. Whilst I was pleasantly surprised by my fruitful hit rate, Helen, who organised the collecting rosters, was less so!

I'm inclined to think that *Tales of a Street Collector* would probably not make an international bestseller, but there were definitely occasions when things got quite spicy and, once or twice, even saucy. In reaching out to new destinations I suppose it was eventually going to put someone's nose out of joint, but 8.45am on a drizzly morning in Leatherhead provided something of a wake up call. Being the instigator of Helen's roster misery, I usually took one on the chin and agreed to do the set-up and first shift. Complete with fluorescent tabard, folding chair, bag of collecting boxes, Samson stickers and the all-important street collection licence, I positioned myself adjacent to the entrance to the Swan Shopping Centre. The early stints were always slow, which merely added to the feeling of being very conspicuous. Most of the pedestrians were either staff or folk rushing to avoid the mass of Saturday shoppers.

It was quiet, but being half asleep myself, I just didn't register the presence of an adversary until he was, literally, right under my nose. Hissing and spitting what sounded predominantly Eastern European obscenities, the only words I could make out were 'Big Issue'. Over the course of the next two hours, at about twenty minute intervals, this strange little man, who could best be described as the love child of Bob Hoskins and a Super Mario brother, would come charging over from his station like a demented warthog, snorting out the same indecipherables. Whilst initially quite unsettling, towards the end of my time slot the ritual had become very entertaining, not only for me but also many of the staff in the shops opposite. With one final snarl, just five minutes before my changeover to one of our more diminutive lady rattlers, he snatched up his stool and strode off, gesticulating wildly as he disappeared into the distance.

"You don't come here often, do you?" shouted one of the guys from a shop on the opposite side of the road, simultaneously chuckling to himself. "That bloke has been selling his mags from the very spot you were standing for the best part of two years!"

"Fat lot of good it did me. Reckon I've collected no more than £30 because of his antics."

In fact, it was £21.92. We never did collect in Leatherhead again!

On the flip side of the coin, collecting at local racecourses proved to be both lucrative and a lot of fun. I was genuinely delighted to receive a very positive reply from Lingfield Park following my request for a bucket collection. Not only would we be permitted to collect at the exits, we would be allowed to mingle with the racegoers on the concourse. Despite the doubts of a few of the trustees, I was convinced that the racing fraternity would be supportive of our cause.

True to their word, Lingfield allotted us a Saturday fixture in mid-August which also had an Abba tribute concert after racing. The latter was a bonus, as many racegoers were likely to stay at the course much longer. On a balmy summer evening our team of six Samson couples assembled on the lawn at the furlong pole for a pre-race picnic. As the racecourse had requested that we defer the start of the concourse collection until after the fourth race, we were able to relax and enjoy the ambience.

When the bucket holders eventually began to circulate it was soon clear that we were in for a good night. As most of the favourites had won in the early races, many of the punters were reasonably happy and beginning to get well oiled. Those that had won, gave freely. Those that had lost, did so in the hope that it would change their luck; if it did, they gave again. By the end of racing, those who'd had no luck just threw their change at us, quite often saying, "You'll make better use of it than I have!" By nightfall, with buckets heavy and clanking, we left the course relieved that the exercise had been worthwhile. On the Sunday I got a call to say that we had amassed over £1200 which, for two and a half hours collecting, was phenomenal. Shortly afterwards, I approached Sandown Park and they were equally charming and helpful, granting us an exit collection. My hunch that horse racing might prove to be a productive avenue to explore had been well founded. However, what I hadn't anticipated was where the racing link would take us next.

I was beginning to find it increasingly challenging to keep up with the weight of enquiries about the campaign and the offers of assistance, but with Helen's and Marion's help, somehow we managed to deal with everything that came Samson's way. It would have been so easy to have left some of the more obscure fundraising approaches to fall by the wayside. Maybe there was still part of the angler in me, wanting to cast out a line and see if something bit. One such enquiry arrived on my desk via no less than Alan May – yes, Alan, he of the stolen shoe and office door caper. It turned out that Alan had mentioned Samson to an old school friend, John Dunbar, whose wife Ann was an MS sufferer. Apart from his main profession as a turf accountant, John also ran several successful racing syndicates for friends and business contacts. Whilst we had an obvious mutual interest through the MS link, John had heard from Alan about my penchant for the nags and the fact that I was trying to raise money and awareness for Samson. His proposal was to put together a charitable racing syndicate in which the members would still get all the trappings of ownership, but where the charity would benefit from each subscriber paying an embedded donation within their subscription plus a percentage of any prize money won and the horse's eventual resale value. Initially, and this may have come from the simple fact that my head was spinning from everything that was going on, I viewed John's idea as too left field to be of interest, but there may also have been an element of déjà vu and a fear of failure in me. I politely sidestepped John's approach without completely declining and promised to ponder it and get back to him.

Here's the déjà vu bit. I set up Trotters Independent Racing in 1999 with a good mate, Dave Bayliss, who had a similar love of racing. Owning a racehorse had been a dream of ours for some years (according to my father, as a child I was convinced I could stable and train a racehorse from our council house!) but my diagnosis early that year had induced a knee-jerk reaction to get on and do it. It was an exciting time but we were out of our league in the financial stakes. Big Gerry at the Club, who was another lover of the gee gees, once asked me how much it was costing. On divulging the approximate figure, he rocked back on his size 16s, widened his eyes and spluttered out, "My God, it's worse than feeding a coke addiction!"

After seven ignominious defeats, Twice, our untrustworthy steed headed to Brighton races on a evening when they were being covered by Sky Sports. Undaunted by our previous abject failures, Dave and I went there with fresh hope as Twice was literally a stone's throw from his box, being trained by Gary Moore on the edge of the racecourse. As our charge's form appeared on screen, Sky Sport's presenter, Jeff Stelling, delivered his withering verdict, "And there's Twice, owned by Trotters Independent Racing. No doubt, yet another of Del Boy's failed bargains!" Needless to say, we came near to last again. However, we could never be accused of lacking hope and perseverance. So, it was with immense pride that Dave and I stood in the winner's enclosure at Lingfield five months later and again at Southwell ten days after that. It had cost a small fortune but my father would have been smiling down on us as we mixed it with the Sheikhs and Knights of the realm.

It should, perhaps, have been a case of 'once bitten, twice shy' but having slept on John's proposition for the best part of a week, I called him and agreed that we should give the charitable racing syndicate a chance. This was on the basis that there would be no financial risk to the charity. For once, providing we got enough subscribers, it would be a 'win, win' situation even if we didn't win! Samson Quest ran nine times for the Samson Centre Owners Group under the watchful eye of Andrew Balding, winning once (at good old Lingfield) and getting placed four times, but the important part was that this bonny little colt raised over £5,000 for the charity along with a pile of positive publicity.

Confidence was now growing within the Steering Group and also within the membership and friends of the charity. This was very welcome as it took some of the pressure off Helen and I and gave the fundraising even more momentum. By our own admission, both of us were bad delegators and tended to nurture and stay with any leads that came our way. One-off donations were hugely appreciated and, other than a phone call and a thank you letter, usually required minimal input from us, but it was the charity fairs, quiz nights, coffee mornings, concerts, sports days and sponsored events run by individuals and organisations indirectly linked to Samson that were the real bonus packages.

An extraordinary example of this came from Ali Payne, a lovely lady and friend of Jackie Britneff, one of our longstanding members. I had got to know Ali quite well through various quizzes held on behalf of the charity but it was something of a surprise when she called me to announce that she wanted to do a sponsored walk for us. Not any old walk, she was going to undertake the El Camino de Santiago, a 500 mile Pilgrims' Walk across the rugged terrain of the Pyrenees, Northern Spain. The great thing was that Ali had planned and booked the whole thing, she would cover all the costs and just needed me to get some sponsorship forms drawn up and publicise it amongst our membership. She ended up raising over £2,500 which, at a time when online giving was not fully established, was a fantastic effort. However, the remarkable thing was that Ali's many sponsorship forms were filled with hundreds of individual donations. When we met as a group to celebrate her homecoming, I politely enquired as to how she had managed to get so many sponsors.

'I just asked everyone I knew, asked them to ask everyone they knew and made sure that everyone got a thank you.'

This may have seemed simple, even obvious, but it proved to be a very useful strategy for me in the many years of fundraising that lay ahead.

Individual inspiration was quickly followed by a massive collective effort.

"Oi, Hammers, how you doing big fella?" an unmistakable voice boomed down the line.

"I'm good thanks, Tugger. How's everything going with you and the lads?"

"Yeah, we're good, my anzum. Listen, me, Duff and a few of the boys have been chatting over a jar, or ten, up at the Belvie and decided we're gonna put on a charity match at the club. Can you make it up to Ealing for a beer and a chinwag next week?"

How could I resist?

The rugby boys duly came together again in the spring of 2006. The Field of Dreams had never been quite as packed. The match was generously sponsored by the McGee Group, the West London construction company that had taken down the iconic Wembley Stadium the previous year, and they brought some real clout to the occasion, literally! Their Managing Director, Brian McGee, and Tugger were former St Benedict's scholars and, more recently, frequent patrons of the Belvedere restaurant on the Hanger Lane gyratory, so from the moment the concept of the charity match had been devised, the gauntlet had been firmly thrown down for each of them to select an Invitation XV who would play for the Samson Trophy. Fiercely competitive, Brian and his Irish contingent enlisted the assistance of international rugby legends Jason Leonard and Zinzan Brooke along with a few former Wasps players. Tugger, true to his Acton roots, selected from within the club, which proved to be the right call. McGee's XV, even with all their stars, struggled to impose their collective wealth of talent against a very determined and cohesive Actonian's XV. The spoils were shared on the pitch, but in the bar and during the auction our Irish friends simply swept the boards.

As with most of the Actonian Club's special days, our Master of Ceremonies was Duff. Ably assisted by Tugger, they made for a powerful duo in elevating the spirits and overall tempo of the proceedings. This was much needed after I'd delivered the sobering bit about why we were all there (Marion still maintains that I should have left out the part about loss of bowel and bladder control!). On the basis that the McGee XV had scored more tries and were the 'away' team we presented the Samson Trophy to Brian. He may have been the supremo of a substantial business empire with all the trappings that went with their success, but he looked truly made up as he triumphantly held aloft the spoils. With a vast array of signed sporting memorabilia, holidays, golf days, etc., it was then auction time. Duff, now in full town crier mode, demanded silence from the band who had masterfully provided cover versions of many 70s and 80s hits from the time of the ref's final whistle. As if not enough blood and sweat had been shed during the game itself, Brian and his band of merry men then set about taking on the Old A's boys on the bidding front. As the bids racked up into their £1000s, I glanced across at Marion, smiled and raised my eyebrows. It was a simple expression that said it all. I had witnessed the wholehearted generosity of the chaps before at the charity dinner, but this was her first time and with the Irish brigade wading in heavily, it was even more uplifting.

Just as Duff was winding things up and priming the band for 'Sloop John B', Brian sidled over, whispered in his ear and placed something in his hand. After the briefest of smiles (which usually signalled mischief!), our MC re-engaged his game face.

"Ladies, gentlemen, boys and girls, shipmates, we have one last very special auction lot for your delight and delectation."

At this point my mind began to conjure images of Duff and Tugger having spent the morning giggling away whilst scrawling absurd Pacific Islanders names on a large pineapple!

"What I have here are the keys to a classic Jaguar XJS. Who will start me off at £3,000?" Duff was suddenly deadpan in his delivery.

Three arms went up straight away, accompanied by a few muffled laughs. I would like to have thought that I'd have been able to spot a prank and call a halt to it before it got out of hand, but as Duff was so focussed and clearly not mucking around, I stood there, gobsmacked, as the bidding hit £6,000. On it went, £6,500, £7,000,

£7,500. . . until the 'hammer' went down at £9,250! There was rousing applause and much hilarity from the McGee ranks which convinced me that it was a stunt. Almost as soon as the commotion had died down, one of their directors emerged from the bar with a tray full of beer.

"Oy, Pat, have you seen my car keys? I had them at the bar five minutes ago."

Cue an eruption of Irish-led belly laughing. Damn, it was a set-up after all.

A week later an envelope containing just a cheque for £9,250 dropped through my letterbox. Samson's star was now rising fast.

Chapter 31

Stars
2nd December 2005

WITH the lights dimmed and the PowerPoint presentation and CD player primed for action, a hush came over the hall. I stood to address an expectant audience with an upsurge of immense pride and satisfaction.

"Ladies and gentlemen, thank you so much for coming along this evening in celebration of the work of the MS Therapy Group (Guildford) and their part in the creation of this wonderful new centre. The last two years have been extraordinary and taken us on an amazing journey which has drawn everyone so close together. Thank you one and all for your support and kindness. I believe that what we see here today is just the start of something very special for our charity. You will, however, be relieved to hear that I am not about to set out new plans and another fundraising campaign – at least, not tonight! Instead we are going to treat you to a reminder of how we have arrived at this point."

I looked across and nodded to Dave Kitching who was hovering over the 'play' button.

As M People's *'Proud'* and Katie Melua's *'Thank You Stars'* boomed out, photos of all the fundraising events, charity dinners, sporting challenges and the emergence of the new centre flowed across the screen. Faces that once stared dispassionately at me in the early days now beamed with the sheer joy of what had been achieved. Some were freely shedding tears. I managed to catch Helen's eye. The smile and a wink were all that I needed but it was Ms Melua's final melody, timed to coincide with the last few images, that brought the applause and cheering to a crescendo with her expressive lyrics of faith and love, guidance from above and thanking the stars.

Everyone involved in the project, in whatever capacity, was one of those stars. Against all the odds, and in double quick time, we had made the dream a reality.

In saying that I felt we were at the start of something special, I really could not have gauged how the charity would develop now that we had a permanent base. It was more a message for us not to rest on our laurels. I need not have feared. Word of our arrival spread rapidly within the local MS community and with it our rate of growth accelerated. We soon found ourselves looking to employ additional physiotherapists to treat new patients and call upon extra volunteers to support the day-to-day running of the Samson Centre. We were very fortunate to have a core group of volunteers, mainly made up of family members and friends, to supplement our physio team, so our development was relatively seamless.

And all this went on whilst I was trying to keep my eye on the ball at work up in Wimbledon. I dealt with fielding calls from the Samson Centre as best I could, but most of my meaningful input as chairman and fundraiser came in the evenings. I had been naive in thinking that my role might become a little less intense once the centre had been established. Joining forces with the Wey Kayak Club and the British Sub Aqua Club (Guildford) brought new demands, in that each member club needed to provide two trustees to form the Board of the Guildford Waterside Centre, which effectively was our umbrella group. As chairman, I had to stand as one of the MS Therapy Group trustees and then set about coercing someone else into joining as our second representative. Cue the re-emergence of my predecessor, Vic Worrall. He was involved with the Guildford Lions, a particularly well organised philanthropic body, which were to hold their monthly committee meetings at the centre. Joining us on the Board were Jim and Dave from the Kayak Club and two trustees from the divers. Unaware of it at the time, these three disparate groups would blend together well over the next 14 years to form a powerful alliance. As with all committees there would be the occasional spat, but given the diversity of our objectives the results of our endeavours would be the stuff of dreams. So together were the clubs that by the spring of 2007, phase 2 of the development saw a superb gymnasium block and new boat storage added.

Shortly after this Vic announced that he was moving away from the area and that the MS Group would need to find another trustee to sit on the Waterside board. Despite the fine work of the Samson Centre Steering Group, at first it seemed as though no one was really willing to take the plunge and devote even more of their time in nurturing our association with the other clubs. The process of forming the Samson Centre had been full on and quite exhausting, so I could understand their reluctance to join another committee involving long evening meetings. The fact of the matter was that I hadn't approached the right person and that person was John Steeds. We may have had our differences over the years but now that the Samson Centre was up and running John seemed even more passionate about the charity's work and the development of our facilities. When I eventually asked John whether he would be interested in standing as a fellow Waterside trustee I sensed an immediate thawing in our relationship. As it turned out, we worked incredibly well together for several years. With my dexterity rapidly deteriorating, John's engineering background and draughtsmanship skills were vital in allowing us to put together alternative schemes for extension of the centre, in particular the provision of extra treatment rooms and our options for a new oxygen therapy facility. His expertise in working up ingenious Excel spreadsheets for the various costings proved crucial in enabling the trustees to understand our fundraising requirements. As Sue was so poorly, John and I would spend many hours in his study refining scheme details until they were approved by the trustees of both committees. And when it came to those committee meetings, occasionally we would play out the 'good cop, bad cop' scenario to get our points across – no prizes for guessing who was who! After my early days at the charity when we so often clashed, it meant a lot to me, and I hope to John, for us to be in harness and able to achieve so much together.

Back to Samson gaining strength and the plethora of opportunities that began to fall into my lap as the charity's quasi-fundraiser. Again, the rugby club were at the forefront, both collectively and individually, devising all manner of events to generate income for us. In the spring of 2006, I received a typically succinct call from Glenn.

"Hammers, hope you're all well. Quick question. Where was your home rugby club?"

"We're all good, thanks Glenn," I said slowly and somewhat guardedly, thrown by the directness of his enquiry. "Uhh, Truro, but why?"

"Thought so. I've got an idea. Call you in a few days."

Invariably a man of few words, perhaps I shouldn't have been quite so surprised by his brief line of questioning. Glenn tended to be direct and focussed on most things that he did. His vast array of scars from our rugby days bore testament to that. Fleetingly I recalled the time in the Rose Room at Twickenham stadium. I had presented him with the 1st XV Player of the Year award on the premise that, in pursuit of the ball, he was utterly fearless and thought nothing of putting his head where the boots were flying.

He called back the following week to announce that he was going to undertake a sponsored bike ride from Truro Rugby Club to the Samson Centre – a mere 242 miles. Nothing particularly unusual in that, you might think. The difference was that Glenn intended to do it in one day. Having retired from the oval ball game, through triathlons and extreme endurance events over the next decade he would come to discover a new way of beasting himself!

At 5am on 10th June 2006, one of the hottest days of the year, Glenn, complete with outriders and support team, set off from Truro RFC. Within the first mile Kim, his brother and fellow Actonian, collided with a sleep walking cat whilst passing under Devil's Arch (ironically, one of the steepest parts of my body changing runs all those years ago) shredding much of the skin down the left side of

240

his body in the process. Kim, who was as equally unhinged as
younger brother, initially refused medical assistance and insisted
remounting his bike. By the time the support team had got him
see sense and force him back into the minibus Glenn was mi
away. And this was the thing with Glenn, he never did anything
half measures. Once he had locked in on a task, there was just
doubting that he would complete it, whether that be 'burying'
unfortunate fly half or competing in an international Iron Ma
challenge. The problem on this occasion, though, was that h
single-mindedness put so much distance between himself and tl
support crew, he went without fluids for a much longer period tha
his meticulous schedule had set out. Thankfully, as he neared tl
border with Devon they caught up, refuelled him and put a ne
outrider onto the road with him. In theory all was now good, excep
that they were dealing with an exceptional athlete. A succession o
outriders were unable to keep up with him for long enough to shar
the workload, so from Stockbridge, Hampshire onwards, Glenn wa
pretty much on his own.

To put his efforts into context, Glenn's average speed for the
entire journey was 16.7 mph, at one point reaching a speed of 41
mph. He lost 9lbs in body weight whilst burning 10,771 calories and
his average heart rate was 140 with a peak of 168. After 14 hours,
33 minutes and 37 seconds in the saddle, Glenn sped through the 60-
strong human sluice that welcomed him back to the Samson Centre.
The banner over-sailing the road read, 'The Iron Man Cometh' –
entirely appropriate for an extraordinary effort by an extraordinary
man. After a shower, a couple of pints of water and an unsuccessful
attempt to get Kim to go to the Royal Surrey County Hospital, the
laconic Mr Karpeta took to the mic and announced that he had
raised £7,500 for the charity. The bar for individual fundraising
feats had been set very high which, of course, the rugby boys, who
were there in large numbers, took as a benchmark to be bettered.

Next up were a remarkable series of sponsored bike rides, half
marathons, skydives, swims, fell runs, etc. – variety was certainly
the name of the game and with it came a lot of publicity which
raised our profile. Marion's file of newspaper cuttings began to
swell rapidly. In February 2008 this reached dizzying heights,

literally, when Ian McLaughlin from the club, along with a group of friends, tackled Kilimanjaro and we were sent an iconic photo of them at the peak holding a large flag with the charity logo announcing '4531 miles to the Samson Centre'. Confirmation indeed that we had arrived on the world stage. It did make me smile though, as I recalled that a couple of years earlier cousin Brian had reached Everest base camp whilst wearing a Samson T-shirt, only for it to go missing one night after he'd hung it outside to dry. Thoughts of Bigfoot marauding through the Himalayas in the charity's colours were perhaps just a little too far-fetched!

However, having mentioned our flourishing profile, I need to step back a year. During August 2007 I popped down to Cornwall to visit my mother for a few days. Trips to the coast and visits to relatives, accompanied by copious amounts of tea and cake, were generally the preferred routine but, without fail, we had to be home or at Marianne's house in time to watch *Deal or No Deal*!

"Do you like watching this programme, John? I know that Noel Edmonds is your favourite," my mother enquired whilst settling down into her recliner.

"No, I can't say I've ever seen it Mum, as I'm usually at work. Besides, the last time I watched Noel Edmonds he was on *Multi-Coloured Swap Shop* on Saturday mornings when I was 15 years old!"

"Oh, you must watch it, it's very popular. The contestants can win £250,000 or just 1p, you know," she insisted, oblivious to my indifference.

Smiling, I put down the newspaper, indulged my mother and promptly fell asleep!

A couple of weeks after returning from the fatherland, my mobile vibrated as I was chairing a lunchtime charity meeting. We were in the middle of discussing finances and since it wasn't a number I recognised I ignored it. When I arrived home, Marion confronted me as soon as I walked through the door.

"Did you speak to the nice lady from Endemol?" she said, grinning broadly.

"Uh, no, you've got me there. Who, um, what are Endemol? Not another drug company looking to get involved in the centre? The number of blinking calls I'm getting, asking for. . ."

Marion cut me off in mid rant and got straight to the point.

"Who's a clever boy? Out of 15,000 nominees, you've been shortlisted to go on *Deal Or No Deal*'s Christmas Stars programme!"

I tried to field the curve ball thrown my way. My mother was the last person to play practical jokes.

"Come again. You're having a laugh, aren't you?" my mind whirring into overdrive as I spoke.

'Got to be someone at the club pulling my chain but where'd they get the Deal Or No Deal *link from?'*

"No, I'm not," Marion insisted, still smiling, "Amanda Bentley is an avid game show fan and put you forward in recognition of all the charity work you have done in the last five years."

"Not a chance, there's no way I am going on to mainstream TV." Just the thought of being in front of the cameras put me into panic mode. "Imagine the humiliation if I cocked up and ended up with the 1p!"

"Oh, come on, it'll be great fun. We can have family and friends as the box openers and we all get to stay together in a top hotel in Bristol for two nights. All expenses paid." Marion sensing my recalcitrance changed tact; "You are always talking about raising the profile of the charity so just think of what this could do for Samson."

As usual, she was right of course!

Mid November 2007, D-Day (or should that be DOND-day?) had arrived. The coach slowly wound its way from Bristol's salubrious Grand Hotel to the outskirts of the city, eventually coming to a halt within a light industrial park – a former paint factory to be precise. Whilst not quite Pinewood Studios, it was a hive of activity as four other Christmas Stars and their supporters were also being filmed over the next two days. I was to be second up in front of the cameras, so thankfully there was little time to get myself worked up into a lather. As Team Hambly disembarked we were ushered through into a large refreshments hall before all 25 of us were given a 'facelift' in the make-up room. There was something surreal in glancing across at Bruv and Glenn as we sat in front of the mirrors getting our faces powdered. Scarface Karpeta would require extra layers to make him presentable enough for family viewing!

"John, please come with me. Filming starts in 40 minutes so we need to brief you and introduce Noel as we warm up your box openers and audience." An attractive young lady, businesslike with clipboard under arm, brought me back to my senses. It was unlike any situation I'd ever experienced before, but somehow I remained unfazed and set off through family and friends as they liberally dished out hugs and kisses.

I caught a glimpse of the bright lights and colours of the set as I was led to a narrow area at the back of the studio. The painted block-work and steelwork of the old paint factory that greeted me, together with propane heater and two chairs, were in stark contrast to what was on the other side of the screens. If it was designed to make contestants chill and lower expectancy, it definitely achieved that! Left alone as muffled voices, laughter and sporadic applause started up a few metres away, it felt like the right time to give myself a 'team talk'. Forearms on knees, hunched over, I stared at the concrete floor trying to envisage what could possibly lay ahead.

"Hello, John." My childhood favourite appeared in front of me soon afterwards. "Are you feeling OK?"

"Oh, hi Noel. Very pleased to meet you." Startled, I tried to stand up and shake his hand but, without my stick, promptly slumped back onto the chair. "Thank you, I'm good. Just getting into the zone. Wherever that is!"

"Don't worry, there isn't one. Just be yourself," our host said warmly. "I've watched the film about you and the charity. You'll be absolutely fine."

Ten minutes later my name was announced and I walked out onto the set amongst a sea of so many familiar faces. It felt good and much less daunting than I had imagined. Settled onto my chair next to Noel and the banker's telephone, they showed a short film about me, the family and Samson which had been shot at home and at the Samson Centre a month earlier. I was then asked to select a box (I went for the one sitting in front of a smiling Tony Two Shirts) that I hoped contained a big sum and would bring sizeable offers from the banker. Niceties over, it was time for him to get stuck into me and, boy, did I give him the ammunition. With the basic aim of the game being to hold onto the big sums as long as possible in order to elicit larger and larger offers from the mystery man holding the purse strings, it was crucial to avoid the boxes with the five largest amounts in the first phase of the game. In revealing three of the 'Big Five' including the £250,000 and £100,000 boxes almost straight away, I knew that I was facing an uphill battle to win a respectable amount, but the banker's offer of £80 was such an insult it irritated me.

"That won't even cover tonight's drinks bill!" I fired back.

"You're right, let's get on with this." Noel was clearly in my camp.

I opted to press on and, despite losing some other high value boxes, managed to get back up to an offer of £5,000. Much to her horror, I asked whether Marion could come up to the top table. Lip readers may well have picked up a couple of expletives as she emerged from the comfort of the sidelines. In truth, she didn't have a clue as to what was going on, but at least by asking her she could take some of the blame if I ended up with pennies! That very thought led me to 'deal' at £5,000. As with many of these game shows, Noel asked me to play through to a conclusion as if I was still in real game time (I guess, the equivalent of *Bullseye*'s Jim Bowen saying, "Come and see what you could have won"!), which revealed that the box Tony had brought to the table actually only had £250 in it, so I had some sense of having beaten the banker.

I had announced at the start of the program that I would be sharing any winnings with the charity, so splitting £5,000 felt like a good result, particularly, as courtesy of Channel 4, so many of us had had a great experience for a few days. However, the program was called *Deal or No Deal* Christmas Stars and, perhaps, in that name I should have known that there would be something else on offer. Once the box opening had finished, Noel announced that there were one or two little treats for us as a family in recognition of all the hard work that we had put into establishing the new Samson Centre. I was genuinely surprised and delighted when Jonny

Wilkinson, fresh from the 2007 Rugby World Cup, appeared on screen to congratulate me on the achievements of the charity, as well as offering a trip to watch the England rugby team train for the Six Nations and then go along to the England v Wales match at Twickenham. At the time I probably appeared happier with Jonny's message then I was with the money! That wasn't the end of it though, as Noel revealed that they would be arranging for Marion and I to go away for a long weekend to celebrate the renewal of our wedding vows and also a trip to the O2 Arena for us (well, the girls!) to watch *High School Musical on Ice*.

As the show drew to a close, Noel announced that there was just one more present 'under the tree'.

"You used to play rugby with this guy. I know you haven't seen him for a while and thought he was in Dublin. Well, he's here today to present you with your Christmas Star trophy."

Baring his pearly whites, Duff strode confidently onto the set, prompting the end credits and the cue for everyone, including the rugby contingent in the audience, to gather on set for a team huddle. Despite my initial misgivings, the whole *Deal Or No Deal* experience had proved to be very enjoyable for all involved and a great shop window for the charity. The programme was screened just before Christmas, giving us national exposure, followed by local newspaper coverage. In the months that followed I began to lose track of the number of strangers who stopped me in the street to chat about the show. My mother's claim that it was popular had been spot on.

Back to the future! Early in 2009 I was approached by Surrey Police who had nominated Samson as the Chief's charity for the year. Obviously we were delighted to be held in such high regard, but there was one element of the nomination that worried me. The charity had been asked to host the Constabulary's annual sponsored walk, affectionately known as the 'Surrey Stumble', which I agreed to without really considering the logistical side of things. We would need to facilitate the administrative support and medical backup, as well as providing hot food and refreshments for the walkers at the finish, and once fully briefed I realised that it was a much bigger event than I'd imagined. Hundreds of competitors, in fact. Step forward Dave Kitching and our friends at the Guildford Waterside Centre. I need not have been concerned, as the day ran so smoothly I even had time to persuade Dave to rig up a big screen for the recovering walkers (OK, for me!) to watch England v France in the Six Nations. Whilst we had worked together on smaller projects, this one really revealed the true power of support which existed in our very midst. It would become one of the hallmarks of the charity and our partnership with the kayakers and divers, culminating in us receiving the Queen's Award for Voluntary Services almost a decade later.

There was just one downside in that I received a public roasting from Marion for my dereliction of duty as a parent. So set on ensuring that everything dovetailed together, I took my eye off our girls for just a few minutes during which time Marion, returning from the 15 mile walk, spotted 7 year old Cerys dangling from a bridge over the river next to the centre – doh, not so much of a star after all!

Chapter 32

So Long Pardner
30th June 2007

"RIGHT, I'm going to make a move, Godders. I've left you a state of play list for all my jobs on the drawing board."

Marc, head down, slowly put his pen on his desk, drew breath and looked across a mountain of files.

"OK Hambers, I'll come down with you."

It was a walk that I had been trying to envisage and prepare for ever since I had come to the decision to retire from the practice six months earlier. Marc and I had worked together for over 20 years, during which time there had barely been a cross word, so inevitably this moment would prove to be hard for both of us. Whilst I would only be 30 miles down the A3, things would never quite be the same without the daily routines, the rapport, the process of problem solving together, bouncing ideas off each other. Yes, there had been difficult schemes, when I would just sit and wonder how on earth I would be able to get on top of a particular situation, but Marc's guidance and calmness always got me through. I wasn't going to miss the cut and thrust of the work. It had become too stressful with a debilitating illness impairing my ability to meet the demands of the job, but I would miss Marc. . . hugely. He could be a closed book when it came to showing his emotions, but as we stood in the reception and shook hands as business partners for the last time, the palpable sense of sadness was very strong. Ten minutes after we had parted I was still sat in the office car park trying to summon the strength to turn on the ignition and pull away. However, as agonising as it felt, there could be no turning back.

Despite the great working relationship Marc and I had had, I have to confess that I was seldom enamoured with life as a chartered building surveyor. Whilst the financial rewards were good, they were not commensurate with the long hours and the constant pressure of having to deal with intractable clients, over-pedantic property professionals and unreliable contractors. That is not to say that there weren't enjoyable and satisfying periods, but so often I would find myself wide awake in the middle of the night with my mind buzzing because of a particular site issue, intricate scheme design, party wall dispute, formal complaint; to name just a few of the recurring worries. So multi-faceted is the construction business, no matter how thorough and diligent your approach, circumstances will contrive to create challenging situations. My sanity was saved by the ability to hang on in there and grind it out. Marcus had instilled this in me during my training years when we were in the West End. Following a short sabbatical in Cornwall after my departure from Cyril Silver & Partners, I had been delighted to re-join forces with him in 1991, eventually becoming business partners in 1994. Suffice it to say, we rolled up our sleeves and achieved a good deal of success, but any attempt to relay accounts of complex construction projects or surveys would be dull at best. However, if there was one thing that Marc and I had in abundance it was the ability to graft whilst retaining a sense of humour and an appreciation for the bizarre. The scenarios that contributed to our amusement and occasional astonishment were surprisingly frequent. Here are a few that stick in the mind.

As I had found out, as a fresh-faced post-grad you generally know next to nothing about the machinations of the construction world and at times appear like the proverbial rabbit in the headlights. As the workload began to grow we made the decision to take on our first trainee surveyor to assist with some of the legwork and in the process gain experience towards his or her professional diary.

Ashley Farrell was a nice chap with good character, a sound grasp of the rudiments of surveying (at least on paper) and an almost complete lack of common sense! As Marc had done with me in my embryonic career, we decided that a few months of work shadowing and providing basic assistance would be the best way forward with him. As luck would have it, within a week of his arrival we were commissioned to carry out a structural survey of a three-bed semi in Wimbledon which appeared to be an ideal opportunity to get him started.

"OK Ashley, I'll open up and quickly scoot around the property to suss things out. You sort out the parking ticket, grab the survey bag and ladders and then bring them up to the first floor landing." These were my simple instructions upon bringing the car to a halt on Hardy Road.

"Got it, no problem John."

Purposefully, Ashley was out of the car and off in search of a ticket machine.

The refurbished property was in immaculate cosmetic order, with the fresh smell of new carpets. My first impression was that the survey would be fairly straightforward and, in truth, it was. Ashley seemed to be on the ball and keen to please, setting up the ladder for the loft inspection and placing the survey bag expectantly at my feet.

"Well done, Ash. Whilst I crack on with the roof space, you take the jemmies and keys and lift the manhole covers in the backyard ready for me to inspect the drains later."

"Uh, yes, of course. You've picked up on that smell too, have you?" he remarked, whilst rummaging through the tool bag.

I hadn't, so was quite impressed by his surveying instincts.

On finishing the loft inspection I returned to the landing and caught a whiff of Ashley's 'drain' smell, except it wasn't. I checked my shoes. All clear. I opened the rear sash window and shouted down to my young assistant who was still struggling with his first manhole cover!

"Ash, check your shoes."

He glanced down then gave me a vacant look.

"They're on the right feet. It's just that the lid is rusted into the frame."

"No, you wally, check to see if you've stepped in dog shit!"

He hadn't.

The survey continued for the next two hours during which time the unpleasant odour persisted in every room and, to a lesser extent, outside. All very peculiar as the manholes, once prised open, revealed nothing sinister.

"OK Ash, we're done here. I'm just going to check that everything is secured and turned off. Please round up all the equipment and stick it in the car. I've got another survey first thing tomorrow."

Still bugged by the fact that I'd been unable to solve the source of the stench I did one last sweep of the premises. After all, I could hardly produce a survey document reporting no significant defects without explaining why the property stank to high heaven!

I dropped Ashley back to the office and set off home. Still I couldn't get my head around the reason behind the afternoon's smelly encounters, to the extent that any fleeting recollection of the pong merely served to prompt my smell receptors into thinking that they were back at Hardy Road. As a result of my newly acquired phantom smell affliction, the escape from the conurbation was much less pleasant than normal. On pulling into the drive 45 minutes later, I was relieved to open the car door and suck in a few lungfuls of sweet Surrey Hills air before gathering up my work files and the survey kit bag, all of which would need sorting out that evening in readiness for the next day's inspection. Marion and the children were out so I flung everything onto our bed and made my way through to the back garden, grabbing the newspaper and a beer on the way. At last, an opportunity to relax and take in some warm early evening sunshine in peace and quiet. Sheer bliss. Well, that is, until I heard the front door slam and wildly enthusiastic footsteps come slapping through the kitchen.

"Daddy, daddy, daddy!" Ellie and Megan flung their arms over my shoulders. "Can you read us a book tonight?"

"Oh, I'm not sure about that. Maybe, but only if you've been good at school today," I teased. "I'll have to ask Mummy about that. Where's she gone, girls?"

"She's changing Grace's poohy bottom," Ellie chirped, already thinking about which weighty tome she would be hauling out of the book cupboard.

"Yeuch, poor Mummy," I smiled, pinching my nose.

"Poor Mummy all right. What a mess!" Marion appeared looking thoroughly cheesed off.

"Hiya, how was your day?" I puckered up for a kiss in a futile attempt to deflect what I sensed was going to be a thorough ticking off.

"It was pretty good until you got home! Just come with me and see what you've done!"

And with that she was off.

"Hum, you're in trouble, naughty Daddy," Ellie's sad face simply reaffirmed my demise.

On reaching the door to our bedroom, a very familiar stench hit me square on my traumatised snout. Marion stood there in her best teapot pose.

"On behalf of the prosecution, I present Exhibit 'A'," she announced with a rueful grin.

There, sitting on our new quilt, was a very large flattened dollop of dog's doings!

"A S H L E Y!"

Initially, the very thought that his first meaningful act as a surveyor had been to place the survey bag smack bang on top of something so revolting made me laugh. However, that soon stopped when it dawned on me that Ashley had slung the offending bag on the backseat of my BMW!

I'm not sure whether it was my council estate background or the fact that other surveyors fancied the high end private sector schemes, but so many of the jobs that landed on my desk were large Housing Association or Local Authority refurbishment projects, invariably with tenants remaining in occupation; and that's where the fun and games started. The diversity of characters and attitudes encountered could test the diplomatic skills of a politician. As a small child I remember how happy and grateful my folks had been when Carrick Council installed basic amenities – gone would be the days of having a bath in the washing-up bowl! How times had changed, as gratitude appeared in short supply on the streets of London, in many instances replaced by an attitude intent on screwing the client, contractor and consultant for everything that could be got.

Over the course of my career I had the 'pleasure' of dealing with several large housing estates and blocks of flats in some of the capital's most deprived areas, which would prove to be a stiff examination of my people skills. One particular estate in Brixton presented the full gamut of human frailty. It seemed as though almost every inspection was conducted in an air of resentment which occasionally extended to aggression. Initially, drawing on my childhood experiences on Trelander's streets and thinking that might be enough to gain trust and acceptance, I did many of the site visits on my own which, in hindsight, was foolhardy. After the estate's rent office was raided and several members of staff subjected to beatings with baseball bats, it was decided that we would not attend the site unaccompanied. Even then we were hopelessly exposed should one of the many mobs take umbrage at our presence, all suited and booted with clipboards and surveying gadgetry. Worryingly, the contractors were equally twitchy when the works eventually got underway. I recall pitching up to site early one October morning with police cars and fire tenders dotted around the estate. On arriving at the site cabin, I was disturbed to find the contracts manager hunched over his desk with head in hands. It transpired that every single scaffold board around four blocks of flats had been removed to create a bonfire to end all bonfires – a salutary reminder not to erect scaffolding for roof repairs within sight of Guy Fawkes night!

We tightened site security but that only served to bring about more bizarre disruptions to progress. Firstly, the contractor's ganger, a thoroughly decent bloke, got carted off by the police accused (wrongly as it turned out) of raping a young single mother. You can study all the contract administration manuals you care to immerse yourself in but I guarantee that none will offer guidance on how to deal with a vigilante group looking for retribution. Thankfully the unrest died down after a few weeks but, somewhat inevitably, was followed by the next hoo-ha. This time the estate caretaker, who had proved a real asset in playing the linkman between us and the residents, was arrested for alleged child abuse.

Unquestionably, the work was testing and character building but it wasn't always aggro. In fact, sometimes it bordered on comical. Take the tenant who insisted that I could only inspect her flat after 6pm. It was inconvenient, but for the sake of harmony I agreed to do so on my way home. When I arrived it was fairly clear why. A voluptuous Brazilian lady wearing a satin negligee and various articles of lingerie greeted me like a long lost friend and took little time in informing me that her husband was away working. Relentlessly pursued from room to room it proved to be a quicker than normal inspection!

And then there was a posh-sounding lady in Wimbledon who insisted that her property had serious subsidence issues and please could I pop in and offer some advice. As it was only just around the corner from the office I took the opportunity to stroll around on a warm sunny day. On glancing at the property from the outside there were no obvious signs of structural problems but I kept an open mind. I tapped on the front door and introduced myself to the owner who turned out to be a diminutive elderly lady. Without prompting, she announced:

"I've lived here for 60 years and never had any problems. This is all very worrying. I'm 83, I'd have you know?"

I raised an eyebrow in acknowledgement then carried out a cursory inspection of the ground floor which revealed hardly even a hairline crack. I was swiftly put in my place and told that the problem was on the first floor. I thought it unusual for there to be subsidence in the absence of any sign of movement to the lower storey but, out of politeness, I persevered. On entering the front bedroom I experienced one of those 'what the heck' moments. Above was what could only be described as a cosmic experience, with the ceiling obliterated by hundreds of tiny multi-coloured stars. It was only when I looked closer that I realised the stars had been precisely placed at the midpoint of each individual crack to a heavily crazed, sagging lath and plaster surface. After giving reassurance that there were no subsidence issues to address, I couldn't help but pose the question as to how the 'planetarium' had been created.

"My trusty friend and I," remarked my sparky octogenarian client proudly pointing to a rickety old wooden stepladder leant against the wall!

Over the many years that Marc and I had worked together we had come across some fairly unpleasant sights. Often sent into rundown properties on reconnaissance missions before clients committed to purchase, we had become used to being exposed to all manner of detritus, but our inspection of a large Victorian house in Highlever Road, North Kensington took us to a new level of 'grot'. Tasked with carrying out structural and measured surveys in the same visit we would need to be both thorough and efficient. Any such ambitions were quashed in the moment that a very rotund, unkempt man, I guessed of German descent, opened the front door, grunted and ushered us into the property. Whilst the stink that hit us was almost overwhelming, it was the sight of piles of rotting rubbish in every corner of every room being picked over by dozens of feral cats that drove home the realisation that this would be no run of the mill survey. Perhaps misguidedly, I had always viewed hoarding as the process of stockpiling items of monetary or sentimental value, but here we were about to witness someone's inability to discard anything at all, even their own waste. It was a dreadful health hazard and we should probably have made our excuses and walked out the door but, aware that our client was keen to acquire the property for conversion to flats, we gathered up our kit and pressed on.

Thirty minutes in, having trodden in countless lumps of something unmentionable, Marc and I met on the staircase.

"Hey, Hambers, have you got the feeling that you're being attacked?"

"Funny you should say that Marc. Originally I thought that this shithole was just making my skin crawl, but I think there's another reason."

"Me too," Marc said with a resigned look. "I think if we drop our trousers we'll find out why mate!"

As feared, he was right. We had been infested by fleas, and not just a few, there were hundreds of the blighters. That brought the survey to a close, but the painstaking removal of the invading army meant that the rest of the day also got. . . well. . . scratched!

This next piece is dedicated to Ellie who, as a child, was fascinated by this tale and all these years on still insists that it is worthy of recounting!

Friday 27th May 2005

The prospect of a record-breaking heatwave for the Whitsun week had enticed many to take the Friday off and head for the coast. Even Marc had broken with his tradition of working through a Bank Holiday weekend and departed for Torquay. As a result, I was left holding the fort as the mercury shot up to 32°C in the capital. The phones were so quiet that I felt it only right to let the staff shoot off home at lunchtime and to stick the office phones onto night service. I intended to give it a couple more hours before making tracks myself. The very thought of escaping the heat spurred me on to complete my dictation in double quick time and get home to Marion and the girls. Ninety minutes later, I was in the process of tidying everything away when the night service ringer stirred itself. Knowing that Marion would only use my private line I ignored it. After a minute, the caller rang off, so I continued with my departure arrangements. Five minutes passed before the outside line started ringing again, this time way beyond a minute. I could so easily have let it be but, such was its persistence, curiosity eventually got the better of me.

"Good afternoon, Scott Godwin Associates, how can I help you?"

"John, it's Riki. God, am I glad to have got hold of you."

Riki Patel was an ambitious developer and a nice guy too, but the fact that he was desperate to get through to me on a Friday afternoon before a national holiday meant that something urgent was in the offing.

"Hi Riki. Great to hear from you. Hope everything's OK?"

"Yes, all good thanks, John." Typically businesslike, that was an end to the niceties: "I wondered if you could look at an apartment in Holland Park?"

"Sure, no problem Riki. When can I get in?"

"Well, here's the thing. I need you to give it a quick once over today!"

My heart sank. I was hot, tired and ready for the journey home. I paused, just momentarily, but long enough for Riki to sense my reluctance to grab the survey kit so late in the day.

"John, this could be a nice refurbishment job if we move quickly this weekend to secure the property. Can I count on you?"

"Of course you can, Riki. What are the access arrangements?"

In trying to please a much valued client I had unwittingly made a fundamental error of judgement.

Around 3.15pm I collected the keys from the estate agents in West Kensington.

"Gosh, you work late," remarked a well-dressed middle aged lady on reception. "We'll be gone by the time you're done so please just post the keys back through the office letterbox."

"No problem. I'll probably only be an hour."

I smiled and put up a hand as I rushed off back to my car, keen to get the job done so that I could get back across the Thames before the start of the weekend's traffic logjam.

Fortunately, I found a parking bay right outside, gathered up my survey kit and skipped up the front entrance steps to a double fronted five storey Victorian property which had been converted into apartments. The pile of letters and junk mail on the floor of the common hall, together with an air of mustiness, gave notice that the building had been unoccupied for a while.

'Oh good,' I thought, *'no residents to slow me down.'*

I bounded up the stairs and let myself into a large first floor flat. I was surprised to find it partially furnished and quite well kempt. Whilst it was in good nick, I could still see why Riki was interested as the space lent itself to further sub-division and improvement.

'Right, come on. Get this done and get out of here. Well, after a quick leak!'

I placed my mobile on the lounge coffee table alongside the survey bag and headed off to the bathroom, which was a lot smaller than I expected given the spaciousness of the accommodation.

Then, I did it. Why I did it, I have no idea. Habit I suppose. After all, I did live with five females. As the overhead closer shut the bathroom door behind me, I turned around and engaged the thumb turn lock before answering the call of nature. The room was airless and uncomfortably warm so I took the opportunity to wash my face and hands. Refreshed, I went to extricate myself, only for the thumb turn knob to come away in my hand. Initially I thought it would just be a case of pushing it back into place but then, as I offered it up, I realised that the end of the metal spindle had sheared off leaving just a jagged stub protruding. I grabbed the lever handle, yanked it down and pulled back. The bathroom door barely budged a millimetre.

A cursory 360° survey of the room and its contents didn't take long. It quickly became apparent that my escape options were limited. Even the usual array of bathroom paraphernalia was sparse. Then it dawned on me. Everyone was on holiday and, in rushing, I had left no details of where I had gone. Instinctively I thrust a hand into my trouser pocket for my mobile.

'Oh shit, no phone, no tools and no one knows I'm stuck here. I could be here for days!'

What had been just a hint of perspiration on my forehead erupted into trickles of sweat. I sat back onto the edge of the bath to try and work out my next move. I suppose I could adopt a brute force approach, reminiscent of the office door caper of Christmas 1987, but then again, my run up would be virtually non-existent and I'd probably end up careering back into the bath! Anyway, even if successful, how would I explain the resultant damage? No, my plan had to be more innovative and subtle. I reviewed the extent of the resources available to me. A couple of old toothbrushes, a pair of tweezers, a roll of dental floss, randomly strewn hair grips, a selection of dried-up flannels and a toilet plunger – hardly items conducive to a modern day remake of *The Shawshank Redemption!*

It felt like the space was getting warmer. I wasn't exactly panic stricken but I could feel my shirt beginning to cling to my increasingly clammy skin. Subconsciously, the thought of becoming marooned in such a small featureless box was having its effect.

'What would be going through poor Marion's head when I failed to show or even make contact for the entire Bank Holiday weekend?'

Looking at the meagre array of inappropriate components I decided that the hair grips and tweezers offered me my best chance of persuading the ironmongery to budge. With trembling hands, I set about trying to bend and wrap the grips around the forlorn spindle before jamming the tweezers into position as a makeshift lever. Sweating profusely, I wiped my brow and braced myself to crank up my invention. For a brief moment, as the mangle of metal bits held under pressure, hope began to rise; only for the whole contraption to yield and fall to pieces. As if to add insult to injury, the tweezers pinged off and ended up in the toilet. I retrieved them, painstakingly reassembled my 'rig' and went for it again. This time, Uri Geller style, the tweezers folded in half.

'Oh God, I'm really in the shit here! How the hell am I going to get out of this hole?'

With an air of resignation, I slumped back onto the bath roll. My shirt was now wringing wet with sweat and, for the first time, I detected MS fatigue beginning to make an untimely intrusion.

'Come on, get your head in gear. What are your options?'

Clearly, they were not plentiful nor particularly workable. I let my head drop, puffed out my cheeks and stared at the floor contemplating my next move. Then it hit me.

'Your shoes, Hammers. Look at your shoes!'

Initially, I wanted to argue with myself! What on earth could my shoes offer?

'The laces, try winding them around the spindle.'

I wasn't convinced but what else was on offer? I whipped off a shoe and hurriedly stripped out the lace. I wondered whether it would be strong enough. Well, there was only one way to find out. I wound the lace as tightly as I could around the pathetically short metal stub (it was getting personal!), leaving two long lengths dangling. This would be the masterstroke. I snapped one of the toothbrushes in half and fashioned the two bits of plastic into toggles by knotting them onto the ends of the laces. Pulling down on the right hand toggle, whilst retaining tension on the other end of the lace, I reckoned that I might just get enough purchase to turn the spindle through the 90° needed to release the deadbolt. I knelt down to give myself a strong base, drew a deep breath and gently applied pressure.

'Fuck, fuck, fuck! There's not enough grip.'

The lace had tightened OK but then, just as hope was riding back into town, it began to glide over the metal. The wax coating on the lace was the new conundrum.

'What's your next move then, smart ass?'

I was close to letting go a full blast of frustration but held it in and retreated the two paces back to the bath rim for inspiration and another team talk.

'Right, sunshine, good effort but no cigar. This prototype door release gizmo needs a rethink.'

I sat quietly for a couple of minutes and tried to compose myself. It had only been about 30 minutes of incarceration but it felt like longer. It had the potential to become much, much longer. It was perhaps that fear that fuelled the light bulb moment.

'Get shot of the wax. That's it!'

I jumped up, filled the basin with warm water and started to soak the lace before scraping it across the sharp edge of the worktop over the vanity unit. I repeated this several times before drawing the lace through one of the rough, dried-up flannels. Eventually, I went back to the spindle and gave it a proper shellacking with the rough edges of the tweezers. Content that I had roughed it up enough and removed all grease and wax, I reinstated the toggle assemblage and sank back to my knees; not quite in classic prayer pose but my innermost feelings were in that direction.

'OK, me 'anzum, let's get this done.'

Slowly, as I increased the tension, the lace began to constrict around my old foe and with a firm tug on the right-hand toggle and a barge from my trusty left shoulder, I heard the most comforting sound – a clunk. Like a safecracker cracking a code, expectantly I grabbed the door lever and slowly pulled it down. Almost as if the whole episode had never really happened, the door silently obliged and I fell forward into the lobby.

*　　*　　*　　*

In the latter part of my surveying days I began to concentrate more on party wall work. I would miss the nip and tuck of site work but as there would be slightly less legwork it made sense to change tack. The Party Wall etc., Act of 1996 had provided a framework for preventing and resolving disputes in relation to party walls, boundaries and excavations near neighbouring buildings. The legislation, previously confined to Inner London, had been reworked and rolled out nationwide. It provided a fantastic opportunity for surveying practices and sole traders to diversify and, in many cases, specialise in this type of work. It was, and continues to be, an incredibly complicated area of expertise, constantly evolving as construction methods and schemes push the boundaries but, in simplistic terms, the Appointing Owners (as opposed to 'clients') instruct surveyors to safeguard their respective interests and from that point the surveyors begin negotiations which eventually lead to the publication of their Award.

All fairly straightforward you might think. Sadly, not so, particularly when acting for the owner keen to get on with the building work. The process of getting to the point of agreement of the Award could be fraught with difficulty, dependant on your owner, their consultants and contractor responding to your requests for information and showing restraint in not prematurely carrying out the notifiable works. And then, on the other side of the wall, there would be the surveyor acting for the neighbour or, in the case of flats, there would be several owners appointing different surveyors. By and large, most surveyors were reasonable, practical and a pleasure to deal with, but occasionally you would come across a pedantic and intransigent individual, seemingly more intent on drawing out the whole process in order to inflate their fee rather than expedite the agreement. One such surveyor could have been the inspiration for the character of Mr Bean, consistently inducing groans when his name appeared on the initial paperwork. During normal negotiations you would expect the travelling draft Award to develop steadily as the surveyors added comments and suggested amendments, but with Mr Bean on the scene the 'red pen' exercise took on a whole new dimension dealing in semantics and grammatical nit-picking. That alone would be infuriating enough but his most irritating trait was still to be revealed.

The inspection of the property adjacent to the works to facilitate preparation of a schedule of condition of the party wall and abutting surfaces could be laborious and very time consuming, especially if the property was in disrepair with a plethora of defects to record. Throw Mr Bean into the equation and you had the stuff of nightmares. Try and imagine the scene. You're in your first room of a five-storey house, eyes peeled, torch in hand and dictaphone at the ready. Big breath and away you go.

"Ceiling. Lath and plaster, painted. There is a hairline crack, approximately 300mm long, starting at the party wall/front wall abutment. . . "

"I'm going to have to stop you there. I think you'll find that it's closer to 350mm long." Would be a typical monotone interjection by Mr Bean.

It was going to be a painfully long day. In fact, this job was going to prove more than a day of pain. A pushy developer as my Appointing Owner, employing an impatient contractor and an overstretched architect, combined with Mr Bean and his vexatious owner on the other side of the wall, the job had all the hallmarks of sleep deprivation. At times I began to wonder if I could be between a rock, the devil, a hard place and the deep blue sea all at the same time! The stress it generated 'poked the bully' and the MS roared back on the scene, but this time it was different. Many of the physical symptoms were bubbling away again but it was the emergence of cognitive fog that really set the alarm bells ringing. Determined to get on top of the job, I hauled myself to the office for 6am only to be confronted by several challenging emails. I grabbed the job file intent on tackling a multitude of new issues. Twenty minutes later I 'came round', catching sight of my reflection in the computer screen, rocking back and forth. In that moment the realisation that I needed to let go of everything that Marc and I had built together hit me squarely between my blurred eyes.

Chapter 33

Oxygenius
July 2007

TWO years after the Samson Centre had been established, I started to explore how we could improve and expand our facilities. One of the treatments offered by other MS centres that particularly intrigued me was baric oxygen therapy. Why would something as simple as breathing oxygen within a pressure vessel be beneficial to MS sufferers? This is how it was first explained to me [GEEK ALERT!]:

In almost every disease or injury, inflammation and a shortage of oxygen in the affected area are major factors. For example, a heart attack or stroke can occur as a result of insufficient oxygen reaching those organs. Asthma or pneumonia prevent the lungs transferring sufficient oxygen to the blood. Major injuries and broken bones result in damage to surrounding blood vessels and tissues which prevent proper blood flow and hinder the availability of oxygen. MS is the same, blood leaks, inflammation occurs and oxygen distribution is reduced and damage follows.

We breathe oxygen every few seconds, but after a very short period of time without it our brain cells begin to die and shortly after we die. In addition to it being the most important factor in all our lives, oxygen also has other important benefits. We now know that oxygen regulates the immune system and programmes most of our genes but it is also a very powerful anti-inflammatory agent and antibiotic. In MS, applying more oxygen can reduce inflammation, increase the rate of healing and prevent infection. That said, just giving 100% oxygen via a mask is not enough to make a big difference. We need to find a way to get more oxygen into our muscles. With oxygen therapy, by putting the person into a baric chamber we can raise the pressure to double normal atmospheric pressure. This enables our blood and muscles to absorb ten times as much oxygen as before. In essence, if you are short of oxygen it makes common sense that having a bit more should help.

As so often with the development of Samson, no sooner had an idea popped into my head than an opportunity presented itself. The UK's leading proponent of oxygen therapy, Professor Philip James, was due to hold a lecture on the subject at the Bedford MS Centre in a month's time. I knew that I had to find time to be there.

Professor James's presentation turned out to be so absorbing and inspirational that I found myself drawn to approach him as he tidied away his papers. After years in the diving industry, followed by the development of baric oxygen therapy at Ninewells Hospital in Dundee and a huge number of MS therapy centres, here was a man who thoroughly knew his subject. Our conversation was brief but I expressed my interest in looking to acquire a chamber and start oxygen sessions at our Guildford centre. I was probably out of line as I had not even discussed this with the Samson trustees nor the Waterside Centre committee, and there was no part of the new building where a chamber could be set up and operated in accordance with the prevailing regulations. However, I didn't have to wait long before I had to address the issue, as within a matter of weeks Prof James called to say that a single person chamber had become available from, of all places, the Isle of Mull!

Transport issues aside, my immediate task was to persuade the trustees that we could actually set up and sustain baric oxygen therapy at the Samson Centre. Inevitably, there was a good deal of apprehension when mention of pressure vessels and oxygen was made. Not for the first time, I got lucky on several fronts. Perhaps most importantly, and thanks to years of lobbying Parliament by Prof James, it was announced that the use of pressure vessels and oxygen as a form of treatment at MS Centres was about to be deregulated so that in effect we would be able to self govern. That allayed some of the concerns but the next dilemma was where and how could we run the installation. Step up to the plate Jim Fardell, a longstanding supporter of the original MS Therapy Group and, collectively, the British Sub Aqua Club (Guildford), our co-lessees at the Waterside Centre. Jim regularly attended the centre with his lovely wife Mary, so that she could have treatment, and somewhere along the line, whilst relaxing in our lounge area over tea and cake, he had been cajoled into running the centre's bar; but what I hadn't appreciated was that Jim had been a specialist engineer for decades in. . . yes, you've guessed it. . . the oxygen industry! Jim would go on to play a vital role in the development of our oxygen treatment facilities and, with him also being an avid angler, we managed to find quite a few opportunities to hone our ideas by the water's edge.

Given that the proposed operation would be based on diving technology, the Sub Aqua Club's interest in helping us to set up and run it was encouraging and very welcome. However, their first intervention in the matter, thanks to a sizeable grant from a financial institution linked to their chairman, helped solve the question of funding the installation. By this time resistance within the board of trustees was receding but we were still scratching our heads as to where to accommodate the system. Time to put on my surveying hat again. Once I'd done so, I realised that it wasn't a case of finding space within the building. The solution lay in the infilling of an open area between the main centre and the gym block. It was not a vast area, just big enough to accommodate two single chambers and the operators' station. The committee agreed, but before we had had a chance to lay a brick I received a call from Scotland to inform me that the chamber would be arriving within a couple of weeks as their MS centre was about to shut down its oxygen unit.

Sure enough, a fortnight later, a tonne of steel about nine foot long, swathed in bubble wrap, rolled off the tail lift of a large delivery lorry. Resembling the cockpit of a light aircraft, the arrival of the chamber onto our rear courtyard signalled a new phase in the development of the centre. This piece of equipment would be something of a departure from the tried and tested treatments provided by our physiotherapy and fitness teams, but just the sight of it fired up thoughts of something much bigger.

Back to the real world. There were only four of us (including the driver) to coax our new heavyweight friend into its temporary place of storage in the divers' boat shed. One of the quartet was Guy Williams, a good mate and fellow MS-er but very importantly a director of a local factory that reconditioned, yes you've guessed it, pressure vessels. The other person was Cyril Lafferty, a friend and former deep sea diving colleague of Prof James. We had spoken over the phone but never met before. Cyril, in his early 70s and recovering from recent cancer surgery, was keen to embark upon an intensive course of baric oxygen therapy to minimise the side effects of post-operative radiotherapy. I was keen to assist him but had to break the news that we were, at best, four months away from getting the facility fully operational at the centre.

"Can I make a suggestion, John?" Cyril offered politely. . .

A month later, on a bright summer's morning, I drew up at the rear of an exclusive riverside property on the outskirts of Walton-upon-Thames. Having got lost several times, it had taken me a fair while to get there so I had pretty much seized up. Slowly I extricated myself from the driver's seat, leant against the car to stretch off my legs then went to grab my crutches off the back seat.

"Morning John, you're looking very stiff. Best I get your treatment started!" smiling, Cyril called across from the entrance to his double garage. Behind him the unmistakable outline of the chamber loomed large. Shorn of its bubble wrap overcoat and now plumbed in with its array of gauges and valves connected to a bank of oxygen cylinders, the set-up looked professional although somewhat incongruous given its garage setting. I hobbled my way across to Cyril and warmly shook his hand.

"This is impressive. You look like you know what you're doing, Cyril."

"I'd like to think so," he said, with a wry smile. "Are you ready for your first taste of baric oxygen therapy?"

I thought I was ready. In fact, having started to suffer from persistent urinary tract infections, I was desperate to know more and get the treatment underway. Up until this point, the thought of incarceration in a cold steel pod barely wider than my shoulders had held no fears, but as Cyril tightened the face mask then slid the seat into position within the chamber my heart rate quickened a little. The clanking of metal as the door was secured behind me completed the entombment. I peered through the front porthole searching for Cyril. Thirty long seconds passed before he settled at the controls just a few feet in front of me and yet his voice sounded very distant and muffled.

"OK John. If you're comfortable I'm going to start the pressurisation process nice and gently and take you to the equivalent of eight feet below sea level. If you feel any discomfort in your ears just put up your hand and I'll ease back. If you feel good we'll continue to 16 feet."

Reassured by Cyril's calming presence, I stuck up a thumb, composed myself and purposefully took a lungful of oxygen and exhaled deeply. Even so, my heart was pounding.

An hour later, with a hiss and prolonged squeal, the rubber seal around the rear aperture relinquished its grip, simultaneously allowing the chamber door to drop noisily to its resting position. Cyril's dulcet tones flooded in, signalling the end of my first session 'in the can'; an exercise that I would repeat over 600 times during the next 10 years.

"Well done, John. Fancy a cup of coffee whilst you tell me how that went for you today?"

And there began a ritual that we repeated every day for six weeks.

About two weeks on from that initial session, as I sat on Cyril's patio looking out across the River Thames, I couldn't help but feel optimistic about the potential that baric oxygen therapy held for users of the Samson Centre. I had been struggling with persistent, debilitating bladder infections for months, but now for the first time there was some respite and, after so many unsuccessful doses of powerful antibiotics, it could only have been down to the use of the chamber.

"You're looking good, John," Cyril remarked as he placed the coffee and biscuits onto the patio table.

"Thanks Cyril. I can't deny that I am feeling a little better each day. Is it that obvious?"

"Well, yes, I thought that you'd got a bit of colour back in your face last week," he said, grinning broadly, "but then you improved again today."

"Sorry, I'm not with you, Cyril."

He continued to smile.

"Aren't you missing something?"

Mystified, I cocked my head to one side and narrowed my eyes as I tried to unravel his line of enquiry.

"Nope, I don't think so," I eventually conceded.

"You forgot your crutches. They're still leaning against the wall in the garage!"

After six weeks, the intensive oxygen therapy had worked its magic. I was totally free of urinary tract infections and the nausea and weakness that accompanied them. During the same period, Cyril had trained me to operate the chamber so I was also able to treat him during my visits. His faith in the treatments was well founded. Carried out alongside regular cycles of radiotherapy, his oncologist had been astonished that a man of Cyril's age had completed the course with no ill effects, not even fatigue. Justifiably satisfied with the results of our embryonic baric oxygen operation, we retired to Cyril's patio for one last time. Having done its work, the chamber was about to go off to Guy's factory for refurbishment.

"Thanks for everything, Cyril. Not only have I regained some equilibrium in my life, but in treating you I have seen first hand the value of using this type of technology for other health conditions.

Wouldn't it be wonderful if we could develop a dedicated oxygen centre at the charity?"

"Now, that would be something, John," Cyril, sipping his coffee, looked across enthusiastically. "The involvement of the Sub Aqua Club could be a real plus."

"Yes, it has been discussed but I'm worried that the set-up might be a bit low key for those guys."

"Not at all, the pressure vessels and plant required to run them are right up their street. Got to be worth having them on board, hasn't it?"

I gazed across the Thames with ideas whirring around my grey matter.

"Talking of divers, Cyril, if this is something that the trustees agree to expand, I don't suppose you'd like to become part of the operation?"

"Yes, I would," Cyril replied without hesitation. "It'd be great to be involved in a new facility like that."

"You said that with some relish, but from what you've told me over the last few weeks, I suspect that you might be a tad over-qualified. We won't be able to offer you anything as exciting as the development of Saturation Diving technology with the US Navy's Sealab III project nor the likes of the Cousteau family, Lt. Commander Lafferty!"

"Oh don't worry about all that. I'd be delighted to help out in whatever way I can, John," Cyril casually remarked, munching on a biscuit. "Anyway, don't make the mistake of thinking that a career in diving was always that glamorous and full of appeal."

"Really, Cyril? Deep sea diving always looks incredibly exciting on the box."

"Take it from me, a week stuck in a hyperbaric chamber simulating a dive to 1,000 ft was decidedly dull and tedious."

"Hmm, I can see your point, but you must have seen some incredible sights out at sea."

Cyril, savouring another biscuit, pondered my query for a few moments.

"Yes, that's true, there were many wonderful times, but also quite a few that I have long since chosen to consign to the back of my mind," he paused again, although, I sensed, not intentionally for effect. "Diving blind through a metre of crude oil in order to inspect an unstable wreck teetering on the edge of a reef, with your rubber suit and hoses perishing by the second, would be a mission I'd like to forget."

"My God, I can see how that might be the stuff of nightmares, but why did you have to take on such a dangerous dive?"

"I had no choice. I received a telegram from the PM ordering my team to make the dive. I couldn't risk my men so I undertook it myself." He stared straight ahead, rubbing his chin reflectively.

"PM? What naval rank was that then?" I jumped in without really thinking.

"Hah, if only it was an officer, I'd have told him it couldn't be done," Cyril continued with his eyes peeled across the river. "No, it was none other than Harold Wilson. The government was under immense pressure to contain the environmental catastrophe wreaked by the *Torrey Canyon* disaster. You're probably too young. Do you remember it?"

"I do, Cyril, I most definitely do," I uttered ruefully. "How could I ever forget the havoc it brought to the Cornish coast?"

Chapter 34

Silver Lining
November 2017

THINGS are getting hard now. It's deep into the game and I'm tiring. No matter how hard I try, there are no chinks in the armour of this opponent.

'Come on, you know the drill, pull yourself together. Breathe. . . focus. . . bind. . . squeeze. . . and drive the legs.'

I close my eyes, visualise the movement and try to raise my game. Still nothing. I'm going to face plant.

'OK, don't panic, straighten your back. Suck it in and re-gather yourself. You've done this thousands of times before. This is not going to be the day that you give in to a bastard like this!'

I re-adjust my feet, hand holds and tense my core. I have to believe in myself. This has to be the one. After a full-on initial thrust I am wavering on the brink. The left leg is on overload, trembling, doing most of the work. I need to lock it out and concentrate on engaging the right.

'Almost there. Slip your binding. Brace the right arm.'

Slowly I get the better of this duel. A huge puff of the cheeks signals success as I thrust my body upwards.

It's taken ten minutes but I'm finally standing next to my bed. Another day going through the wringer is about to begin.

The MS that so rudely interrupted family, business and sporting life almost twenty years ago is ravaging my central nervous system.

No amount of determination or defiance seems to stem the physical deterioration now. The reserves of strength that once sustained a hectic lifestyle are badly depleted. Mentally, there's clarity and a willingness to stay involved in the work of the charity but it's getting harder to keep bouncing off the ropes when I get knocked back. Spiritually, I'm still strong and in the zone. My faith and the love of my family and friends have taken good care of that and the Samson Centre has kept my sense of purpose and expectation intact.

However, as positive as I strive to remain, it seems as though almost every facet of my being is becoming affected to some degree. From intense muscle spasms, loss of mobility and dexterity to bouts of incontinence, twitching eyeballs and overwhelming fatigue, this neurological predator knows no bounds as it indiscriminately devours the precious myelin sheath around my spinal cord and brain at an alarming rate. How prophetic had I been all those years before when setting out on the fundraising trail? Asked to explain what MS was to a school assembly of 7-11 year olds, I had likened it to a family of mice nibbling through the electric cabling in a large house, causing fuse blowing and circuit failure. It felt like a clever analogy at the time but, now my condition is so unfathomably complicated and unpleasant, it should perhaps give the impression that the house has been infested by rats!

I remember a classic Clint Eastwood line in *Unforgiven. 'It's a hell of a thing killin' a man. You take away all he's got and all he's ever gonna have.'* These days virtually nothing is as it was. MS has taken that life away and it's become increasingly difficult to look too far ahead. The sense of loss, of missing out, is always there. It could envelop and suffocate me if I dwell on it for more than a passing moment. I avoid Facebook like the plague. Even though I am not an envious person, I no longer want to see the fun everyone else is having. I just need to live in my world and fix my attention on things which are realistically achievable. And then there's the bit that really rankles me; Marion and the girls have also had to settle for much less. Their incredible love, patience and support deserves a great deal more. MS has not only left its indelible mark on me but their lives too. That said, when they were young, Marion and I did our best to shield the children from the fact that there was potentially something looming in the background. In periods when the illness intervened and disrupted family life it was just because 'Daddy's got poorly legs. Don't worry, they'll get better'. And invariably they did, but gradually a rolling gait became a limp, a walking stick became crutches and a self-propelled wheelchair became a motorised one. As the girls matured, we slowly introduced them to the world of MS, which hopefully, through Samson Centre events, was fun and less daunting than being sat down and given a right scare by the cold, hard facts. It was without doubt the right approach. The girls along with Marion are now heavily involved in fundraising for the charity. It has made them particularly well rounded and kind to others, which has been so good for me as the illness has tightened its grip.

That last word 'grip' could not be more apt as I return to my tablet after an enforced three week absence. MS on its own is a handful, but throw in a virus or an infection and we are talking of a whole different ball game. For many years, despite having a weakened immune system, I had managed to dodge the bullet as various bugs and ailments wafted through the house. I suppose it was just a matter of time before I copped something nasty, but the speed that it took hold and poleaxed me one evening after dinner was alarming. Rigors to bedridden in a matter of minutes.

By the early hours, the muscle spasms had become so intense that I was unable to move at all, not even a finger for the bed controls. My ritual of rugby themed visualisation to get me up and weight bearing was utterly futile. Save for twitching and sudden jolts in my legs through nerve pain, I realised that I was almost completely locked into my own body. In the pitch black and silence of the early hours, the helplessness of my situation sent a chilling wave of panic through me. Determined not to disturb Marion, for the next hour I remained prostrate trying to compose myself. My mind flitted and flashed from one worry to the next – bodily functions, outstanding paperwork, student grants, diary appointments, mortgage issues, fundraising events, an unpaid credit card bill, Mum's house move, huff, huff, huff and then, completely out of the blue, up popped George Muller! God only knows why my subconscious mind should dredge up good old George. I am certainly no evangelist, nor would

I ever claim to be in his league of philanthropy but, in hindsight, I can only think that my overworked coping mechanism had somehow remembered that George had been desperately ill several times, yet recovered to continue his incredible feats later in life. With the body failing under extreme duress, mind and spirit appeared to be taking up the battle and conducting my own pep talk.

Ten days after it had all started, and following countless visits by the district and continence nurses, GP, social care team and paramedics, I turned a corner and tentatively began to re-join the ranks of the human race. It had been an alarming insight into just how desperate my condition could become in such a short period of time, but what the episode did more than anything was to push me down the path of accepting the fact that I was badly disabled. It seemed odd to be saying that after all the years of struggling along with the disease but undeniably I was losing the battle on so many fronts. Whilst I had never been an advocate of the commonly spouted phrase 'I've got MS but MS hasn't got me', I had defiantly pressed on in order to get things done for the family and the charity. Perhaps for too long I had kept my head down and ignored something that was so obvious to everyone around me and now I was paying a price. It had got me after all.

And then there was Marion. The strain of having to look after a disabled husband and four daughters whilst continuing to be the main breadwinner must have been immense. Quite how she managed to smile and greet every childminding parent each morning without a hint of her inner turmoil was beyond me. I owed it to this remarkable woman to stop pushing myself to my physical and mental limits which so often were leaving her to sort out the resultant chaos. Nevertheless, acceptance would mean a drastic change in attitude insofar as letting go of so many things that I was involved with and at a time when the Samson Centre was looking to raise close to £900,000 towards the final phase of our development. How on earth could I step back when inevitably I would be heavily involved with the design and construction of our new oxygen therapy suite? With perfect timing my mobile sprang to life.

"Hi John, how are things with you, Marion and those lovely girls?"

It was the unmistakably chirpy voice of Tony Two Shirts.

"Hiya Tone, great to hear from you. We're all good thanks. How about you and Lucy?"

"Yeah, all good with us thanks, mate." I could almost see his broad smile across the ether. "I'll be quick as I'm about to meet with my fellow directors."

"No problem, what can I do for you?"

"Well, it's simple really. Silver are doing rather well these days and we are now required to meet certain corporate social responsibilities. If you don't mind I'm going to put forward the Samson Centre as our charity for the year along with a proposal that we step in and, subject to your trustees approval, help you all out with the design and management of your next building project. If I get agreement from the directors, our consultancy role will be on a pro bono basis. How does that sound to you?"

A few seconds passed whilst I took in what Tony had said.

"Are you still there John?"

"Uh, sorry mate, I'm blown away by what you've said. It's incredibly kind of you to think of the charity for one, but it might also just save my sanity!"

"Brilliant, let's get this on. I'll call you as soon as I have approval from the directors."

At a time when I was all but ready to stand down, Tony's intervention would prove crucial in getting me over the finishing line.

Chapter 35

Knight of Inspiration
25th January 2019

THERE'S still a bit of tidying up to be done but essentially the construction of the building is complete, so many years after the persistent nocturnal nudging to set about creating a dedicated MS therapy centre in West Surrey had prodded me into submission. I take a moment and glance around our new conference room. At the head of the table Tony, professional as ever, is running through the outstanding snags and paperwork, the directors and site manager from Exel, our contractors, look justifiably pleased with the project they have delivered, Jim and Dave from the Waterside Centre have the satisfied glow of two trustees who have played major roles in achieving something extraordinary, and then there's Martin Dent and I, Samson's Chair and Vice Chair, hugely proud of what the Samson Centre now stands for but both absolutely exhausted from the effort it has taken to get the charity to this point.

If someone had asked me back in 2003 how I thought the Samson Centre would look when complete and what sort of service it would deliver I just could not have foreseen the sheer scale of it on either front. Of course, I had a vision in my mind's eye, but never in my wildest dreams could I have imagined the groundswell of support that would come our way and ultimately propel the charity to the dizzy heights of 10,000 physio/gym/exercise/oxygen treatment sessions per year, with over 200 members, 11 paid staff and the 40-

something volunteers who had so deservedly earned us the Queen's Award in 2018. I may have instilled the belief and got the project rolling, but the last ten years have been a massive team effort with Jackie Payne, our Centre Manager, and Martin as Chairman, right at the forefront in terms of putting the charity on a business footing. Even though this process had been essential in order to safeguard Samson's development, I have no doubt that our growth owed as much to the fact that we had managed to create a feeling of inclusivity. Samson had become a well oiled machine, full of synergy; its whole being greater than the sum of its parts. The T.E.A.M. acronym, 'together, everyone achieves more', seemed entirely appropriate in our case and that extended to our association with the other Waterside Centre member clubs.

As I reflect it is obvious that the team environment is where I have felt most comfortable and within which I have operated best. From humble beginnings at Langdon's and the Truro Trout & Freshwater Fishing Club to my introduction to the Cornish rugby scene, the repressive stranglehold of self-doubt and introversion that had so blighted my early teenage years was gradually released, to the point that I ended up leading various initiatives. Then, after years stuttering along away from my beloved Kernow, as corny as it may sound, it was my arrival at a junior rugby club in West London in the late '80s that provided the springboard for so many positive elements of my life over the ensuing 30 years. The fulfilling sense of achievement pervading that final construction meeting was the culmination of that process.

Fulfilling, yes, but in truth I felt like an empty vessel. Despite the superb job that Tony and the Silver team had provided in shepherding us over the finishing line, I was spent. I had been hanging on in there for most of the building contract. Week after week of sleep disrupted by excruciating night-time spasms and neuralgic pain had eroded my resolve. I was desperate to see the project finished but the energy and ability to multitask, to problem solve, had all but gone. Somehow, during one of the hottest summers on record, I had got through five months of three hour site meetings and committee discussions (relevance noted below) but then with the end in sight I really began to struggle. It may not have been obvious to my fellow trustees and the construction team but I was acutely aware that I was contributing less and less. Thank God Tony was at the helm and proving the ideal linkman. Living with progressive MS, I had learnt to cope with the myriad of 'system failures' my body was suffering. However, the danger with managing a multitude of problems is that you can easily miss the ones that are draining away your resilience. And so the cascade commenced.

Sat 13th October 2018 – Marion and Meg had organised a disco for Samson and the Brain Tumour Charity at our local village hall. From daybreak the house was buzzing as the girls set about getting everything organised. For several weeks I had been feeling distinctly off colour but this was most acute on waking. That morning was probably as bad as it had been, but knowing how busy the day was going to be I forced myself out of bed and plonked myself into an armchair next to it. I vaguely remember voices echoing around the room and black spots blurring my vision before passing out. Ten minutes later, covered in sweat and prone on the floor, I slowly came to as Jose, our neighbour and a former ICU nurse, pounded away on my chest. I had stopped breathing. Embarrassingly, I had also wet myself. Meg, normally so unflappable, was in a terrible state. Even Dan, my 6' 6" Romanian carer, was crying, having arrived as the paramedics were taking charge. Initially my 'obs' weren't great but gradually oxygen sats, blood pressure and breathing regularised and with that the blue lips and grey pallor dissipated. As alarming as the episode was I politely declined their kind offer of a trip to the Royal Surrey. The pungent smell in the bedroom told me all I needed to know, or at least I thought so.

I was partly right. I did have a bladder infection, but what I hadn't considered was whether that was solely responsible for the feeling of sickness, not only in the mornings but sometimes in the middle of the night. I had also missed the significance of the cognitive fog, shortness of breath and ridiculously high pitched voice that greeted me at the start of each day. At first Marion and I made light of the voice thing, putting it down to '[Joe] Pasquale Syndrome'. However, it was no laughing matter. A referral to the respiratory clinic revealed that I had developed chronic sleep apnoea (on average I stopped breathing 18 times an hour) along with scoliosis of the spine which was restricting lung function. No wonder I felt knackered. One consolation though, unlike my old foe, sleep apnoea was a treatable condition. I just had to dress up like Hannibal Lecter and do Darth Vader impressions every night!

'For heaven's sake, what else?'

Well, how about trying incontinence? Now there's something I never thought I would have to address in my mid fifties, let alone double incontinence. And to think I used to laugh at David Walliams's depiction of Mrs Emmery wetting herself in *Little Britain!* Looking back now I can see how I had contributed to the problem over a long period. I had always been told to drink at least 2 litres of water a day to maintain healthy bladder and kidney function. That would be all well and good with reasonable mobility and an ability to weight bear. I no longer had either so drank sparingly. During visits to the Samson Centre and those long site meetings I took no fluids on board, so on the swelteringly hot days I was arriving home weak and dehydrated, invariably leading to falls and poor Marion having to mobilise a neighbourhood rescue team to get me off the floor and mop up. Sounds bad enough, but unwittingly I had entered a vicious circle. Massively swollen feet (oedemas), I could just about tolerate but I was about to discover how dysfunctional the gut could become without adequate fluid intake. Suffice it to say, the effects were unpleasant, humiliating and, given the exceptional weather, utterly depressing, to be spending hours stuck in the smallest room in the house racked with stomach spasms.

Fast forward to early January 2019. Something had to change, not only for me but for Marion's sanity, so I agreed to undergo surgery to fit me up with a suprapubic catheter. All went well and I was discharged after an overnight stay. The following day remains a blur. I vaguely remember Marion and Ellie, in full Community Nurse mode, clucking around me as I lay in bed sweating, deliriously spouting total gobbledygook. Ellie, worried that I might develop sepsis, took control and made the 999 call, and I was readmitted to the Royal Surrey where I spent four very uncomfortable nights fighting off an infection. It was by far and away the most challenging and upsetting spell I had endured with the disease. Contorted with spasms and unable to move, talk or get a full breath, I needed care throughout the first two nights. The NHS gets its fair amount of criticism but none of it will ever come from me after that experience. The team of staff nurses and care assistants, nearly all from the Philippines and Eastern Europe, were incredibly attentive and compassionate. As a small child I used to suffer from a recurring nightmare of helplessness, drifting away alone into the dark recesses of deep space. My mother and father used to recount how they had to gently coax me out of my traumatised state. Fifty-three years on, the nightmare was back. Like that desperately confused child, I was so grateful to those lovely people for staying with me.

I was relieved to get home, but having been bed bound for almost a week, my leg and core strength had all but disappeared, so the first few days were very trying. Day by day, thanks to Team Hambly, a new overhead hoist and my trusty Motomed bike, even allowing for my new plumbing appendages, I regained some semblance of normality. Allowed the luxury of immersing myself in box sets as I peddled my legs back to life, I ploughed through all thirty episodes of Netflix's *Narcos* before coming to my senses! Unsurprisingly, revved up after all that cocaine by proxy, I turned insomniac and resorted to surfing catch-up TV. It was there that I stumbled across *Billy Connolly: Made in Scotland*. At a time when I felt quite disorientated, the tone of the programme really struck a chord. I even woke Marion with the sound of my snorting as the sleep apnoea machine fought with my laughter and my tears. So much of what Sir Billy said evoked emotion within me.

Sitting in what looks like a theatre, with a mixture of humour and solemnity, he opens up about what ill health is doing to him. He remarks that it's like looking down the wrong end of the telescope. I get that. Things feel like they're getting away from me too.

The programme changes tack. A statuesque Sir Billy is on stage during a recent world tour. He cuts straight to the chase by telling his audience that he's got Parkinson's Disease and 'wishes to f*** that he'd kept it to himself!' Classic Sir Billy; if there is an elephant in the room it's just been given a good kick up the arse.

The scene changes again. He now looks longingly across a beautiful sandy bay somewhere up in Scotland. You could be mistaken for thinking that it is Cornwall. The glint in his eye is still there but I can sense that he is about to deliver a sobering summation.

Life is slipping away and he feels as though he's near the end. And yet, it doesn't frighten him. In his inimitable way, he sees it as an adventure. He talks of losing his balance, his senses, his energy and, then the really hard-hitting facts, his memory and his talent. He can't even pick up and play his banjo anymore.

Then, for me, he really hits the mark. He believes that his gradual loss of critical faculties comes from a higher force, as if to say, 'Right, I gave you all those abilities and attributes as a youth but now it's time to remove them and prepare you for the next part of your journey.' He likens this stage of his life, the shedding of 'stuff', to climbing the dark side of a hill but, ultimately, he believes that he will emerge into the light on the other side – the next episode of the spirit world.

Cut back to the theatre. There's even more gravity now. Unlike many of the common ailments we get and then recover from, his Parkinson's is not going to go away. He knows that it will only get worse. He pauses and walks away from the camera to regain his composure. When he returns his 'game face' is back on. Life is harsh at times but you can either implode and bemoan your lot or rise up and make the best of what you are and have a go at it.

As I lay there gently nodding, I questioned whether I'd had my 'go at it'. Seldom had I felt inclined to curl up and lament my situation but, at that moment, I was probably at my lowest point. I could empathise with Sir Billy's comment that things were slipping away. For the last couple of years I had begun to view the acceleration in my disability and loss of function as if I was literally dissolving in public. The return of that nightmare in hospital had merely served to reinforce the feeling that my physical being was regressing to infancy but, now fully awake and inspired by what I had just heard, I wondered whether I could raise my game just one more time.

The following morning I dictated an email and clicked send.

"Calling Actonians across the globe. . ."

Chapter 36

Crown the Day
Saturday 7th September 2019

IT'S almost 16 years to the day since I nervously rose to my feet to deliver the opening speech at the inaugural Actonians charity reunion and my first as Chairman of the emerging Samson Centre project. Things are very different now though. There are no nerves, none of the trepidation that I am promoting the unachievable and no worries that I will end up looking the fool for following a fanciful dream. As the London Welsh Rugby Choir and the club bring a rousing rendition of 'Sloop John B' to a close, I rise slowly to my full height and turn off the wheelchair.

"Well I feel so broke up, I want to go home. . ."

I take a few seconds to glance around a sea of familiar faces as the final spine-tingling harmonies fill the air. I may be broke up but I feel like I am already home. We are in the main hall at the Samson Centre. There is no coincidence to this evening. I had always planned to share this moment with the guys who had dragged me out of the suffocating quagmire of doubt and confusion that had accompanied my early days with MS. The event is all the more uplifting having Marion, the girls and so many close friends present to form a willing team of volunteers. They are our 'Samsons' and 'Delilahs' for the night. By my side is Ian Darke from the BT Sports' commentary team. His wife Liz, one of our trustees, had confirmed Ian's availability as our MC just a couple of weeks before. After his opening address and a few hilarious sporting anecdotes, Ian turns to me.

"John, I've known you for almost 20 years and I'm aware that the rugby club are pretty special to you. Can you sum up why?"

Bobby, my carer, unsuccessfully fiddles with my clip-on mic before Ian holds the main microphone to my mouth. The impromptu silence fails to unnerve me as I realign my chair to face the room.

"Thanks very much Ian. It's quite simple really. Without these fellas, I very much doubt whether I would have had the confidence to embark on this journey. When I first rolled up at Popes Lane in the summer of 1987 I could have had no idea of the major part that Actonians RFC would have on my life over the next 30 years. The ten years I had as a player and skipper were some of the best I had, and if the others were anything like me at the time, we never quite fully appreciated how good those days were. However, that was only part of the Actonians story. How many junior rugby clubs can proudly say that they've raised £100,000s to assist in the development of a facility as special as this? It has been an astonishing achievement."

I pause and dip my head slightly to draw breath.

"Be in no doubt that your kindness and generosity have massively improved the lives of hundreds of MS sufferers in London and the South East. For that everyone here at Samson will forever be in your debt. The bonds established in rugby – on the field, in the clubhouse, on tour – can be incredibly strong. In the case of our club, rugby's core values have always been in abundance – respect, integrity, solidarity, discipline, passion – but to these you can now add philanthropy. That, gentleman, pretty much sums up rugby and what we all stand for. Throughout the world we are a unique band of brothers."

As my voice tails off with fatigue and emotion, the lads rise to deliver an uplifting round of applause. I am virtually spent. It has been a demanding week at times, one that I had almost contemplated shying away from, but how could I? This was the culmination of almost two decades work. Three days earlier, attended by Her Majesty's Lord Lieutenant of Surrey, Professor

James, the construction team and many of our benefactors, trustees and members, the Samson Centre had held the official opening of the new oxygen therapy wing. It had been a magnificent occasion, starting with a lecture on the benefits of baric oxygen in our new conference room, then speeches and a buffet lunch. Meticulously choreographed by Jackie and Denice, our fundraiser, the event which spanned over four hours, had been a roaring success, but by the evening my batteries were very low. Just a few days later I was tapping into my hidden reserves again. The effort was taking its toll and this was probably clear for all to see.

Our midriffs may have expanded and the hair turned grey and thin but the buzz and the cacophony of sound are unmistakable. I now entirely understand Dave's words about needing to return to the wooden shed (our clubhouse) at a time of anguish. Except on this occasion the clubhouse and its magical air have been brought on tour to Guildford. The memories quickly come flooding back. Oh, how I hanker for those halcyon days of the 80s and 90s. My discomfort and tiredness are temporarily swept aside as a wave of warmth and understanding rolls in and picks me up. It feels like I am being carried shoulder high from the Field of Dreams.

After Ian has chatted with our Guest of Honour, Simon Shaw of England and the British Lions, about the forthcoming Rugby World Cup (South Africa were his pick, by the way), the event goes up another gear as Duff takes the vanguard and does what he does best. As on numerous tours, depending on the severity of the alleged crime, ad-libbing his way from case to case, he is both hilarious and menacing as The Judge during Players Court. For once I have the luxury of knowing that I will remain with the chanting mob as the miscreants are grudgingly dragged to the front to receive their sentence, the appropriately named Purple Nasty; a mysterious concoction of Guinness, Pernod/vodka, blackcurrant and chocolate. Duff, now in full flow, rips up Ian's running order and goes straight into fundraising mode. The evening is meant to be free and a celebration of the club's contribution towards the creation of the Samson Centre. By the time he's auctioned off a 2012 Olympic GB 7's shirt and Meg has fleeced almost everyone for drinking with the 'wrong' hand, there's a substantial sum in the buckets, but in the days to follow, with the alcoholic haze slowly dissipating, donations appear online. In typical Actonian style the evening generates over £15,000.

Fittingly, as the formalities drew to a close, I had the great honour of presenting Stumble and Simon Taylor with a plaque which read 'This oxygen therapy suite was made possible by the kind and generous support of players from Actonians RFC'. It would be mounted adjacent to the entrance to the new oxygen suite in recognition of the Rugby Club's extraordinary contribution to the cause.

The euphoria of the reunion sustained me through to the early hours of Sunday morning. It had been such a remarkable evening that I was buzzed up and sleep became impossible. Eventually, as the adrenaline ebbed away, predictably the MS came roaring back, filling me with spasm, numbness and nausea. Clearly, after all the fun, it was time to pay the price. In familiar nocturnal pose, flat out and rigid, I stared at the ceiling. The display from the sleep apnoea machine dimly shed light on the overhead hoist. The bed control pad illuminated the metal railings between Marion and I. Perhaps it's a good thing that we no longer share a marital bed. I'm just too restless these days. Week after week, the interminable deterioration has crept up on me.

'How the hell have you allowed yourself to get into this state?' I ponder regretfully before rounding on myself, *'Come on you sad bastard, pull your finger out and get on top of this.'*

Resentment at my incapacity stewed within me for the next four hours. As the faint light of dawn began to creep around the curtains I had begun to see things a little more clearly. So many times people had told me to ease back and start looking after myself and the family. By passing the chairmanship to Martin ten years earlier and with Jackie joining us as centre manager around the same time, I had thought then that the process was underway but, as Vice Chairman to both the Samson Centre and the Guildford Waterside Centre, I was kidding myself that I would be able to fade into the background. Three large Samson building projects had followed my so-called stepping back, all of which I'd had a major hand in, so the pressure to raise the funds and deliver the schemes had never been released.

In addition, I was still the person that friends, and friends of friends, identified as the face of Samson so, invariably, I would be their first point of contact and then stay with the matter through to its conclusion. Quite rightly, those who raised funds for the charity needed thanking so I would attend the cheque presentations and do the acceptance speeches. Even though Jackie, and latterly Denice, eventually took on many of these duties, I was struggling to raise my game for the more formal occasions when I was the front man. I loathed having to address audiences from a wheelchair, and now with my voice faltering, at times I could sense that I was losing the room. Many of my fears and doubts about public speaking resurfaced and I would end up beating myself up about what I should or shouldn't have said.

No, there was only one way forward and that was to take an even larger step back. I would resign my trusteeship on the Guildford Waterside Centre board as well as relinquishing the Vice Chairman's seat at the Samson Centre. I hadn't planned it whilst putting together the Actonians reunion, but by the morning after the event, I had come to the realisation that it had served to neatly bookend my journey in establishing and helping to develop our bespoke facilities. Unlike the uncertainty of when I announced to Marc that I was retiring from the surveying practice, this time there was more conviction. If I was to stand any chance of stabilising my condition, I knew that I had to be completely focused and start being more selfish. I had managed to muster the much vaunted 'strength in adversity' for the charity on many occasions but this would be a much more different challenge. This time it would be for me. In essence, I would attempt to halt (hopefully, even reverse) some of the effects of an aggressive incurable illness to which I had submitted for far too long. I could be in no doubt that my dwindling reserves of energy, my mental resolve, my hopes and my faith would be tested to breaking point but one particular throw away comment from a neurologist a few months earlier had simmered within me and inadvertently bolstered my determination.

The comment I am referring to came during a telephone consultation as I was being assessed for a drug trial for secondary/primary progressive MS. Having endured the usual barrage of scans and tests, including the ever popular lumbar puncture, I was optimistic that there would be a positive outcome; something on which Marion and I could rebuild our hopes and dreams.

It went something like this:

"Unfortunately you are not going to be a suitable candidate for the trial. Your latest scans indicate that there are many new lesions on your brain and spinal cord. Your MS is too advanced. I am sorry to tell you this as you must be having a rough time. Goodbye."

'Having a rough time? A rough time!' I choked over his words, *'You're bloody right I am. I know that, I don't need you to point out the bloody obvious. I have to grapple with this day and night.'*

And then there was a second thing that drove me on, perhaps appropriately, relating to the publication of this book. A number of friends with contacts in the literary world had read the odd chapter and mentioned that it might be worth approaching a few publishers to get their initial feedback. I'm not sure whether the latter were just being polite to a first time writer but nearly all of them commented that, whilst my reflections were reasonably well written, I wasn't famous, so there would be very limited interest in my story. Since I'd never wanted to be in the spotlight, that seemed to present a substantial impediment to getting the book out there. Over recent years when being presented with awards for my involvement in creating the Samson Centre, I had always said how grateful I was and what a great honour it was to be there, but without wishing to appear ungrateful, for me 'charitable work was more about making a difference to others and not about achieving personal recognition'.

I wasn't about to abandon that particular belief, so either I would have to self-publish or do something extraordinary that would make a publisher's ears prick up. Could it be that an intense period of oxygen, traditional and holistic therapies, light exercise and a large dose of stubbornness might just possibly enable me to get one over the insidious beast inside me and make me stick out from the crowd?

The truth is that I don't know but, then again, when I look back I can see how all the wonderful people and the remarkable events I have written about here have been the beacons in life's game of dot-to-dot; the ones that have guided and shaped me and the things I have strived to achieve. Who's to say that there aren't other beacons out there that I can head towards, enabling me to turn things around, to fulfil dreams that have been in cold storage for so long. It would fly in the face of what we know and expect of MS, but when I consider all the incredible things that have happened to me and the family as a result of the disease being in our lives, I know that anything is possible.

The old man's voice is with me again:

"Be patient, boy. Remember what your Aunt Doreen used to say."

'I know, Father. The evening will crown the day.'

Epilogue
April 2020

Why write an epilogue when, by and large, you're happy enough with the ending of the preceding 36 chapters? Well, frankly, the evening has not crowned the day. The expectancy of a period of improved health and mobility has been all but extinguished by the Covid-19 virus. When I started out on this journey of reflection, like the tides pulsing in and out of Mount's Bay regardless of the weather and everything else going on in the world, I had imagined that, when pieced together, the key chapters would show life's ebb and flow. However, what I had not foreseen (and to be honest, who could have?) was a global pandemic of such enormity that it would, literally, halt the tide of everyday life. Those reassuring daily rhythms of the sea, seemingly discharged from duty as the country braced itself for a tsunami of medical, emotional and economic turmoil, the enormity of which had not been witnessed for generations, perhaps ever. At the time of penning this, the disease is spreading rapidly and indiscriminately across the country, wreaking havoc on families and businesses and leaving its indelible mark on life as we know it.

Shutting down the Samson Centre a month ago, in order to safeguard our members, was a difficult decision and may have been viewed by some as premature, given that the government's graduated lockdown had not yet been imposed. Despite the financial repercussions, we can now be in no doubt that it was the correct call for the charity, but in the intervening weeks the full impact of this invisible killer has been rammed home. And by that, I mean our family 'doorstep'. Firstly, Ellie, our own NHS hero, was advised to move out because her vital work as a nurse was potentially putting me, a vulnerable person, in danger of the virus. *'Me? Vulnerable? How can that be? A few months ago, mentally, I still felt capable of running through a barn door!'* Within 48 hours, somehow, we managed to locate, furnish and move Ellie into a one bed flat in Guildford. Being so under the pump with work, she was understandably distraught at being wrenched from the family bosom to go 'off to battle', ostensibly in isolation. If that was a punch to the solar plexus, then the next was the uppercut that put us all on the canvas.

Janet 'Gaga' Reeves, Marion's lovely mother, having been admitted to hospital in February following a fall, somewhere along the line had picked up the virus. I will never forget the moment that an inconsolable Marion, and then the girls, staggered crestfallen into my office to give me the awful news. We remained on tenterhooks for the next week, fearing the shrill beckoning of the telephone each time it rang. On day nine, incredibly, Gaga appeared to be rallying and, with it, our hopes of a remarkable recovery began to rise. It was therefore even more shattering to receive the call that we had all been dreading just the next day.

Eighteen days later, the gravity of grieving within the stranglehold of the coronavirus hit us full on. We would not be allowed to attend the funeral service, nor, through self-isolation measures, would we be able to visit Marion's father, John, to comfort him. On 17th April at 2:45pm the family gathered together in our respective homes, and online across the world, to pay our last respects to our beloved Gaga. We held a funeral liturgy at home, entitled 'A Simple Reflection', which had been provided by the vicar taking the service in West London. It was incredibly emotional but somehow we held ourselves together, that is until we received a WhatsApp video showing John placing a bouquet of flowers onto Janet's coffin. The funeral directors had kindly agreed to allow the hearse to pull up outside the family home for two minutes en route to the crematorium. The sight of Gaga's funeral cortège of one silently moving away, with John, dignified as ever, looking on, will live with me forever.

The morning after, as I am sitting on the patio in the early summer sunshine reflecting on the events of the last few weeks, Cerys appears at my shoulder and quietly places the following reading onto my lap before strolling down the garden to stroke Oreo, her cat:

> *God saw you getting tired*
> *When a cure was not to be.*
> *So He wrapped His arms around you,*
> *And whispered, "Come unto me."*
> *You didn't deserve what you went through,*
> *And so He gave you rest.*
> *God's garden must be beautiful,*
> *He only takes the best.*
> *So when I saw you sleeping,*
> *So peaceful and free from pain.*
> *I could not wish you to come back,*
> *to suffer that all again.*

As I tilt my head back to take in what my youngest daughter has just delivered, a solitary, wispy cloud in the clear blue sky drifts serenely across the sun and then slowly dissipates. Bye, bye for now Gaga.